CHRISTMAS 1997

TO: ELLY
WITH LOVE Ron
x

STRAWBERRY FAIR

Strawberry Fair

A Biography of
Frances, Countess Waldegrave
1821–1879

by

OSBERT WYNDHAM HEWETT

JOHN MURRAY
FIFTY ALBEMARLE STREET
LONDON

To
LORD STRACHIE

First published 1956

Printed in Great Britain by Latimer, Trend & Co. Ltd., Plymouth
and published by John Murray (Publishers) Ltd.

CONTENTS

ILLUSTRATIONS

* By kind permission of Lord Strachie.

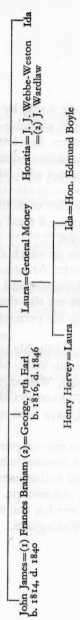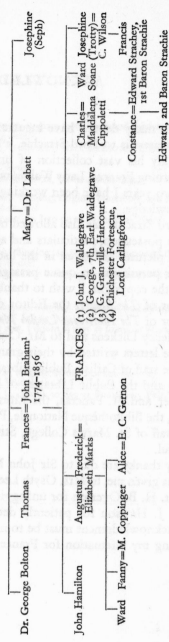

John James, 6th Earl Waldegrave = (1815) Annette King = (1839) Algernon Hicks

John James = (1) Frances Braham (2) = George, 7th Earl
b. 1814, d. 1840   b. 1816, d. 1846

Laura = General Money

Horatia = J. J. Webbe-Weston
= (2) J. Wardlaw

Ida

Ida = Hon. Edmund Boyle

Henry Hervey = Laura

George Bolton of Ardwick = Elizabeth Wilson of Manchester

Mary = Dr. Labatt

Frances = John Braham¹
1774–1856

Josephine (Seph)

Dr. George Bolton

Thomas

Augustus Frederick = Elizabeth Marks

FRANCES
(1) John J. Waldegrave
(2) George, 7th Earl Waldegrave
(3) G. Granville Harcourt
(4) Chichester Fortescue, Lord Carlingford

Charles = Maddalena Cippoletti

Ward Josephine Soane (Trotty) = C. Wilson

Francis

Constance = Edward Strachey, 1st Baron Strachie

John Hamilton

Ward Fanny = M. Coppinger Alice = E. C. Gernon

Edward, 2nd Baron Strachie

¹ John Braham had by Nancy Storace an illegitimate son, William Spencer Harris Braham (later Canon Meadows).

INTRODUCTION

On 6 January 1862, the *Europe* arrived off Queenstown, bringing the news that the Federal Government had agreed to release the Confederate Commissioners, Slidell and Mason, whom they had seized aboard the British steamer *Trent*. The danger of war with the Northern States of America was over, and the British, in their relief, began at the same time to recover from their grief at the death of the Prince Consort, all the more sincere for their lack of appreciation during his lifetime. Five days after Prince Albert's death, old Mr. Harcourt had died at Strawberry Hill, but in their anxiety about the Queen and about the Trent affair, few had realized it.

Now it became the one topic. Lady Waldegrave was widowed for the third time. Who would be her fourth choice? No one doubted her remarrying, although they were amazed to learn how genuinely she mourned the old man who for the last fourteen years had made her life none too happy. The odds were shortest on the Duke of Newcastle, the Colonial Secretary, whom Frances Waldegrave had vowed to make Premier, and who had openly adored her since he had divorced his wife eleven years before. Lord St. Germans obviously thought his own chances were good, but the more romantically minded backed Chichester Fortescue, much as they may have been amused by his hopeless infatuation during the past ten years. As Fortescue was Newcastle's parliamentary under-secretary and was thus the colonial authority in the House of Commons, the fact that they were both enslaved by the same woman intrigued everybody.

The publication of old Harcourt's will greatly increased the discussion. As her other husbands had done, he left her everything he could dispose of, and his testament ended: 'The unspeakable interest with which I earnestly regard Lady Waldegrave's future fate induces me to advise her earnestly to unite herself again with someone who may deserve to enjoy the blessing of her society during the many years of her probable survival after my life. I am grateful to Providence for the great happiness I enjoy in her singular affection, and I pray and confidently hope that she may long continue to possess the same esteem and friendship of those who are intimate with her and can appreciate her admirable qualities and the respect of all with whom in any relation of life she is connected.'

The only thing that was certain was that she would never be allowed to remain a widow for long. In 1847 her choice of George Granville Harcourt had astonished society, and now, since young men such as the poet Julian Fane and octogenarians such as Lord Lansdowne were equally devoted to her, any forecast was problematical.

The daughter of John Braham, the greatest singer of his time, Frances, Countess Waldegrave, though inheriting his intellect, wit and superb health, owed her wonderful colouring, her great, deep blue eyes, and wealth of fair hair to her mother. Her grace of movement—*incessu patuit dea* was invariably quoted of her—and radiant vitality made it difficult to believe that she was born in 1821. Newcastle and Fortescue would have married her had she been penniless, but her income of £20,000 a year scarcely discouraged the others. Lady Palmerston's Saturdays at Cambridge House, her parties at Broadlands and her position as the Premier's wife, made her the principal Liberal hostess, but the members of no cabinet had so cordially disliked each other as the members of Palmerston's last administration, and Lady Palmerston herself exerted little political influence.

Lady Waldegrave had for years been striving to end the dissension within the Liberal Party, and her fabulous hospitality at Carlton Gardens, Strawberry Hill, Nuneham and Dudbrook, together with her intense interest in politics—Disraeli insisted that had she been a man she would have made a brilliant Prime Minister—had made her at least as important a political hostess as Emily Palmerston.

The social columns of the daily press were no longer full of lists of Lady Waldegrave's guests, but the public could read that she had left Strawberry Hill for Dudbrook. Naturally she had wanted a change of scene, but she had also wanted to get away from the over-attentive sympathy of the Orleans family. Although the Duc and Duchesse d'Aumale were her most intimate friends, it was

rather alarming for her household to have royalty appearing un-
announced at any time of the day. Her own utter lack of any sense
of protocol simplified everything when she was herself at hand,
but the innumerable in-laws by her various marriages, who continually surrounded her, had a more Victorian respect for the
exalted.

Her Essex home proved to be no refuge. The Aumales invited
themselves to Dudbrook and persuaded her to visit them at
Wood Norton. Harcourt and Waldegrave relations also insisted
on her visiting them, until poor Frances in despair returned to
London. By then Fortescue had arrived from Ireland, Newcastle
from Clumber, Lord St. Germans from Port Eliot, and before long
there was a stream of callers at No. 7 Carlton Gardens. Palmerston,
Clarendon and Lord John Russell temporarily forgot their ani-
mosities to discuss the great problem as eagerly as any gossip
columnist. Whom would the most fascinating widow in London
marry?

THE ACTIVITIES of her village were by no means Miss Mitford's only interest. In a letter dated January 1816, to Sir William Elford, she wrote: 'From marriages to scandal is the most natural transition imaginable. Only think of Braham having at last run away from Storace and her wig. I am very sorry for it, since it may deprive us of Braham's sweet notes. I hope you like Braham's singing, although I know among your scientific musicians it is a crime *de lèze majesté* to say so; but he is the only singer I have ever heard in my life who ever conveyed to my very unmusical ears any idea of the expression to which music is susceptible; no one else joins any sense to the sound. They may talk of music as married to immortal verse, but if it were not for Braham they would have been divorced long ago. All the rest might just as well sing backwards, as the Chinese write, or indeed sing in Chinese or Otaheitan, for any benefit they derive from the poetry.'

It was a sensational scandal because the twenty years the liaison had lasted had given it such a respectable air of domesticity that most people had forgotten the two were not married. In 1795 Nancy Storace had gone to Bath on a visit to Rauzzini, her old singing master. The original Suzanna in the *Nozze Di Figaro*, she had, while in Vienna, married the violinist Doctor Fisher. Within a few weeks his behaviour became so intolerable that the Emperor of Austria, Storace's devoted admirer, had banished him and arranged some form of separation. Fisher survived till 1804, so that when the *prima donna* met Rauzzini's brilliant young Jewish pupil at Bath, she was not free to marry.

John Braham was eight years her junior and his squat ugliness was remarkable, but the beauty of his voice, which made him, for the next thirty-five years, the greatest tenor in Europe, completely infatuated her. Signora Storace was then at the height of her fame and somewhat florid beauty, and her brother, the composer Stephen Storace, was all-powerful at Drury Lane and Covent Garden. She proposed that Braham should make his operatic

début in her brother's new opera *Mahmoud* and, after his resounding success at its production at Drury Lane, the two singers left
for a prolonged continental tour.

For the young tenor it was a triumph all the way. In Paris
Madame Bonaparte patronized his concerts. In Italy, the Italians
admitted that *'non c'è tenore in Italia come Braham'*, and Cimarosa
wrote his opera *Artemisia* especially for him.

The year 1801 marked their return to England, the birth of
their son, Spencer, and for Braham the beginning of thirty-five
years of unparalleled success. His popularity both as singer and
composer was enormous and, to some extent, led him to misuse
his great gifts. In opera he infuriated the critics by dazzling and
delighting his audiences with totally unnecessary and meretricious
displays of the incredible range an flexidbility of his voice. As
Leigh Hunt said of him, 'He lights up, as it were, fifty wax candles
to exhibit a nutshell.' In oratorio, however, he was unsurpassed.
He had, as a young man, become a Christian, a fact that roused
Charles Lamb to write an essay upon his apostacy, though Lamb
had elsewhere called him 'angel, gentleman and Jew'. Despite his
early dissipations, he was a devout man and his rendering of
sacred songs was intensely moving.

His return to England was warmly welcomed by his early
patron, the great financier, Goldsmid, whose musical parties at
his Morden house were the talk of London. There began Braham's
long friendship with the musical royal brothers. The Goldsmids
advised him wisely about the disposal of the fortune his voice was
bringing him, and introduced him to every musical notability.
Storace was still popular, but in 1809, realizing that neither her
voice nor her figure had the beauty they had once possessed, she
retired to her pleasant country house near Dulwich. Braham and
she were still devoted to each other and to their son, so her retirement from the stage caused no separation.

Nancy Storace was friendly with a Mrs. Wright whose husband
was a purser on one of the East India Company's ships. Braham,
of course, was introduced and was soon as intimate with the
Wrights as was his mistress. Mr. Wright was charmed that his
wife should have such wealthy and important friends. To show his
approval, he would retire to bed leaving his wife to entertain the
singer till three or four in the morning. Braham gladly took ad-

vantage of the hospitality so generously extended to him. Wright's generosity, however, was limited. At the end of 1815 he returned to England to find his wife involved in a chronologically tactless pregnancy. Without delay he brought an action against Braham for criminal conversation, claiming £5,000 damages.

As soon as they heard the news, the more sanctimonious of his public determined to destroy Braham. During an oratorio at Drury Lane in March, he was hissed. At the end of a song he came forward and addressed the audience.

'I am now before you as a public character. If, in that situation, I have given offence, you have an undoubted right to call for an apology or defence; but if I have erred as a private individual, the nature of that error cannot, with discretion, come under your notice. It will be properly investigated before a court constituted to hear both the accuser and the accused, and where justice only can be done. I, therefore, only claim from you the privilege which the meanest subject enjoys, that is, of not being condemned before heard; and I trust the result will acquit me of any aggravated offence that can deserve your displeasure.'

The case came up for hearing on 23 July 1816. Serjeant Copley, the future Lord Lyndhurst, was briefed for the defence. The Lord Chief Justice, in his summing-up, left no doubt that he considered it was blackmail, but the jury awarded Wright £1,000 damages. Storace, who must have been accustomed to Braham's infidelities, would probably have forgiven him this, too, but he chose to take her anger as final and went off on a provincial tour.

His engagements in Liverpool had for some years brought him in contact with an odd character named Wilson. At one time, Wilson had taught in his brother-in-law's Manchester dancing academy where he had met and married a very handsome widow, considerably his senior but with a little money. On his brother-in-law's death in 1809 he had set up in Liverpool as an organizer of concerts, through which he had met Braham. His gay, malicious eccentricity amused the singer who was frequently at their house. As Braham was singing in Manchester, Wilson introduced him to his widowed sister, Mrs. Bolton, who was only eleven months Braham's senior, extremely good-looking, and finding it difficult to educate two sons and three daughters on her very small income. The eldest girl, Fanny, was at seventeen already a beauty and, though very tall, had such grace of movement that her height was an added attraction. The difference in age, and more striking still, the difference in height, in no way daunted John Braham. He must and would marry Fanny Bolton.

Probably she was influenced by his great fame and wealth but, unquestionably, Fanny was deeply in love with the ugly little man though he was more than old enough to be her father. For the whole family it was a miracle. Braham settled £15,000 on her and promised to assist her two brothers. He was all fire and impatience for the wedding and, towards the end of November, the musical world was amazed to read of the marriage of 'On November 11, at the Collegiate Church, Manchester, John Braham of Tavistock Square, London, to Frances Elizabeth, daughter of the late George Bolton of Ardwick'.

For young Mrs. Braham, her new house at 3 Tavistock Square was a fantastic world where luxury was taken for granted, where royalty was treated as casually as any other acquaintance and where the intoxication of the theatre was always accessible. Her husband knew everyone of interest in England, musicians, writers, painters, politicians—she had to entertain them all and did so with the strange mixture of *naïveté* and poise that was so appealing. Jewels, carriages, clothes, anything she or her family wanted, Braham was delighted to give. The great Regency ladies, already intrigued by her husband's indifference to them, were anxious to meet her, but, at first, all she wanted was to spend her time in a stage box in the enchantment of the theatre, listening to the delirious applause that greeted Braham. She was well aware that Storace was still living at Herne Hill and had no desire for any reconciliation in that direction, nor had she the least intention of allowing any more Mrs. Wrights.

Any fears she may have had about Herne Hill were groundless. Signora Storace had retired with a fortune of over £40,000 and the sixteen-year-old Spencer was already shrewd enough to see that his financial prospects would be strengthened if his mother and father were kept firmly apart. Spencer was disillusioned very quickly. In August the following year Nancy Storace died, and the only will that was found was one made before her marriage to Fisher, leaving everything to her mother and sisters.

It soon became obvious that, however successful she might be

4

as a hostess, Mrs. Braham's talents were not suited to the management of a household and, before they had been married twelve months, her husband was writing to his mother-in-law, Mrs. Bolton, beseeching her to let her house in Manchester and to come with her two younger daughters to run the house in Tavistock Square. The elder son was already studying medicine in London and Braham offered to find some opening for the younger one.

Their first child, Hamilton, was born on New Year's Day, 1819, and the second, Augustus, in December the same year. Thereafter Braham supplied his wife prolifically with pregnancies, but she still continued to be with him on almost all his provincial tours. When she was quite unable to travel she sent her uncle or a brother to chaperon him.

On 4 January 1821, the first daughter, Frances Elizabeth Anne, was born at Tavistock Square. The second child had not yet been christened and it was decided to make a double event of it. The christening, followed by a large dinner party, was held in August. The Duke of Sussex was godfather to Augustus Frederick Braham, and Doctor and Mrs. Morris of Liverpool were the baby girl's godparents. Sir Francis Burdett was another guest and amused them with accounts of his imprisonment in the Queen's Bench and the rooms he had occupied there in the Governor's lodge.

During the twenties Braham's triumphs continued unbroken. His old patron was now on the throne and as fervent an admirer as when he was Prince of Wales. One evening, when he had Braham to sing to his guests, the King's enthusiasm was such that he was with difficulty prevented from knighting him then and there. On another occasion, finding that a state concert had been arranged on the same night as Braham's benefit, he had his friend advised that the royal concert had been postponed lest it should interfere with the other.

In view of Braham's great success in *Der Freischutz* on its first performance in this country, Weber wrote his *Oberon* with Braham, whom he considered the greatest living singer, in mind for the role of Sir Huon, and was himself a witness of the tenor's triumph on the first night of *Oberon* at Covent Garden.

At the end of 1822, Mrs. Braham had a third son, Charles Bampfylde, and a fourth, Ward Soane, arrived in April 1824. Although Fanny Braham was singularly lacking in the more usual forms of maternal affection, she found it no longer possible to devote her entire life to her husband and to her passion for the theatre. She had always enjoyed the admiration and appreciation her husband's guests had shown her but had, hitherto, really enjoyed her social success mostly because it pleased him. Now that her increasing family tied her to the house, she suddenly developed a passion for entertaining that had the same impulsive zest as her enthusiasm for the theatre.

The Royal Academy of Music was founded in 1823 by Lord Burghersh, the soldier-diplomat-musician. His wife, a niece of the Duke of Wellington, had gained some reputation as a painter. One of her sisters had married Lord Fitzroy Somerset who, as Lord Raglan, was to achieve fame in the Crimea, and another sister had married Sir Charles Bagot, Ambassador to St. Petersburg and The Hague, and later to be Governor-General of Canada. Lord Burghersh had known Braham for years, and Lady Burghersh was delighted with his beautiful young wife. She and her two sisters took Mrs. Braham everywhere and made as much of the children as they did of the mother.

It proved too much for the young woman. Braham's fortune, which had seemed so splendid, would scarcely provide each of the children with an income sufficient to marry a Fane, a Bagot, a Wellesley or a Somerset. The house in Baker Street had somehow shrunk, now that it was a question of entertaining the wives and children of her husband's patrons. The birth of a second daughter, Josephine, in June 1829, finally decided it.

The village of Brompton was an easy walk from Hyde Park Corner. Opposite the old church, between Yeoman's Row and the road that led through market gardens to Fulham, stood a large house with considerable grounds. Braham at once signed a lease of twenty-one years at £250 a year commencing Michaelmas Day, 1830, 'for the house called The Grange and the fields in front on the Fulham Road, and the Kitchen Garden . . . tenant to thoroughly repair the house, cottages and stables and other outbuildings and the fence surrounding the fields and to maintain them in repair'. A short distance away was Blemell House, Mr. Pollard's academy for the children of the nobility and gentry, where Frances and her brothers could be educated.

6

Mrs. Braham's sister Josephine (Aunt Seph) had taken over the housekeeping so it was decided that their mother, Mrs. Bolton, should have her own establishment in one of the cottages. The old Wilsons were also offered a cottage at the Grange, but they eventually took a small house in Chelsea. Frances spent most of her time with her grandmother or with the Wilsons. Her great-uncle and aunt were childless and utterly spoilt the little girl. It was an enchanting house to visit and their parrot was so talkative that it was to achieve the distinction of a long description in the *Morning Post*. Great-Uncle Wilson could dress dolls far better than Frances herself and there was nothing he could not teach her about dancing. His wife was a magician at telling one's fortune with the cards and, better still, could never resist a passing gipsy. Their great-niece was soon able to tell the old lady's cards herself and, as a reward, a gipsy was found to read her palm. It was all very exciting, four husbands, wealth, rank, fame, but it would only be the last husband she truly loved.

Mr. Pollard's academy was to Mrs. Braham one of the attractions of Brompton. With six children cluttering up the house she had little time to devote to her beloved John. To her, he was still the greatest man in the world and, in the passion of his love-making, she envied no other woman a younger husband. His conversation and wit were brilliant and she could listen happily for hours while he talked with his friends. The only regret was that she could not make him understand that the Duke of Sussex and such men as Lord Maryborough or Lord Burghersh were more important than Hazlitt, William Jerdan or Leigh Hunt. At the Grange she could probably change all that. They had let the Baker Street house furnished as she was determined that her new home should be really splendid, and she spent thousands on the decorations and contents. She knew her extravagance was justified as they would soon make the princely fortune that would enable the children to marry into the first families of England, and force society to realize her dear John was not only the greatest singer, but one of the greatest men in every way.

Braham's illegitimate son, Spencer, Vicar of Willisborough, Kent, and minor Canon of Canterbury Cathedral, with whom his stepmother was on friendly terms, had married in October 1829. In honour of the event the Duke of Sussex had made him his domestic chaplain. At the Grange it was at last possible to show their appreciation of this royal favour. In July 1831 the decorations and furnishings were finished and Mrs. Braham's first great party there was to meet His Royal Highness. It was a magnificent success, but Braham was a little worried at so much money being spent on a man who was not really a very good musician, and who had just tried to borrow £4,000 from him.

His wife's passion for royalty, and titles generally, was quite incomprehensible to him. The Emperor of Austria was royal but Nancy Storace had preferred him, Braham, as a lover. Lord Burghersh had rendered very great services to music, was an able general and diplomatist so John was genuinely puzzled to find Mrs. Braham only valued him as the heir to the earldom and son-in-law to another earl. Though prepared to indulge his young wife in every way, he had not the remotest understanding of her valuation of society, and Augustus was the only one of her children who inherited his mother's appreciation of rank for rank's sake.

Since Trotty's birth (Josephine, the youngest child), Mrs. Braham had put on a good deal of weight and found stairs a difficulty. Her husband, therefore, always stipulated in his engagements that she should have a pit tier box for his first nights. At the beginning of November he was to sing in *Fra Diavolo* at Covent Garden. When his wife arrived at the theatre she found that her box had, by mistake, been let to Lady Harrington, formerly the actress Maria Foote. As she was an old friend, Mrs. Braham made no protest and accepted a first tier box. On her way up she slipped on the stone stairs and, falling heavily, dislocated her ankle. Braham was naturally furious and vowed to build her her own theatre where such mishaps could never happen.

All his life he had ridiculed anyone insane enough to go in for theatrical management and had sworn that nothing would persuade him to do so. Probably his promise to his wife was made in the excitement of the moment and forgotten as soon as said, but Mrs. Braham never forgot for a moment for the rest of her life.

At one time Braham had hoped that his sons would inherit his love of music, but his passionate young wife easily persuaded him that the Church, the Army and the Law, were the only suitable professions for gentlemen. He felt that his savings of some £90,000 would amply provide for their careers, and thanks to the continued friendship of the Goldsmid brothers, the money was wisely invested. He did, however, see that his singing days were drawing to a close and that in a few years it would be no easy matter to earn his £10,000 a year, but he could not bring himself to spoil her wild happiness by trying to cut even her rashest extravagances.

The next three years passed in a blaze of triumph and prosperity. Despite his age Braham was unrivalled and, since he was devoting more time to oratorio than opera, he was less inclined to dazzle his admirers with those vocal gymnastics that had formerly so offended the critics. With Malibran, Grisi and all the great visiting *prime donne* he sang throughout the kingdom. For over thirty years now he had reigned undisputed king of song.

His wife, too, was full of triumphs. The brilliant assembly of musicians, dramatists, actors, poets and critics attracted even a few dukes, and their hostess welcomed them ecstatically. Her hospitality was a little impeded by continual pregnancies which, after Trotty's birth, all ended in *fausses couches*. It was probably as well, for she had no time to spare for the children she already had. They were perfectly content to be neglected. For her sons there were the butcher boys and 'tigers' of Yeomans Row to fight with, or in more amicable moods to drink, smoke, swear and bet with.

Frances had celebrated her eleventh birthday by swearing eternal fidelity to Hutchinson Carroll, the schoolboy son of a musically minded Irish general. With Grandmamma Bolton's cottage or the Wilsons at Chelsea as refuges she could easily escape from the wearisome gentility of the girls her mother liked to invite. Visitors considered her a 'singularly pretty and fascinating child' but, like her father, she found her mother's conception of social pleasures an enigma.

The question of the immense fortune to be gained still worried the lady of the Grange. The Goldsmids were far too conservative in their financial advice, and it was impossible to make her husband buy one share of which they did not approve. She had never forgotten the first night of *Fra Diavolo*, and was constantly reminding the old man of it.

Among the many dramatists who frequented the house at Brompton was Samuel Beazley, the author of innumerable plays. Mrs. Bra-

ham had no particular affection for him; his blood was not noticeably blue and he moved mostly in the odd colony that lived round
Soho Square. The drama, however, was not his principal interest.
He was an excellent architect and specialized in theatres. One
evening he casually mentioned his latest project to her, and immediately her whole plan crystallized. He must draw up a plan of
'the prettiest playhouse in Europe', a theatre which should be the
home of English opera, where Braham's many compositions
could be fully appreciated, but it must not be in the Strand.
London was steadily moving westward. With the Pimlico fields a
maze of new houses, and Tyburnia a town in itself, no one lived
further east than Regent Street.

It was his obituary notice that finally convinced Braham himself.
He arrived in Cardiff, where he was to sing, on 13 August 1834, to
find the theatre closed. All the morning papers had contained
accounts of his death of cholera. Having, with considerable difficulty, persuaded the manager that he was still alive, he settled
down to read his obituary notices. They were all extremely flattering but for one thing. None was astonished that the 'veteran
singer' was dead. 'Veteran' was a little strong as he was only sixty,
but he had been for so long the greatest living tenor that he was
believed to be much older. Most pointed out that, though his loss
was irreparable, his fame was secure because he had died before
his powers had *further* declined.

In the meantime Beazley and Mrs. Braham were scouring the
west end of London for a good site. It was several months before
anywhere suitable was found. On the south side of King's Street,
within a stone's throw of St. James's Street, was a deep vacant
plot with a good frontage. It was a splendid position but almost
too splendid. The question of licences for theatres was a very
tricky one indeed, and they both realized that there would be considerable opposition to the granting of a licence for a playhouse
in so august a neighbourhood. Mrs. Braham was less nervous
than the architect as she knew she could rely on the support of the
Burghershes, the Duke of Sussex, even the Duke of Wellington
himself.

A theatrical acquaintance, Yates, hearing of the King Street
venture, approached Mrs. Braham about another speculation. The
Colosseum, a vast pseudo-classical temple in Regent's Park, was

in the market, and Yates hoped to take it in partnership with Braham.

Mrs. Braham had exhausted her husband into agreement about the King Street theatre and now with despairing resignation he gave way about the Colosseum. A cheque for £30,000 transferred the management of the Regent's Park temple on 18 May 1835 to Messrs. Yates and Braham. Two days later Beazley, on Braham's behalf, bought the King Street site for £8,000.

Mrs. Braham and her architect wasted no time. The theatre, with a house for themselves, was to be finished by Christmas. All available strings were to be pulled to obtain the licence, a brilliant cast engaged, libretti and music to be commissioned—the immense fortune was just round the corner.

II. THE FIRST MARRIAGE 1835—1839

BRAHAM was too busy with concerts to devote himself to either concern. He arranged that most of his engagements were in London, but some absences were inevitable. In September he had to sing at the York Musical Festival, when his success particularly pleased him. In March the 'Antient Concerts' had been under the aegis of the Archbishop of York, who had, with great condescension, written a number of little notes, suggesting to Braham the best way to sing his various songs. The fantastic conceit of it had tickled the incomparable singer.

At the York Festival the Archbishop was again all-powerful and had most of his family with him, including his eldest son George with his beautiful but not over-faithful wife, Lady Elizabeth. Lord Esher has described Archbishop Harcourt as 'a very sumptuous prelate' which was, apparently, also the Duchess of Kent's opinion as with her daughter Princess Victoria she was staying at Bishopthorpe for the Festival. On most days the royal and archiepiscopal party lunched at the Deanery, one or two of the principal singers being invited to meet them. John Braham was so delighted to find that Grisi, Lablache, Rubini, and his former pupil Adelaide Kemble were singing with him, that he quite forgot to mention in his diary that he had lunched with his future Queen and her mother. His letter of September 8 must sorely have vexed his royalty-conscious wife, as he merely says among a host of other details, 'Princess Victoria and the Duchess of Kent at lunch'.

A musical critic who greatly appreciated Braham was the Scot, George Hogarth, who with his delightful wife and daughters welcomed and encouraged any struggling young musician, writer or artist in their impecunious household. Their latest protégé was a rather vulgar, flamboyant youth whose 'sketches', signed Boz, were attracting some attention in the newspapers. Both Braham and Hogarth were also interested in a young musician, John Hullah, so it was decided to commission the two young men to write the libretto and the music of an operetta for the new theatre. The

12

first production, however was to be an opera, *Agnes Sorel*, libretto by Gilbert à Beckett and the music by his wife.

The Colosseum, under its new management was, at first, a success. Yates was a shrewd business man, and trusted nobody in the theatrical world. He had been in management too long to have any illusions. Mrs. Braham on the other hand had almost no business experience at all, was full of optimism, and prepared to trust any plausible rogue. With Braham so frequently out of town, his wife was continually at the Colosseum suggesting improvements and alterations, which Yates invariably opposed. Braham concluded his diary for 1835, 'Separation between Yates and me, thank God.'

The St. James's Theatre opened on 14 December 1835 with the à Beckett opera, *Agnes Sorel*. Malicious little Creevey considered it 'by far the most beautiful Playhouse in London', and even Chorley, the Athenaeum's atrabilious musical critic who loathed Braham, was to admit it was the 'prettiest of all theatres, at home or abroad'. Its position in the heart of clubland and away from the crowds and smells of the Strand sounded excellent, but it took nearly forty years to make the theatre a success.

The initial setbacks in King Street worried Mrs. Braham not at all. Although the existing seating capacity did not justify it, she engaged casts regardless of expense, and was always commissioning new plays and operas. The Hullah-Boz opera was still not complete by August '36, though in July Mr. Dickens had written to tell Braham of the enthusiastic reception it had had at a private hearing in his rooms at Furnival's Inn. The thrusting young journalist was glad of this introduction to the great world and already in March had written to Catherine Hogarth urging her to go with him to the theatre and 'meet a set of people in which we are likely to be so interested'.

Braham had been amused by Boz's *Great Winglebury Duel*, and wrote suggesting that Dickens should use it as the basis of a two-act farce. He replied at once:

Furnivals Inn
Thursday afternoon

'Dear Sir,

We enclose you the parts of the Village Coquettes, complete, with the exception of the chorus, which will be ready in a few days.

'I beg my compliments to Mrs. Braham for whose satisfaction I have written a formal note on the other side, in which I accept your offer for a farce in due form. I have christened it *The Strange Gentleman*. Harley will be the strange gentleman of course and there will be several little points about his first appearance which I think both you and he will like. I will call on you, with the piece complete, and ready for the Performers, *next Sunday week*. But if you should intend leaving town before that day, I will make an additional effort to get it finished earlier, so that you may see it, before you go. I think, however, I recollect you to have said that you would not be absent until the 8th.

'I have not filled up old Vernon's part with the name of any performer because, in the absence of Strickland, I do not know to whom you propose giving it.

I am,

Dear Sir,

Very faithfully yours,

Charles Dickens'

'Mr. Hullah will be most happy to write another song for Miss Rainforth, if you continue to wish it. Our only anxiety is not to overburden the piece with songs. She has two already—one very showy one—and a good deal to do, in the concerted music.'

The enclosure read:

Furnivals Inn

25 *August* 1836

'Dear Sir,

I accept with pleasure your offer of *Thirty Pounds* for the copyright of a farce in two acts, called *The Strange Gentleman*, to be produced at the St. James's Theatre on the first of October, and paid for on the third night of representation.

Dear Sir,

Faithfully yours,

John Braham Esqre. Charles Dickens'

It was produced on 29 September 1836, and ran for over fifty nights, with Madame Sala as Julia Dobbs. Whatever its success, a two-act farce was only a small part of the programme and the other items did not draw.

After months of delay *The Village Coquettes* was announced for December 6, with Braham himself as the wicked Squire Norton. At the end of the piece Boz created a precedent by appearing on the stage. The vulgarity of such an innovation scandalized the critics, including the critic of the *Examiner*, John Forster, with whom this was young Mr. Dickens's first contact. The operetta had some success. Braham considered it 'triumphant' and found the notices 'except *The Times*, speak well'. He asked Boz to write another farce, this time for £100, and *Is She His Wife* appeared on the stage of the King Street theatre on 6 March 1837. It was not a success, though well received on the first night.

From 1836 on, life was a continual lawsuit for the Brahams. They were swindled right and left, the licences for both houses were constantly in jeopardy, and they were always either selling some of their house property, or borrowing to sink more money in another of Mrs. Braham's fantastic schemes.

At the Grange, Mrs. Braham still blithely entertained on a grand scale. She considered her staff of fourteen a minimum for running the house in comfort, and when in April '37, her eldest son Hamilton entered Worcester College, Oxford, she felt the expense of it was more than justified. Augustus and Charles were destined for the army. Ward was a strange child with an incomprehensible character and poor health, whose attendance at Mr. Pollard's academy was erratic. Trotty was also delicate, but Frances, who had inherited her father's splendid health and her mother's beauty, would have been a most satisfactory child had she not lived so entirely in a world of her own. She had the most charming, tender little voice, and was for her age an accomplished pianist, yet no one could persuade her to sing or play outside the most intimate family circle. The admiration which her fair, lovely colouring and tall graceful slenderness attracted at all the balls, to which her mother dragged her as soon as she was sixteen, made no impression on her. She was only happy with her grandmother, the old Wilsons, her beloved governess, Miss Grant, or, when he was on holiday from his school at Hofwyl, with Hutchinson Carroll.

When Hutchinson left school and appeared in uniform Frances was enchanted. They were inseparable, to Mrs. Braham's annoyance, as it was quite obvious that their affection was utterly fraternal, yet the fact that the girl so blatantly preferred his company discouraged other less fraternal admirers. Despite all their reverses, the Brahams' way of life showed no signs of financial strain, and Mrs. Braham meant her eldest daughter to marry before anyone could realize that her dowry had sadly shrunk.

Lord Frederick Beauclerk, the heir presumptive of his brother the Duke of St. Albans, was Frances's slave and, as no one knew how the Duchess of St. Albans would leave the Coutts millions, Mrs. Braham rather favoured the match, though her husband insisted that Lord Frederick was dissolute and only interested in marrying money. Unluckily for the young suitor the Duchess died in 1837, and it was soon known that she had left almost everything to the daughter of Braham's old friend, Sir Francis Burdett. Though Lord Frederick was still persistent Mrs. Braham did all in her power to discourage him.

Travelling about the country as much as he did, the finest holiday, in Braham's opinion, was a few weeks at the Grange, especially in August when London was empty and all his wife's friends in the country or at the sea. For his family it was dull, and they were glad of the few friends who had country houses within driving distance. Sometimes they would drive down to Beulah Spa for the day, or to a fête at the Duchess of St. Albans' at Highgate. Richmond was a pleasant drive and meant a day's boating or swimming for the boys. Mrs. Braham and her sister Josephine were, therefore, very glad to accept an invitation to a garden fête at Strawberry Hill in August 1833.

Horace Walpole had left his Gothic villa to his cousin, Mrs. Damer, with remainder to his great-niece, the widow of the fourth Earl Waldegrave and herself the daughter of the second earl. The lovely central figure in Reynolds' 'Ladies Waldegrave', she was a lachrymose creature, much given to bewailing the early death of her husband, the loss of her eldest son who was drowned at Eton, the unhappy state of the family finances and the wildness of the sixth earl. Her one consolation was her younger son, William, a strongly evangelical, naval man, most suitably married to the daughter of the wealthy Samuel Whitbread.

The last months of her life were darkened by a fear that her elder son would marry Annette King, the woman with whom he was living at Paris, where his regiment was stationed. In October

1814, Miss King had given birth to John James Henry Walde-grave, but it took a second pregnancy to persuade the earl to marry her, which he did at last in Paris exactly twelve months later. The news was too much for his mother, who died in the following January, ten days before Viscount Chewton drew his first breath.

The earl and countess arrived at Strawberry Hill in May 1816. Chewton was christened in Twickenham Church on June 11, and on June 12, 'John James, Earl of Waldegrave', married 'Anne, Countess of Waldegrave'—surely one of the oddest entries ever made in a parish register. Annette was determined that her position should be unassailable but, as the remarriage made everyone doubt the story of the Paris wedding, it led William Waldegrave, on his brother's death, to bring the question of the seventh earl's legitimacy before the House of Lords. The Paris wedding was proved to be valid but the young earl, naturally, never forgave his uncle.

In 1835 the sixth earl died. He left his Essex estates to the eldest boy, John, but the rest of the property went with the title to the second son, George, with due provision for Annette and the three daughters. The dowager found herself in a serious position. All the estates were heavily mortgaged, and needed years of careful administration. Neither of the boys was capable of managing anything but a four-in-hand, and John was scarcely capable of managing even that. He was remarkably good-looking—William IV considered him the handsomest young man in the kingdom, but he was epileptic and spent his life drinking with grooms and stable boys. George, the new earl, was at Oxford and could not be made to understand that there was simply no money to pay for his wild extravagances.

A young doctor, Algernon Hicks, was found to act as medical adviser and general Mentor for the boys. The eldest girl's health also caused constant anxiety and made a resident doctor almost essential. He was of quite good family and made an agreeable addition to the circle at Strawberry Hill and Dudbrook. At first it seemed to work admirably, but Hicks soon found that a little laxity towards his principal patient was rewarded by a handsome loan, and that he could get anything he wanted from the dowager by threatening to leave. She had few friends. The Waldegraves' relations, such as the Graftons, the Radstocks and the Seymours, were prepared to take some interest in the young earl, but they could not overlook Annette's early life.

George's career at Oxford was brief. He was soon back at Strawberry Hill making himself almost as notorious as his crony Lord Waterford and the whole Waterford set of rowdies, but Waterford was a large, bold, ruthless Irish marquis and the public found it easier to forgive his escapades than those of his slightly built, youthful companion, with his face of a mischievous child, who always had an attack of remorse when the adventure had gone too far.

Waterford's effrontery even carried him through the very unpleasant early months of 1838 when the lonelier outskirts of London were rendered unsafe for any woman by 'Spring-heeled Jack', widely acknowledged to be Waterford himself.

In August 1838 the Dowager Lady Waldegrave gave an alfresco dinner at Strawberry Hill. For her to get a full complement of guests was always rather a highways and hedges affair, and a number of oddities were asked.

Rogers, the poet banker, thought the occasion might provide him with some gossip for his next breakfast party. Lady Morgan, the Irish novelist, was in London, so was asked, as was another friend of the Brahams, a musical spinster, Flora McLeod. After the party in '33, Annette and her husband had dined at the Grange and a desultory sort of acquaintance had been kept up. Lady Morgan's and Miss McLeod's names reminded her of the Brahams so they, too, with the older children, were invited. The prospect bored Frances, but she went, looking charming with her lovely colouring, dressed in white with a feathered white chip bonnet and a pink satin cloak. There was no one she knew, so she wandered into the quaint house, up to the Long Gallery, and stood watching the guests below from one of the Gothic windows. The two hosts, from the lawn, saw the fair slender girl and ran up to find out who she was.

Before the party broke up Mrs. Braham felt all her troubles were over. John Waldegrave was even better looking than Hutchinson Carroll, infinitely wealthier than Lord Frederick, and was patently enslaved by Frances. Lady Waldegrave promised to bring her eldest girl and John to dine at the Grange in a month's time, and by then Frances could be persuaded to be a little more polite to them. As it was, she spent the drive back amusing her brothers with imitations of poor John Waldegrave's uncouth manners.

Annette wanted the match quite as much as Mrs. Braham. A daughter-in-law would take the appalling responsibility of the young man off her shoulders and, as the Grange was still run in great style, not even Flora McLeod realized that John Braham's fortune had vanished. Hicks had again threatened to leave, the mortgages on the Essex estates were crippling—a marriage between her eldest son and the rich Miss Braham was the one solution.

At first, however, nothing would persuade Frances. To her he was simply a drunken clod with none of Hutchinson's dash and none of Beauclerk's charm. Flora McLeod did all she could, Mrs. Braham stormed, and Charles, who also lived in a world of stables, pleaded for such a sympathetic brother-in-law. It was not until Mrs. Braham was badly shaken by a rumour that John was much poorer than she had been told, that Frances's attitude changed. As soon as her parents assured her that she need not consider herself bound by any understanding there might have been with John Waldegrave, she decided that there was an understanding.

She had never wanted to become Lady Frederick Beauclerk, but the way her mother had treated Lord Frederick had been humiliating for everybody. She would not be branded as a jilt to suit her mother's convenience. On her eighteenth birthday there was a dinner party at the Grange, and John who, since he had been frequenting the Grange, had been leading a sober and rational existence, persuaded her to accept him, but the engagement was not to be announced until the Brahams were more reasonable. Mrs. Braham was furious and raged at Frances, who retired to the refuge of her grandmother's cottage. From there she wrote separately to her father and mother.

'My dear Father,
    From the conversation which took place this morning, I am deeply grieved that you should have formed so erroneous an opinion of my sentiments towards Mr. Waldegrave—That I did not in the *first* instance (that is at the *time* when Miss McLeod made us acquainted with Mr. Waldegrave's intentions) feel any

particular regard for him is most true, but a more acquaintance with him and a firm belief in his affection for me, added to the high opinion I have of his amiability and honourable character, have converted that indifference into greater love and esteem for him than it appears I am thought capable of—and *that* perhaps arising from my old fault of showing a coldness in my manner very foreign from my Heart. I own to the Love and Habit of quizzing which often leads me to imitate where I am aware it would be more prudent to desist, but this, I assure you does not arise, *as may be thought*, from any dislike or disrespect to the Person. With regard to music, little as the whole of the Waldegrave family appreciate or care for it, added to my own particular dislike to exhibit as a performer on the piano still, if I thought it were likely to strengthen Mr. Waldegrave's affection for me, I would endeavour to surmount my own objections—This confession must prove to you how far I am from wishing to break off the engagement with Mr. W.—I am quite assured that my dear Mother's doubts and anxieties about me arise from the most affectionate motives and only regret that she should be made uneasy by any misconceived ideas respecting me, which lead her and you to suspect me of a worse disposition than I feel I possess. I hope my dear Father this explanation will satisfy you respecting my Feelings towards Mr. Waldegrave and that you will drive from your mind any belief in the cold and calculating nature of, my dearest Father,

Your ever most
affectionate daughter
Frances Braham'

The Grange
Wednesday, 9 *January* 1839

'My dearest Mother,

I am much grieved to hear of Mr. Abbot's conduct but whatever Mr. Waldegrave's Fortune may prove will make *no difference* to me as the love and esteem I bear him will, through life, either in adversity or prosperity be always my principal feeling.

Ever your affectionate daughter,
Fanny Braham'

Meanwhile Annette was none too happy. Lawyers on each side had begun discussing settlements, and it appeared that Frances would have little but Dee Side House, near Chester, worth about £5,000, which her godfather had left her in 1829, and eventually £2,500 from her mother's marriage settlement. No one, however, could believe that there was not a great deal more money to come from Braham. Lord Waldegrave, who was devoted to his brother, had, strangely enough, become far wilder ever since John had proposed. With Lord Waterford he was appearing sadly often at the police courts for beating-up night watchmen, upsetting hawkers' barrows and every variety of hooliganism. The eldest girl, Lady Laura, disliked her mother and was always ill. Annette felt friendless and despondent and, if Hicks went, there would be no one to help her.

At the Grange, things seemed, generally, a little brighter. Braham was having an enormous success in *William Tell* at Drury Lane, and neither the St. James's nor the Colosseum was doing too badly. Charles found John Waldegrave's dogs and horses better company than the butcher boys in Yeomans Row, and was delighted to go off to Dudbrook with him at the end of the month. They got back to the Grange on February 3 and John, for the first time, slept there, as the next night they were going to Drury Lane when the young Queen was to attend the thirty-third night of *William Tell*. It was a splendid occasion. Their box attracted nearly as much attention as the Queen's which pleased them until they found that the attention was caused by the latest scandal. Annette had married Hicks two days before.

Both her sons were furious and refused to receive her. With Dudbrook and Strawberry Hill closed to her, she settled with the three daughters at Doctor Hicks's house in Henrietta Street. It brought on one of John's attacks, and gave Frances a foretaste of what her married life would be, as he was too ill to be moved from the Grange for days. News of the Hicks's wedding reached Ireland where the officers in Augustus's mess were so full of the scandal that he had not the courage to tell them of his sister's engagement.

John's convalescence at Brompton and his mother's remarriage gave Mrs. Braham an opportunity to interest him in her theatrical affairs. She might have succeeded had her brother, Doctor George Bolton, not been called in to attend the invalid. Bolton had somehow acquired a reputation with the young men about town, and his consulting room at 9 Pall Mall was gratifyingly crowded. He was gay, easy-going and popular, but was prepared to sacrifice anyone, with the single exception of his mother, to his own interests. A great part of the trouble, both domestic and financial, that changed Mrs. Braham into a quarrelsome, scheming, querulous invalid, was caused by her brother's endless mischief-making.

At the end of February Mrs. Braham was delighted to hear that the Dudbrook estate was worth £20,000 more than they had been told. In April she had more definite news for her husband who was on tour. 'The settlement will be ready in less than three weeks and the wedding, Fanny wants on the 23rd May, Waldegrave this day week, but I say about the 13th. Lord Frederick Beauclerk came to our box last night at the St. James's. He told Augustus, Fanny behaved like an angel because she politely answered him when he spoke to her and shook hands with him. He said he could have twisted Waldegrave's neck round and that I broke off the match from seeing him so tipsy at the sale. Lord F. was quite sober, gentleman like and agreeable and Fanny continued to be as amiable as I could wish her to be. . . . The following is the amount of settlement made on *Fanny*. Dudbrook House and £1,000 a year; should she marry without having children, the house goes but she retains the £1,000 a year, but should she marry and have had children then she not only loses the house but has only £600 a year. Her own property is left to herself entirely to do what she likes with. Navestock and Langenhoe are settled, also Borley upon the children that are to be or I should rather say to the eldest son but he will have to pay off the estate £7,500 to each child to the amount of six but, if more, then £5,000. I think this is the correct account I had from Nicholson last night, he thinks it is a very fine settlement but it seems Waldegrave has a great deal more property to increase the settlement or I should rather say to leave by will.'

Although the strictest economy was essential in the Grange finances, the thought of so much money coming into the family encouraged Mrs. Braham to broadcast invitations to the splendid wedding breakfast she was determined to give. Hamilton at Oxford was finding Little Go an insuperable obstacle, and his gambling debts had, the previous year, involved him in a duel, but even to him his mother was benign.

'I have sent you, by this day's post, £45 and I am very glad you are able to come to the wedding . . . any young friend you should like to ask to the wedding we shall be happy to see. The Maryboroughs, Bagots, Fitzroy Somersets, Burghershes, etc., will be here, altogether about 150. Lord Waldegrave is one of the groomsmen. He sends Fanny flowers, etc., nearly every day. He is particularly amiable at present.'

As Hamilton had hopes, if he ever graduated, of one of the fat livings in John's gift—Borley, Langenhoe or Peldon—he tactfully chose a Bible as a wedding present. Augustus was on leave at home, and there was only one cloud in the Braham sky. The Waldegrave lawyers had heard rumours of financial difficulties at the St. James's Theatre and at the Colosseum, and had insisted upon John Braham renouncing his guardianship of the bride, should she be widowed during her minority, in favour of his friend and business associate Doctor Daniel.

III. MÉNAGE à TROIS

ON SATURDAY, 25 May 1839, at Holy Trinity Church, Brompton, near London, John James Henry Waldegrave was married to Frances Elizabeth Anne Braham. The congregation crossed the road to a magnificent reception in the grounds of the Grange, and watched the young couple drive off to Brighton for the honeymoon. The excitement, as usual, was too much for John, and brought on an attack which his wife hopefully diagnosed as only bilious. However, he soon recovered and Frances could assure her dearest Mamma that 'my dear husband is remarkably well and really looks five years younger' and John wrote to say that 'my dearest little wife is quite well and I try everything I can to make her happy and she does the same to me. I have grown quite steady and forsaken the bottle.'

After a fortnight they arrived at the Grange where Mrs. Braham broke up the party by miscarrying of twins, so bride and groom left the next day for Strawberry Hill where 'Lord Waldegrave had provided a beautiful dinner for us consisting of A Haunch of Mutton, A Beefstake Pudding, A Duck, Green Peas, Esparagus, New Potatoes, every kind of fruit, Champagne and all choice wines—We waited as long as we could for him and would have waited longer had not Mrs. Willis told us that he had left orders to all the servants that we were to be considered Master and Mistress of Strawberry Hill and that if he and Mr. Harbord did not arrive in time for dinner, they were not to be expected until the evening. Lord W. told Mrs. Willis that he hoped we would never think of leaving this place but to consider it entirely our own Home. From the minute we entered Twickenham they have not ceased ringing the bells. . . . I cannot tell you how beautiful Strawberry is looking—My rooms are most delightful and every pains seem to have been taken to make them comfortable.'

Three days later Frances tells her mother: 'I would not have imagined anyone could have been so kind or so like a brother

24

as my new dear relation. Ever since he has been here he has been as sober as a judge. . . . George seems to have made up his mind that we are *never to leave him*. I am quite mistress here, at least so they please to say . . . you have no idea how gentlemanly or how amusing his Lordship is. John is very well and very happy, he desires his best love to all. . . . I think when you write to me at Strawberry Hill you had better not style me The Honourable as his Lordship might, if he saw it, take it into his head that John would try for the title which of course would break the harmony that now exists between them.'

The fantastic *ménage à trois* had begun.

Frances found it difficult to realize that she was a married woman. Hay-making, pillow-fights, hide-and-seek in the shrubberies at Strawberry Hill, or wild dashes up to the Grange in Lord Waldegrave's four-in-hand with his friend Harbord, 'a complete stage coachman', in the box, parties on the river when her own brothers were on a visit, and all the time long-faced lawyers preaching economy, was the tale of their life that summer. In July they left for Dudbrook, Lord Waldegrave with them. Rent Day came at the beginning of August, and was all too welcome. The mortgages and John's debts swallowed up most of it, but they decided to give a tenants' ball and in a burst of philanthropy offered Frances's old great-uncle Wilson and his wife a cottage at Dudbrook. Piqued by this, the circle at the Grange decided to be malicious and was so unpleasant to the old couple that they tearfully refused to accept it. It was all very trivial but was, indirectly, to cause Mrs. Braham years of unhappiness.

Writing to her mother in August from Essex, Frances's attitude to her own household was clear. 'George, John and myself will dine with you on Sunday next at 7 o'clock if not inconvenient —pray write and let me know as soon as you can. Will you ask Uncle George to meet us as my two little children Johnny and Geo as well as their venerable Mamma would like to see him. . . . Revd. and Mrs. Linzee and Miss Linzee have just called— Kelvedon Hall—I don't know a bit in the world who they are— John says they are one of the oldest families in Essex. People, you will be glad to hear, are calling every day—but our most frequent visitors are the Creditors—a *remarkable old family* and John's most intimate. . . . John and Geo just rang for North and Edward to dress them when to their astonishment they heard that the 2 Gentlemen's Gentlemen *were gone out shooting.*'

Braham was not so cheerful as his daughter. He was singing in Ireland in September at a time when the Colosseum was doing well, but the optimism in his wife's letters tried his patience and he wrote: 'I have this morning made a correct account of what I individually earned this last 10 months.' The amount, neatly tabulated was £1,773 18s. 0d. 'Is this not frightful to contemplate that such a sum should be absorbed without being able to keep out of debt and, with the income from the Colosseum, not to be able to pay the interests due to the different parties? This sum alone ought almost to have kept the Grange and family expenses. You see, my love, what an indifferent calculator you are. Does it not show the necessity of a tremendous reduction in our expenses?' When he arrived back at the Grange he found the usual extravagant way of life there, and when, a few days later Frances, John and George (Lord Waldegrave) dined there, he enters in his diary, 'singing, drinking and yelling'.

In November the St. James's Theatre opened under new management, but the theatrical slump continued, and within a fortnight Braham's diary reads: 'Only 2/- in the house tonight and one of them a bad one.' Four days after that entry the new manager went bankrupt. By the middle of December Mrs. Braham was forced to pawn her jewels for £500, but she still would not agree to move to a smaller house. Frances and John were in no position to help and the visits to the Grange became so embarrassing, that they were only possible if liberally assisted by wine. Although Braham was an abstemious man, his sons drank quite as hard as the Waldegrave brothers, and George Bolton encouraged them all. Probably it was too gay a life at Strawberry Hill, for by Christmas John was in a bad state.

Braham began his diary for 1840 'disappointment from every quarter'. It was not much brighter at Dudbrook. John Waldegrave was being dunned for bills amounting to £4,560, and that only represented half his outstanding debts. With the interest to pay on the mortgages there was no chance of any income for the next nine months, and, as the advowson of the Rectory of Borley was tied up in the marriage settlements, he could raise no money by that. His lawyers besought him to sell some of his horses, but he simply retired to his brother's at Strawberry Hill and forgot about it. His health was steadily deteriorating, and even one glass of wine was too much for him.

Lord Waldegrave was, as always, gentle and considerate with Frances. He could still be as great a hooligan as any of Lord Waterford's cronies, but in her presence, he was invariably a kind, perfect host. Young Ward Braham spent most of his time at Strawberry Hill, which he preferred to the Grange where his mother lived in a constant turmoil of plans and business. Her optimism was unflagging. The Queen's marriage inspired her. The St. James's should be renamed the Prince's Theatre. All her more eminent friends were commissioned to arrange it. On March 12 Prince Albert graciously gave his consent and the Queen agreed to a Royal Box. The house adjoining was promptly pulled to bits to make a suitably Royal entrance, and as usual Mrs. Braham expected 'an immense fortune'.

On March 25 Ensign Augustus Braham sailed for the Mauritius where his mother, though sad at his departure, was convinced he too would make the inevitable fortune. She admitted to her husband that she had become very irritable and 'passionate' with all the responsibility, but far more was her bad temper caused by the endless mischief made by her brother, George Bolton, and her old aunt and uncle, the Wilsons, who always hoped to increase Frances's affection for themselves by alienating her still further from her parents.

On March 28 she told Braham, 'Fanny, I am happy to say, is going to Court on the 9th April'. By April 6 she was refusing an invitation to Flora McLeod's party as the Waldegraves would be there. She had tried to interfere in the youthful *ménage à trois* and Frances had been annoyed, but a few days later she wrote:

'My dear Mamma,

Pray do not let us look black at each other any more and forgive and forget my temper the other day and, let us, for the future, always meet with the love we bear each other in our faces and then I am sure you will always feel pleasure when, my dear Mamma, you meet your affectionate daughter,

F. Waldegrave'

To this Mrs. Braham made no reply and studiously avoided any meeting with her daughter. Frances followed her example, but, as she was determined still to see her brother Ward, she met him at his tutor's. Mrs. Braham expressed her indignation at this, and John Waldegrave at once wrote to George Bolton.

'Dear George,

Fanny wrote a very kind and affectionate letter to her Mamma which she has not had the good breeding to answer and I am determined therefore not to allow Mrs. Waldegrave either to write or visit the Grange until an apology has been offered—This letter you are welcome to show. With best love from Fanny and myself,

I remain,

Every yours most truly,

J. Waldegrave'

On April 12 Mrs. Braham, in a letter to her husband, mentions that 'Ward called upon Lord Waldegrave who told him that John Waldegrave had had a fit and was very ill, dangerously so. Ward is going down to Strawberry Hill to see them. I, therefore, may perhaps see them. Lord W. said this is the second fit he has had, both in 48 hours; he cannot live long and they dread his being worse. G.B. [George Bolton] had just been sent for; a Doctor Clark of Richmond is attending him.'

On April 16 'John Waldegrave is out of immediate danger for which I am very grateful'. Encouraged by the recovery, John, Frances and Lord Waldegrave drove down to Dudbrook, but, by the twenty-fourth, John's health had so deteriorated that they set off for London in a carriage and four. At Woodford, John had a fit, but appeared to recover. They drove on to London, direct to George Bolton's surgery at 9 Pall Mall. As they arrived John had another fit. No. 9 was apparently closed and, while their manservant was hammering on the door and Lord Waldegrave was trying to hold his brother down, Frances in terror ran from house to house trying to get a glass of water for her husband. Another doctor was found and John was taken to 38 Jermyn Street where they had occasionally spent a night or two. His brother drove off to look for Bolton, and Frances found herself alone with a raving imbecile. He could not recognize her, and was convinced that she was some woman of the streets who was keeping him from his beloved Frances. She dared not look away from him for a moment because he kept trying to get past her to his dear wife. She knew it would not be for long as George Bolton would arrive at any moment. Unfortunately Bolton thought Lord Waldegrave was exaggerating the case, and did not appear till the next morning, by which time the poor girl was in a state of collapse.

Twenty-four hours later John Waldegrave was dead.

John Braham was singing at Derby when he heard the news. He at once returned to London, and went directly with his wife to Jermyn Street. The nineteen-year-old widow was too exhausted and miserable to have made any plans. She was even too tired to resist her mother's outburst of tenderness. Flora McLeod was with her, and Frances was more at ease with an intimate friend of the Waldegrave brothers than with the woman who had invariably criticized her.

It was difficult however for Mrs. Braham to give her whole mind to sympathy, as one of her dearest plans was about to be realized. The Queen had announced her intention of attending the Prince's Theatre with Prince Albert and the Duchess of Kent three days later to see *Don Juan*. On the evening of her triumph, she heard yet more splendid news. John Waldegrave had left everything to his widow.

At last there would be money enough to realize all her schemes for both the Colosseum and the Prince's Theatre. Doctor Daniel was, by the marriage settlements, Frances's guardian during her minority, but that could surely be set aside in favour of her own father. An optimistic lawyer was found to agree with her, and by the next day she had persuaded her husband that it was his duty to reassert his claim to the guardianship.

Once again Mrs. Braham had over-reached herself. Frances learned of it and immediately sent Doctor Daniel to the Grange to announce that she had decided to pay Flora McLeod an indefinite visit at her house in Wilton Place. As usual the worst sufferer was the old singer. His wife went into one of her almost apopletic rages and had to be 'cupped'. She was too ill for him to leave her, which resulted in his not being present the following day at his son-in-law's funeral.

Flora McLeod was a strange creature. She had known the Waldegraves all her life and the Brahams for nearly twenty years.

Since her mother's death she had been living at 9 Wilton Place and giving rein to her passion for the theatrical world. She was as full of plans for the Colosseum and the theatre in King Street as Mrs. Braham herself, and this had caused the first coolness. The Waldegrave brothers had always treated her as if she was an indulgent maiden aunt, and she had always joined good-humouredly in any of their rather childish games at Strawberry Hill or in her own house. She never preached economy, and never told Frances that her high spirits were unbecoming to a married woman.

During John's illness Frances had come to depend entirely on her brother-in-law and Flora, and was so accustomed to Lord Waldegrave's presence that she took it for granted that she should still see him as regularly. From the beginning John had left all arrangements to his wife and his brother, and the two of them grew to think of him as their joint responsibility. The trio had been inseparable. Doctor Hicks's behaviour on the one hand and Mrs. Braham's on the other had forced them into a kind of isolation, and had strengthened their dependence on each other. For nearly a year Lord Waldegrave had looked on Frances as the chatelaine of Strawberry Hill, and for as long she had relied on his gentle, chivalrous tenderness.

He came regularly to Wilton Place. There was so much to discuss about the Essex estates and the problem of Doctor Daniel's trusteeship. The easy-going Flora saw no harm in it, and was glad that anyone should help her to make the young widow forget her unhappiness for a little.

It was unfortunate for Frances that the gutter press of the early forties had reached such a degree of scurrility. Their gossip writers were delighted that the notorious young earl should be attentive to his brother's widow. Their attitude was highly moral. John Waldegrave's death of delirium tremens was a warning to all frivolous young men. They expressed amazement that the widow should still associate with so disreputable a character as her brother-in-law.

Mrs. Braham read each and every paragraph. She knew that her friends were all discussing Frances's refusal to live at the Grange, and she felt they were all reading these scandals. When Frances heard that her mother had recovered, she wrote:

'My dear Mamma,

It has made me very happy to hear you are so much better and I trust you will soon be quite recovered. Miss Flora McLeod unites in kindest love to yourself and all at the Grange with

your affectionate daughter,

Frances Waldegrave'

Mrs. Braham promptly replied insisting upon Frances's returning to the Grange. Frances refused, giving her reason. Then her mother lost her temper completely.

'This is no occasion for falsehood, Fanny, but that you should descend to such means merely to throw off the restraint of a mother's love does not augur well for your future happiness. You might have been a pride and blessing to your family, let me pray you may not be their shame.

'Poor John Waldegrave knows now I was his only friend, had he followed my advice for the last six months, you need not be deploring his decease and alas I fear the world suspects it too.'

She goes on to reproach Frances for having allowed her husband and his brother, during a pillow-fight at Flora McLeod's 'to enter her [Flora's] room when she had only on her night chemise and race her about with pillows'. For Mrs. Braham, this enormity put Frances forever beyond the pale.

'When I asked you to stay one week I did so with the hope of checking, if possible, the reports in circulation. Bells Life in London I am told, announced his death as a victim of intemperance and held him out as a warning to his brother and others—this my dear child does not place you in an amiable light and doubly requires great circumspection on your part. . . . Strange rumours are afloat, your own heart, if you possess one, which I very much doubt, will answer this question.'

Frances never spoke to her mother again. It naturally meant a separation from her father, and she was more than ever thrown on the affection of Miss McLeod and Lord Waldegrave. Flora, however, was at last aroused by Mrs. Braham's letter to the indiscretion of having Lord Waldegrave so frequently at Wilton Place. Obviously the best thing for her guest was to marry, and Lord Reidhaven was only too anxious to acquire so beautiful and wealthy a wife. Frances refused to show any interest in him, and could not understand why Flora would not receive the man who, for over a year, had been the dearest and best of brothers, the man who 'looked like a Prince and treated her like a Goddess'. She particularly wanted to see him as Flora was growing more persistent about Lord Reidhaven. Another thing was embarrassing her. The living expenses at Wilton Place were increasing week by week, yet she hardly liked to ask her hostess for an account of how the money was spent. Never had she needed the earl so much, and she was miserable without him. When, the year before, she had written of the three of them as 'my two little children Johnny and Geo as well as their venerable Mamma', it had partly expressed her feelings. Her brother-in-law had the most engaging look of a mischievous small boy that made even her youthful heart maternal.

She was worried about him, as she heard that he was again with the rowdy Waterford set, and that, since Flora had banished him, he was drinking heavily. For the Derby he had various men friends with him at Strawberry Hill who on their way back from the races had somehow purloined a racegoer's hat. On the Thursday they were again at the races, and in the evening Lord Waldegrave and three friends in masquerade drove to Kingston Fair, which outdid Greenwich in riotousness. Soon after midnight, on the way to Twickenham one of the party—they had all wined plentifully—decided 'to knock up a woman who kept a mangle' at Hampton Wick—door knockers had an irresistible fascination for Lord Waterford—and a policeman was rather tactless in the way he tried to quieten them. There was a struggle outside the Swan Inn. Police Constable Charles Wheatley got badly knocked about, and, though for a time he managed to hold the smallest of the party, they all succeeded in getting away, but left behind the hat they had taken on Derby Day.

The owner of the hat was traced and through him the police were able to identify Lord Waldegrave and his friend, Captain Duff. On June 27 they appeared before the Twickenham magistrates and were committed on bail to the Assizes. They refused to divulge the names of the other two, but the newspapers were careful to announce that Lord Waterford had left that day by sea for his castle in Northumberland.

The public was thoroughly tired of the hooliganism of the Waterford set, and everyone wanted to see an example made of one of them. Frances was in a frenzy. Her poor George who was so gay, so light-hearted, so generous and so kind was now as friendless as herself.

She wrote expressing all the sympathy she felt and, defying Flora, insisted upon his calling. To her astonishment he came, not the dejected creature she expected, but half delirious with joy. His lawyer had at last established that as John was illegitimate in the eyes of the law, he did not count as George's brother and that he, George, was thus free to marry Frances if she would accept him. Before she realized what she was doing, Frances had rushed upstairs for her Prayer Book. There it was in the table of Kindred, 'deceased husband's brother'. Lord Waldegrave explained all over again and she had to listen to an incomprehensible account of the Act of 1835, which forbade marriages with deceased husbands' brothers and deceased wives' sisters, though grudgingly admitting the validity of such marriages as had been solemnized before the passing of the Act.

In the excitement of the whole thing, she had had no time to analyze her own feelings. Her first thought had been that it would mean the old happy Strawberry Hill and Dudbrook life, but now she realized that she did most desperately want to marry him. She was completely dazed. She had never thought of marrying him, though so often during the previous twelve months she had wished that John could somehow be changed into another George. In any case she would never marry him if he wanted the marriage only to protect his brother's widow. George reassured her. From the moment he had seen her in the long gallery at Strawberry Hill he had meant to propose, and was horrified to find his brother had forestalled him. He had forced himself to accept the situation and had resigned himself to devoting his life to her as the perfect brother-in-law.

It was all useless. There it stood in the Prayer Book that in the eyes of the Church it was forbidden whatever the legal position might be. At last Lord Waldegrave persuaded her to agree that, if there was nothing in the Bible to forbid such a marriage, she would accept him, but, in any case, she must leave Wilton Place at once as he would hear no more talk of Lord Reidhaven. They agreed that she should engage a companion, and go down to Dudbrook with Great-Uncle and Aunt Wilson and begin her Biblical

33

research. Painful as it was for her, Frances stipulated that he should not visit her again till she had the Bible's sanction for the wedding.

They had both entirely forgotten that he had been committed to the Assizes. They had, however, not forgotten that Frances was a minor and that everything would depend on Doctor Daniel's ability to maintain his trusteeship. The old Wilsons were delighted to go to Dudbrook, they both loved the earl, and loved even more the prospect of spiting Mrs. Braham. Both of them joined in the hunt through the Bible, though it is doubtful that they would have mentioned any unfavourable find. Frances assiduously read and read, sending regular progress reports to Strawberry Hill. Lord Waldegrave was almost daily with his lawyer, and had the wording of the Marriage Act of 1835 as word perfect as Frances had her Bible. John's marriage had not been consummated in view of his health. The disastrous Act of '35 excluded Scotland. John had had no legal status. The lawyer, Mr. Pearson, found every proof that this marriage would be valid.

The lawyer's arguments had not the slightest effect on Frances. If there was nothing in the Bible to forbid it, she would marry him. Nothing else would persuade her.

Her father was badly upset by the quarrel between Frances and her mother. He himself, had no desire to see her fortune disappear into the bottomless sack of his wife's theatrical projects, and he knew too well how bottomless it was. He, who had made never less than ten thousand a year for over twenty years, had to tour the country singing anywhere that promised a few pounds towards the ghastly debts—if he was lucky, making a bare two hundred pounds a month. He was well into his sixties and wanted rest. He was still infatuated with his wife and when they were together, she could persuade him to anything, but his letters to her began to betray a weary impatience. Hamilton could no longer hope for a Waldegrave living, so he decided that the law was his destiny. It was sadly obvious that his genius would never flower at Oxford and his mother was convinced that Cambridge would solve all problems. His father had no illusions and was, for once, severe with Mrs. Braham:

'I am sorry to find you touch upon the *insane point* of Cambridge. Is not one disappointment sufficient? You know I was always against the vain project of sending any of my children to the University—the result proves I was right. But the dazzling *vulgarity* of the thing blinded me. John knows more than is necessary of the Classics for the legal profession, whereas upon the point of Law, History and Politics he is as innocent as nurse Goodchild. What has Horace or Homer to do with law proceedings? but merely as now and then an ornament by way of quotation?'

He already foresaw that their creditors might drive them abroad when their only hope would be an American tour, but he was a very tired man and most of his arguments ended 'but do as you will'.

His one consolation was that Mendelssohn would be at the Birmingham Festival in September and that he, Braham, was to sing his *Lobgesang*. Even the presence of the composer did not detract from the great tenor's personal triumph and to his audience his voice was as superb as it had been twenty years earlier. In London, however, it was no tale of triumph for his wife. She suddenly lost her nerve and, remembering Braham's prophecy, decided that their only chance lay in America. On September 24 she wrote to Birmingham announcing her decision, and on October 1, Mr. and Mrs. Braham, little Josephine, Aunt Seph, Charles and Braham's personal servant sailed in the *President* from Liverpool.

They had heard a rumour that Frances had, some weeks before, gone to Edinburgh with Great-Uncle Wilson and her companion, but they were too much occupied with their own affairs to be interested in where young Mrs. Waldegrave chose to spend the autumn. Frances also had no time to worry about the household at the Grange. She had, at last, convinced herself that whatever the Anglican Prayer Book might say, the Bible nowhere forbade her marriage to Lord Waldegrave. On the Monday before the *President* sailed for America, at a ceremony in Edinburgh that would have been quiet had the best man, Captain Billy Duff, not been a little tipsy, George Edward, seventh Earl Waldegrave was married to Frances Anne Waldegrave, widow, of Navestock, Essex.

FRANCES learned of her father's departure from the newspapers, but did not know that so many of the family had accompanied him. She at once sent Charles and Ward four sovereigns apiece, telling them that 'whenever either of you want anything do not fail to write and ask me'. To this Ward replied with the smugness of his sixteen years:

'Not having been allowed to receive money without the sanction of our good parents I should not feel comfortable to avail myself of your generosity, now that they are absent. When I can inform them of it and am favoured with their approval I shall with gratitude accept any kind favour from my always beloved sister.' Since he spent the next thirty-six years living exclusively and extremely well on kind favours from his always beloved sister, it was probably as well that he left himself the loophole of the last sentence. In a letter to his parents the same week, he admits he has heard that 'Lord W. never drinks nor has so indulged for the last three or four months or she would not have married him, that they go to church regularly—play whist every night and afford a perfect example of domestic felicity'.

Lord and Lady Waldegrave spent the next three months in Edinburgh. Their wedding had aroused a great deal of comment —Mrs. Braham, reading of it in the American press, wrote bitterly to Grandmamma Bolton that the Americans knew more about it than she did—and George and Frances preferred to let the discussion die down before they returned to the south. Edinburgh had the advantage of keeping her husband away from his more riotous friends. Captain Duff's behaviour at the wedding had provided her with an excuse for discouraging him. As both he and George were out on bail together, until the case came up for trial they were bound to be to some extent in contact. He was an amusing companion but a dangerous influence for Waldegrave. His passion for the underworld brought him in touch with half the thieves and pickpockets in the kingdom, and he had quite a prosperous career recovering stolen goods since he charged a handsome percentage. One night he was searching for a watch in one of their dens, when a Birmingham professional who didn't know him doubted his word and was uncivil. Duff knocked him down, on which his London colleagues remarked, 'You're rayther 'ard on 'im, Cap'n, but I must say 'e did not speak very gentlemanly.'

Frances's first marriage had scarcely been a marriage at all. She had never felt more than a pitiful affection for John, and her attitude had been rather that of a devoted nurse to a delicate child than that of a wife. She had had to show all the care, consideration and tenderness. Now she had a husband who devoted his entire life to her, who was determined to make her forget the months of anxiety with John, and whose happiness lay in being always with her. The gossip about them, since it affected her, entirely changed Waldegrave's attitude to society. The familiarity he had allowed all his companions was at an end. Frances was the Countess Waldegrave, and must be treated with all the honour and respect due to her rank.

To Frances it mattered very little. She had never enjoyed her mother's vast parties, and although she loved dancing, Waldegrave was a very indifferent dancer and was miserable at a ball. Their life alone together was so happy that their comparative isolation never struck her. She was in such a good humour with the world in general that in a letter to her grandmother she told her, 'When next you write to Mamma, give her, Papa, Charles, Aunt Seph and Josephine my love and tell Mamma if it would give her any pleasure to hear from me it will make me very happy.' Mrs. Braham's reply was, however, so sanctimonious, full of the long suffering martyrdom of a mother's heart, that either Mrs. Bolton had not the courage to pass it on, or Frances was too irritated by it to do anything more.

Early in '41 they were back at Strawberry Hill where Ward was staying with them. In March there was splendid news for old Mrs. Bolton. 'I hope Papa and Mamma and all my Family are quite well. When next you write pray give them my kindest love. I trust in six or seven months if all goes well with my health to introduce to you your little Great-grandson Lord Chewton.' Unfortunately the Court of Queen's Bench was awaiting Lord Waldegrave, where with Duff he was to appear on April 29. The next day *The Times* announced, 'The court was crowded to excess this morning in the expectation of Lord Waldegrave being brought up to receive the judgment of the court, but the curious were doomed to disappointment.' *The Morning Herald* had published the prosecution affidavits with libellous comments under the heading of 'The Waldegrave Outrage', and, presumably in some connection with that, the defence had the trial postponed to Monday, May 3. Once again there were enormous crowds with their usual ghoulish delight in the degradation of a public figure. Both Duff and Waldegrave pleaded guilty and were sentenced to six months' detention in the Queen's Bench, with fines of £20 and £200 respectively.

Frances awaited the result at Thomas's Hotel, Berkeley Square, and from the court her husband wrote:

'My own Darling,
6 months Queen's Bench. I will send Beavan to tell you when we have arranged our appartments. For God's sake take care. Be under no fear that I will do anything or look at anybody.

Your ever fond Husband,
Waldegrave'

Even the provincial newspapers were full of it. 'When Lord Waldegrave arrived in the Queen's Bench on Monday week, he proceeded to the coffee room of the prison. He has the apartments over the lobby of the prison, occupied by Sir Francis Burdett when he was committed to the custody of the marshal. He has a numerous retinue about him, sees a good deal of company and lives in excellent style.' The public, having thoroughly enjoyed the sacrifice of their victim, were now remorseful and full of sympathy for him. They were therefore enchanted when Frances insisted on sharing her husband's imprisonment, and the young earl and countess became the hero and heroine of the day. She at once invited Grandmamma Bolton to visit them.

Queen's Bench
Tuesday

'My dear Grandmamma,
You will be glad to hear we have very comfortable rooms in the Queen's Bench and are very well and as happy as we can be under

the circumstances. We shall be most happy to send our carriage for you any day you would like to come and see us. With our best love believe me dear Grandmamma

Ever yours most affectionately
Frances Waldegrave'

They gave delightful dinner parties and led a far more social life than they had led since Frances's first marriage. She sent her brother Charles in America an account of their life.

Queen's Bench
July 16, 1841

'My dearest Charles,

Your letter gave me very great pleasure and I am delighted to hear that my Father is getting on so well and I hope and pray you will all keep your health and be as happy and prosperous as I wish you to be—I suppose you have heard by this time we are in the Queen's Bench owing to the unfortunate policeman affair but we are as happy as we can be considering the horrid confinement and all our relations and friends have been most kind—The Queen takes the greatest interest in us and is most anxious to find an excuse to let us out. Of course as we have been in here two months I have not much news to tell you—I have not heard from dear Augustus but hope he is going on well—Ward has just returned from Dudbrook where he has been staying during a fortnight of his holidays, he has been very happy riding Peggy and fishing and driving out with Morris, he has grown very tall and so much improved I hardly think you would know him. I suppose you know Lady Laura is married to a Colonel Money he is sixty five and Laura twenty three, neither Lord Euston or any of us quite liked the marriage on account of the great difference in their ages—You will be glad to hear Grandmamma and Aunt and Uncle Wilson are quite well—You cannot think how sorry I was to hear you had so much illness amongst you but I hope and trust you are all by this time quite recovered—With very best love to Papa, Mamma, Aunt Josephine, Trot and yourself.

Believe me dearest Charley ever
Your most affectionate sister
Frances Waldegrave'

'You must excuse this hasty scrawl. Waldegrave says you may show this letter to anyone you please as you know someone who said he only married me for my fortune. You know as well as all *his* relations and all the world except them (who never could feel love for anything in the world except money and title) how he adores me. Burn this with my note. You need not say he told you to show it and you need not show it unless you like but if you ever hear my family cast any doubt on his love and affection for me then Waldegrave desires you will show it. So you had better always keep it by you.'

She enclosed a letter from her husband:

Queen's Bench
July 16, 1841

'My dear Charles,

Here we are your blessed sister and myself confined for an assault which could not have been proved had we not pleaded guilty on a policeman last year. I say we as my darling wife has not left me *one moment* since our marriage and whether in a palace or prison our love for one another only increases, we hope soon however to get out through the kind exertions of our dearly beloved cousin Vic. I. who is deeply interested in Fanny. We are as comfortable as can be have our own servants—friends to dinner, relations paying continual visits in fact a perfect hive of *Condolents* I confess not so much on my account as to show their admiration which is felt from the highest to the lowest for the exemplary conduct and devotion which your sister (you ought to be proud of her) has shown in sharing with me the confinement in this prison. I regret to hear that you have all been so unwell but I trust by this time that you are recovering your health. At Strawberry Hill and Dudbrook last time we were there everything was looking beautiful the horses and dogs in high form. Flint is quite well. Othello was obliged to be shot on account of old age—Morris and Billy are quite well. Jimmy and all our pets are in the enjoyment of good health. The horses at Strawberry are in Physick to be ready for our release. We have had to kill a grey horse which used to go in the team and two cows have died the only casualties. This is all the news of our home affairs which will interest you.

'By the time you get this scrawl our party the Tories will be in, the elections have driven the Pigmy Lord John Russell half mad, he is obliged (the only wise step he has taken lately) to have recourse to matrimony as a solace, he is to be married to a daughter of Lord Minto next week. The Rads will be in a minority of 86 when Parliament meets. Vic is to be in the straw again in October or beginning of November. We have not heard from Augustus I hope he is well he must soon get promoted there is only one Ensign before him on the list. Ward appears quite well, I doubt if you would know him again he has been staying a fortnight at Dudbrook, he is a most excellent amiable boy and I am very fond of him and am fully persuaded from what Fanny has told me that I should have the same feeling for you if I knew more of you. My dear Charles I have told you all the news I can think of the only thing I regret is that owing to *some* letters *now* in my possession *containing accusations and abusing in the most horrid terms* my dearest wife which I can never forgive or forget prevents me from adding my kind regards to your parents but at the same time I wish them every success and health.

Believe me,

Your very affectionate brother-in-law,

Waldegrave'

Their time in the Queen's Bench passed happily enough, but they had two disappointments. Frances's anxiety about the trial brought on a miscarriage, and, despite her desire to help, 'Vic. I' could find no reasonable grounds for obtaining Waldegrave's early release. When they finally left, showering Bibles and other presents on their gaolers, they were given a tumultuous send-off.

In January 1842, Frances attained her majority. Although John Waldegrave's will was not proved until May, it was now far simpler for their lawyer Pearson to deal with the combined estates. The debts and encumbrances generally were crippling, but, with the strictest economy and care for a few years, the Waldegraves would be a very wealthy couple. They were certainly being dunned right and left, and there was no cash in hand for anything but the simplest life. Three or four years in comparative retirement in Essex or Somersetshire would put everything right. A quiet life in England, however, in no way attracted Lord Waldegrave. His friends were accustomed to his prodigal, open-

41

handed ways, and he cared for neither their sympathy nor the prospect of eating humble pie in front of his creditors.

He had taken a violent dislike to Twickenham. He, his father, his grandmother and Horace Walpole himself had invariably been very liberal in their dealings with the parish, yet it was the Twickenham bench that had committed him to the assizes. Walpole's lath and plaster villa was in a sad state of disrepair and would, if neglected, be a total ruin in a year or two. It was, however, full of the treasures Walpole had collected, in which the young earl had not the remotest interest. They should all be sold, and the shell of Strawberry Hill left to remind Twickenham of its ingratitude.

The announcement of the sale caused a tremendous sensation. Much as the press disliked and distrusted the auctioneer, George Robins, they could not resist leading articles on the subject. Even the sedate *Athenaeum*, week after week, enlarged upon it. Enormous marquees appeared on the lawns at Strawberry Hill, and all London crowded there. The sale began on April 25, and was to last twenty-four days. Even the family portraits were included but Frances, unknown to her husband, had them bought in for her. The list 'to be bought in' in her handwriting still exists and includes Reynolds's superb 'Ladies Waldegrave', 'Maria, Lady Waldegrave', 'James, Earl of Waldegrave', and Ramsey's 'Laura and Charlotte Waldegrave'.

The sale at Strawberry Hill realized £33, 468 and provided Mr. Pearson with the means to pacify the creditors. Their acquaintances were therefore rather surprised when Lord and Lady Waldegrave left England while the sale was in progress. Frances vaguely announced that they would be travelling abroad 'until a Bill in Chancery is passed to settle all our affairs', but it was generally assumed that their debts must be larger than anyone had imagined.

It was, however, John Braham's debts that they were trying to escape. The affairs of both the St. James's Theatre and the Colosseum had grown more involved than ever, thanks to Hamilton's incompetent management. The American tour had not been as financially successful as Braham had hoped, and Mrs. Braham insisted on living on far too grand a scale to leave much to send to the English creditors. Her friend Sir Charles Bagot was now Governor-General of Canada, and Mrs. Braham felt she could not embarrass him by petty economies while in the colony. The

Charles Dickenses arrived in America in 1841 and, though neither Braham nor his wife much cared for him, they found Mrs. Dickens delightful, and, for the sake of her company, had to lead the same flamboyant life that the young novelist favoured.

Mrs. Braham, unwisely, saw to it that the English press was kept liberally supplied with accounts of her husband's triumphs all over the United States and Canada, with the result that even their friends such as Frances's guardian, Doctor Daniel, began to press for repayment. They were thousands in Daniel's debt and, at last, he decided to sell up the Grange. The sale had been announced while the Strawberry Hill sale was in progress. It was a most unpleasant situation for the young Waldegraves. If they stayed in England they would be expected to buy in almost everything that was sold at the Grange, yet, to pay their own debts, they had to sell their own treasures for half their value. The position was not improved by Doctor Daniel's being Frances's guardian and being on reasonably good terms with her.

Mrs. Braham had so thoroughly alienated her eldest daughter, that both George and Frances now believed her capable of anything to save her beloved theatre. Those months of searching through the Bible had not completely reassured Frances; George was her deceased husband's brother; she, a minor, had married him without her father's consent, and nobody seemed to have much faith in the validity of Scottish marriages. From his mother, with her determination to make her own marriage doubly secure, and from the painful proceedings on his succession, Waldegrave had an almost pathological dread that his marriage to Frances could be set aside. They were both certain—quite unjustifiably—that if Mrs. Braham thought she could get control of the Essex estates by upsetting the marriage, she would do so.

They arrived in Hamburg on the day of the disastrous fire that destroyed half the city, and from Lübeck, where they stayed until Hamburg was again habitable, Frances sent Ward a highly coloured account of the catastrophe and of their journey—'our courier travels before us in a carriage and pair of Post Horses—in one place we had six horses, they are dressed in scarlet and gold and when we enter any town or a carriage is before us, they blow their horns for the people to know we are coming'.

At the end of the month 'Lord Stuart de Rothesay, the Russian ambassador called upon us . . . on his way to England. His daughter is going to be married to Lord Waterford.' Another rake was to be reformed, and Waterford soon found himself reading a chapter of the Bible a day to his Louisa till his death out hunting some fifteen years later.

After a month in Dresden they returned to Hamburg to meet their devoted lawyer, Pearson, and his wife, and then in the autumn went to Frankfurt and Switzerland. They wintered on the Riviera and, as soon as the Mont Cenis road reopened, they drove to Geneva.

The Canton of Neuchatel did not become completely Swiss until 1857 and, though almost entirely French speaking, the inhabitants were by nationality Prussian. The whole position was anomalous as, in 1841, the Canton joined the Confederacy, but the King of Prussia remained the monarch until 1848. In this Canton, surrounded by forty acres of old oaks, looking across the Lake of Bienne to the Juras, was a charming house, Boisrond, the property of the Comte de Pourtalès. In July the Waldegraves took it and had Pearson out to arrange for its purchase. At once they set about acquiring Prussian nationality as the first step towards Pearson's carefully prepared plan.

Frances was delighted with her new home. 'It is the prettiest place we have seen on the Continent,' she assured Ward. 'We have sent to England for the phaeton and one of the English grooms and three horses. We are also going to have Faithful, the large dog, 2 very handsome setters for Waldegrave to shoot with and a rough terrier for me. George [Waldegrave's personal servant] is now made Steward and we shall have an English Under Butler and head Footman also an English cook and kitchen-maid, Housemaid, Lady's Maid and perhaps 2 laundry maids, also another groom who is a Swiss.'

By the New Year the purchase of the Boisrond estate was concluded and for her twenty-third birthday, George Edward Earl of [*sic*] Waldegrave did 'present the same as a birthday present to my adored wife, Frances Elizabeth Ann to be held by her as her own irrevocably'. It was a gay birthday for her. Pearson, who came out every three months, to further the great plan, was with them. In a letter to Ward, his sister told him 'we were very much flattered at the head People from the village of Cornaux coming,

44

of their own accord, at eleven o'clock at night and serenading me. They then, with the Captain at their head, took an oath of allegiance to us and swore they would shed every drop of blood in our defence whenever we called upon them to defend us. Moss then gave them some Punch in which they drank our healths with very many cheers and marched away. It was really a beautiful scene, the moon shining on the ground and trees with the Jura at the back covered with snow. This is very agreeable as they often have revolutions in Switzerland and these men have taken a solemn oath to defend us to their last breath. We were rather alarmed early in the morning by hearing a cannon under our windows. Mr. Moss and all the servants ran down with their guns intending to fire as they imagined we must be besieged when, luckily, they discovered it was some of the Cornaux who had fetched a cannon from Cressy, some miles off, and were firing in honour of my birthday.'

In the spring of 1844 they spent a few weeks in Geneva and Lausanne, but were again at Boisrond at the end of April. The great plan had, at last, materialized. On June 4, on the advice of the Attorney-General, Sir W. Follett, they went through a ceremony of marriage at the little village church of Dombresson. Frances was now no longer a minor. They had both acquired Prussian nationality, and Pearson had seen to it that in this case no one could, by any means, upset the marriage.

Meanwhile, in America, the Brahams at last had realized that they must return and face their creditors if anything was to be saved. They had been away for over two years, and American enthusiasm for the ageing singer was wearing thin. Charles's début, as a tenor at eighteen at his father's side had aroused an ephemeral interest, but it was going to take years of study to make anything remarkable of his voice. Hamilton, too, appeared to think that his deep voice could be turned to a greater advantage than his qualities as a student or as a business man. The thought of a British concert tour, with two of his sons, appealed to Braham, and on January 25 Mr. and Mrs. Braham, Charles, little Josephine and Aunt Seph landed at Liverpool. A fortnight later the old man and Charles gave their first concert at the St. James's Theatre, and were rapturously received.

Arrangements were made for the concert tour. Hamilton was

to have some training, and appear in public in the autumn. All Mrs. Braham's optimism returned. Her friends welcomed her back. Lady Mornington called two days after their arrival, and asked them to dinner, where Mrs. Braham tried to interest Lord Fitzroy Somerset in Augustus's military future. Braham had met his creditors who had 'behaved very handsomely', so his wife felt quite justified in house-hunting with a less economical eye.

Nothing can be found to show whether the Brahams were told of the Dombresson marriage, but at the end of the month, Frances was writing to her father, 'your kind letter has given us the greatest pleasure. I wish to God you had always yourself expressed so openly your sentiments to me as then we never should have been estranged.' Braham's letter had been a 'truly candid exposure' of his affairs, and to that side of it Waldegrave replied offering to pay £100 a year towards Ward's education, and regretting that 'we are, as you must be aware, not in a position to do more'.

The next news of the Waldegraves is in a letter to Ward dated Brussels, August 2, 'that we have taken a sudden fancy to come to England' where they arrived a week later, and, after a night in London, set off with Ward to Harptree Court, their house in Somersetshire.

The arrival at Harptree Court was a tremendous affair. All the tenants turned out, triumphal arches appeared overnight, Waldegrave's yeomanry were there in force, and at the top of the beautiful tower of Chewton Mendip church a man with a telescope was stationed to warn the bell-ringers both at Chewton and East Harptree, of the carriage's approach.

Lord Waldegrave was a popular landlord, and everyone felt that his high spirits had been too harshly punished. Even had Frances been old and ugly, her share in his imprisonment would have won their hearts, and the sight of her radiant young beauty completely enslaved them.

The whole neighbourhood called. They were genuinely glad to see the young earl among them again, and their curiosity about his wife brought them to Harptree immediately. After the retired life at Boisrond it made the young couple nervous, and, if they happened to be caught indoors by callers, they usually hid under a table until the disappointed visitors left. Most of their time was

46

spent out of doors. Except for the six months at the Queen's Bench, since she had first married most of Frances's life had been spent in shooting, fishing, or boating. Both her husbands had liked her to be permanently with them, and, as neither of them cared for society, Frances had almost forgotten her way about a drawing-room.

Waldegrave adored her and she was very happy with him, but, at times, she rather missed those long discussions she had had at the Grange parties with the more serious minded of her father's friends. Sir William Beechey, Sir Francis Burdett, Jerdan, Hunt, they had all been prepared to listen and advise while she thought things out aloud, but neither Waldegrave had ever been able to see any reason for thinking anything out beyond planning the next day's sport. Her husband promised her a season in London the next year, as she had not yet been presented on her second marriage, and then she might meet some of her more intellectual friends.

Their return to England interested the public all the more as, in the same year, John Mills published his *D'Horsay or Follies of the Day* in which two prominent characters were the 'Marquess of Riverford' and his satellite 'Betsy, Earl of Raspberry Hill'. That there should be no mistake in identifying the characters, Mills brought in George Bobbins, the auctioneer, who discusses the Raspberry Hill sale. It was particularly annoying for Frances, since her husband had completely broken with the Waterford set and had, for the last three years, lead a very steady life. The book revived all the old scandal, but at the same time reminded the world of the excellent influence the young countess had been.

Although Ward's tutor was an eminently suitable man, he lived in London which meant that Ward saw too much of his brothers Hamilton and Charles, and was learning to share their interest in horses and alcohol, instead of devoting himself to theology. As the Waldegraves were paying for his education, and as it was their living that he was to be given, they found a parson at Bicester who was prepared to coach him, and for the next two years he divided his time between Bicester and Harptree. The half-brother, Spencer Braham, had lost his patron, the Duke of Sussex, the previous year, so Waldegrave appointed him his domestic chaplain. Spencer had now six children, and would have preferred to be offered the living of Peldon which was reserved for Ward, but was grateful enough to accept the chaplaincy.

Waldegrave still found it hard to forgive his Uncle William for the legitimacy case, but Mrs. William Waldegrave, who had been largely responsible, was now dead, and Frances persuaded her husband to invite his uncle and cousins to Harptree. The Moneys came at the same time, and gradually contact was established with all the relatives except for the two mothers, the Dowager Countess and Mrs. Braham. This meant that Waldegrave could see nothing of his two younger sisters, but he preferred that to meeting his stepfather.

Mrs. Braham sincerely regretted her past behaviour and sent endless messages by Ward, once even writing direct to her elder daughter:

'My dear Fanny,

I couldn't let Ward depart without a line to you. It has been the interest of many to keep us apart but I am sure you have never seen me commit any act that would lessen your respect and esteem for me.

'There is no action of mine during my whole life that I have cause to blush for either towards you, Lord Waldegrave or the world, and as to my letter (the copy of which I thank you for having sent me to peruse) it was my *duty* to tell you what the slanderous world did say. There are two or three things (as for instance the commencement of the letter) which I regret having written but that anyone could believe that I could think a daughter of mine other than virtuous and pure can know little of your mother's proud feeling.

F.B.'

But Great-Aunt Wilson and George Bolton had made too much mischief for Frances ever to forgive her.

In November news arrived that Augustus had been very ill in the Mauritius, with rheumatic fever, and was returning to England with the next detachment. During his years there, he had scarcely ever heard from his family, and the little money they had sent him had mostly been stolen by a postman. He landed at the beginning of December, but was too ill to go to Harptree Court till the New Year. There he found Ward, the old Wilsons and the

Pearsons, and January passed pleasantly for them all. As he had left for the Mauritius while John Waldegrave was still alive, Augustus had heard little of the quarrel between his mother and sister. The stay at Harptree enlightened him:

'Dear Mother,   *Jan. 22. 1845*

I recd. your letter yesterday and will explain about Ward on my arrival in town—likewise everything concerning our family affairs. I do not think that you will ever see Lady W. unless with great pain on both sides but I will see you soon and explain exactly how you stand etc. Give my love to my dearest Father and tell him *no* hopes of the £. s. d. he hinted at from Lady W—but will explain all on my arrival—Give my love to Sapho, Jack, Charles and dear Trotty and with kind remembrances to George Bolton and all the cottage

Dear Mother

Your affectionate son

Augustus'

'*Private*

Mind

Do not mix yourself in *any way* by *word* or *deed* with *George Bolton* or I cannot answer for the consequences, he has already ruined the name of the family and Lord W. does not care *a damn* about exposing our family and you have compromised yourself most dreadfully by your *letters*—were it not for the handwriting I could not believe they were yours I really thought my dear Mother that you had more forethought than to commit yourself *so completely* even if writing in moments of passion—but I will see you soon and tell you all, but *keep clear of George* for God's sake

Your affectionate son

Augustus'

In February Waldegrave fell ill. There was something wrong with his liver, but, after the horror of his brother's epilepsy, Frances found him no problem to nurse, and by the second week in March had him sufficiently well to leave for a month at Torquay and Plymouth. By the time they arrived at Thomas's Hotel, Berkeley Square, in April, he had quite recovered. One thing, however, worried his wife. Every day they drove in the parks, but they drove with the carriage curtains drawn so that no stranger should look at Frances. He was charming to all their friends, they gave innumerable dinners and went to endless parties, yet the public gaze was not to rest on the lovely young countess. Nevertheless she enjoyed herself, and her letters to Ward were cheerful enough.

'I have seen Augustus who is full of Pilbean's Atmospheric Railway. It seems, as fast as my father sends money to your Mother, she sends it all to G.B.B. [Uncle George Bolton] for shares in this bubble. He says that there is not a pound in the house to pay the Bills of the rating etc., as she sends every sixpence to that swindler, G.B.B.'

A few days later came the earliest hint of her future career. 'Waldegrave again attended the House yesterday. When the Maynooth question comes before the House of Peers, Waldegrave, I am glad to say, intends voting for it.

'It is only just as the English took away the lands belonging to the Irish Church and gave them to the Protestants. We have no right to force our religion on the Irish people and that plan has never been known to prosper in any country. Sir Robert's motion is most *noble and just* and his plan is the *only* way of quieting Ireland. Do you know we keep up a Catholic Church in Canada, and make *no scruples* about it?

'I think it very bad taste in the Clergy interfering so much in this question. They are constantly preaching about it and bringing up politics in the Pulpit which I think disgraceful in God's ministers.'

Then, 'This morning I am going to order my Court Dress as Lady Clinton is going to present me at the Drawing Room on Friday next. . . . The train is of very rich white satin lined with white silk and trimmed with ribbon and net. The dress of net over white satin and trimmed with Honiton lace and pink and white roses, for my head a plume of feathers, Honiton lace lappets, a half wreath of Flowers made in diamonds, diamond and large pearl ear-rings and Brooch—Diamond and Emerald bracelets.'

The Waldegraves stayed in London to see the Maynooth Bill through the House of Lords, but, by June 11, Frances was delighted to be back at Harptree Court which 'is really looking too beautiful to describe. . . . I can assure you it is more like fairyland than anything else.'

FRANCES, COUNTESS WALDEGRAVE, 1850
From a lithograph after Swinton

Mr BRAHAM in the character of ORLANDO.
To Mr THOS DIBDIN (the Author of the CABINET &c) this PRINT
is inscrib'd by his FRIEND.   ROBT DIGHTON
Drawn. Etch'd & Publ. by Dighton, Char Cross. March. 22. 1802

JOHN BRAHAM, 1802
A Caricature by Robert Deighton

The summer and autumn passed peacefully at Harptree. The financial situation was steadily improving, Ward was over as often as his studies would allow. Augustus, whose ill health, or possibly the friendship with Lord Fitzroy Somerset, procured him indefinite leave, paid several visits, and Lord Waldegrave's health appeared to be improving. Mrs. Braham almost too casually mentioned to Ward a rumour she had heard at a dinner party at George Bolton's: Lady Horatia Waldegrave was said to be engaged. The Harptree family was forced to ask for further information and she obviously enjoyed doling it out, morsel by morsel. At first they were aghast, as the man was a connection of Algernon Hicks, but it was only a connection by marriage. He was James Webbe-Weston, a captain in the Imperial Army, and the owner of Sutton Place, a beautiful house near Guildford.

By the New Year Lord Waldegrave's health was beginning to cause Frances some anxiety. They had arranged to take a house in Upper Eccleston Street for the season, and she felt that the distractions of London might arouse him from the strange mood—almost of vacancy—that had settled on him. In the month of February she was shocked by the news that her mother had died of heart disease. Fortunately Aunt Seph was with the old man, and he had all his children to comfort him.

In March the Waldegraves set out for Ramsgate with Ward. Frances felt that both her husband and Ward needed sea air to put them on their feet. At Canterbury Waldegrave had a fearful attack, but, after a week of his wife's devoted nursing, they were able to move to Ramsgate for the rest of the month. On returning to Harptree they found more bad news. Augustus wrote to say that he had sold out of the army and on the proceeds was marrying a little Jewess, Miss Elizabeth Marks. She was Christian by religion and made him an excellent wife, but, as he had no means beyond whatever his lieutenancy had fetched, Frances was furious with him for marrying at all.

The house in Eccleston Street brought her little pleasure. Waldegrave grew more peculiar daily. Doctor Cutler assured her that it was only the liver trouble, and that careful living would soon put that right. To distract her a little, Frances had her sister Josephine to stay, but she, too, promptly fell ill, and the whole household had to go down to Somerset until the convalescence was over. Braham, Hamilton and Charles were singing in the north of England, and Seph was looking after Braham's house. Grandmamma Bolton, old Mrs. Wilson and Great-Aunt Carshore, Mrs. Bolton's widowed sister, were living in a cottage at Starch Green near Hammersmith, and at the end of July the Augustus Brahams settled in a little house near by.

It was fortunate that the lawyer Pearson and his wife and the Cutlers were on such intimate terms with the earl and countess as Waldegrave was quite incapable of attending to his affairs. He would have no one near him but Frances who, but for the devoted companionship of Ward, would have collapsed from constant attendance on her semi-imbecile patient. By the beginning of September, Cutler, in consultations with other doctors, admitted that it was cirrhosis and that there was no hope.

On September 8 Frances wrote to all his relations, the Duchess of Grafton, the Radstocks, the Seymours, his Uncle William, the heir to the earldom, and to his mother, though when Annette and her younger daughters arrived, Waldegrave refused to see them. Doctor Symonds of Bristol was summoned and never forgot the contrast between the radiant beauty of the young wife and the ghastliness of the dying man.

Lord Waldegrave died on 28 September 1846, the sixth anniversary of his wedding. Frances's splendid vitality, which had carried her through the last eight months of anxiety and devotion, gave way. Spencer came from Canterbury and, with Ward's tutor, the Vicar of Bicester, accompanied the coffin to Navestock. The young wife was scarcely aware of what was happening. Even when Pearson told her that she had been left the whole of the Waldegrave estates, it made no impression. It was not till she had letters of condolence from the Evangelical Radstocks that she could be aroused. Their assurance, that such trials and tribulations were excellent for her spiritual welfare, stung her back to life. 'Some day they will be horrified to find that God is good.' The handsomest letter came from the new earl. He had realized, that as the estates were not entailed, there was little chance of their coming to him. Waldegrave, when a bachelor, had always intended to leave them to his Seymour cousins. Moreover, William Waldegrave had married the favourite daughter of a wealthy man who would presumably provide adequately for the children. At the time of his nephew's death, William had been contemplating remarriage with a wealthy widow, but rather feared to offer her quite so impoverished a coronet, yet he wrote:

Oct 2. 1846

'My dear Niece,

Yesterday in the street, I was addressed by a Person who told me that he knows that all the Waldegrave Estates were left by my nephew to you, this information did not surprise me nor do I regret that my nephew had so done but I request one thing of you which is to consider me as your uncle and let us be upon the best and most friendly terms—should you wish to enquire of me pray to do in the most open and friendly manner—do not let any person come between us but write and speak openly and freely to me.

All your cousins at home sent their love to you.

Your affectionate uncle,
William Waldegrave'

Frances wrote offering to make his eldest son an allowance of £300 a year, but forgot to address the letter to the Earl Waldegrave. When a second note followed by hand again only to 'My dear Uncle', the poor man at once presumed that Frances was pregnant, and made frantic enquiries through the female relations.

Towards the end of October Lady Waldegrave and Ward left for a little tour through Wiltshire, Dorset, Hampshire and the Isle of Wight, after a few days in London where she arranged to take a house for the winter. Before the tour was finished she was planning some sort of allowance for her father, and on November 30 she advised him of it.

'My dearest Father,

I have been for a long time most anxious to see you retire from public life, and have regretted that the state of your affairs prevented the possibility of my making any arrangements which would enable you to do so. I am now, however, happy to say that my solicitor informs me that £2,000 to which I am entitled under my mother's marriage settlement will more than discharge your debts and leave you an income of £400 per annum from your own property.

'To this I propose adding £200 per annum making your income £600 which sum will, I trust, now that I have provided for my sister and younger brother, enable you to live in comfortable independence for the rest of your days.

'That you may long enjoy them in health and happiness is the ardent wish of

Your ever affectionate daughter,
Frances Waldegrave'

32 *Curzon Street*
Mayfair

Her father replied from Gainsborough where he was singing with his two sons. It was not over gracious.

Dec. 2nd. 1846

'My dearest Daughter—

You have indeed made your Father happy, and God will reward you in this world and in the world to come. The income I shall enjoy will, *I hope*—excuse the word hope as I am a bad calculator —suffice to make me comfortable. I would, were it in my power, return to London immediately, but I am bound to remain in the provinces until the 23rd., and on Christmas Day I shall have the happiness to see you my adored daughter, and my dear son Ward —Trotty and Saph, and, please God, we will have a happy meeting.

'May Heaven preserve you in health and prosperity prays your ever devoted Father,

John Braham'

On December 8, the earl remarried and, though his younger children were a little bitter to Frances about the estates, the new countess had money enough to besprinkle the south coast with strictly Evangelical churches.

At the end of the year her affairs at last in order, her health and beauty completely restored, on good terms with all her family except Augustus and George Bolton, the twenty-five-year-old dowager had the leisure and courage to consider her future.

V. MR. HARCOURT   1847–1848
OF NUNEHAM PARK

FRANCES had always disliked the gentility and young-ladyism of the friends her mother had tried to inflict on her, nor could she understand her modishly ailing contemporaries who spent half their lives fretfully on a sofa. They, in turn, resented her superb vitality and the easy natural grace that the open-air life, which she had lived with her two husbands, had given her. Mrs. Braham had never concerned herself with her children's education. She had sent them to expensive schools and given them expensive governesses and tutors, but there had been no supervision, and the children had consequently run wild.

Since April '39, Frances had had the advice and example of no older woman to guide her, and the years at Dudbrook, Strawberry Hill, Boisrond and Harptree, though they had made her an authority on all outdoor activities, had not taught her the refinements of small talk. Her interest in things was never politely indifferent. It was either vehement or non-existent. Her first contacts with society in 1847 made her painfully conscious of her lack of airs and graces. In a fashionable drawing-room she felt and looked like some splendid young savage at bay. She could no longer hide under tables when people called and unaccompanied hiding would have been a dreary occupation. In any case she had had more than enough of isolation. For the last year of Lord Waldegrave's life his mind had been practically a blank, and she felt that, unless she had the stimulus of intelligent companionship, her own mind would go. Neither of her husbands had ever read a book for pleasure, and both were profoundly bored if she wanted to read. For them, no abstract problem had existed, and her periodic desire to retire to a corner and think things out was quite beyond them. There was seven and a half years of 'thinking things out' to be done, but she had lost touch with the brilliant elderly men who had explained her problems to her at the Grange.

Cutler, Lord Waldegrave's London doctor, was an Essex man and had known the family all his life. He was a great man of fashion, shrewd and good-natured, so it was to him Frances turned for advice. Unfortunately he was better qualified as a medical or social adviser than as a moral guide, his own morals being of a distinctly Regency order. He, at once, saw her difficulties. He had a patient, a Madame de Bruntière, a very cultured French woman who, as she had been a Mademoiselle Tallien, was violently Bonapartist and, therefore, found London pleasanter than the Paris of Louis Philipe. Her finances were straitened and she would make the ideal companion and guide. Lady Waldegrave was delighted, all the more so as Boisrond had made her realize her shortcomings in French. Waldegrave, who detested everything non-English, had quite sympathized with his English servants when they hit the Swiss for being so stupid as not to understand them.

Madame de Bruntière decided that matchmaking was included in her duties and her first candidate was, of course, her idol, Prince Louis Napoleon, who had the year before escaped from the fortress of Ham. Despite his faith in his imperial destiny, throughout 1847 he had, or claimed to have, fits of gloom when a quiet life in England with a rich wife seemed tempting. As late as the autumn, when he was staying in the Isle of Arran with his cousin, Lady Douglas, he told Lord Lincoln, a fellow guest, that he had given up the idea of Empire, and was looking for a rich wife. How much he wanted to settle down is doubtful, but a rich wife at the moment would equally have helped any imperial ambitions.

Frances, however, had had enough of adventurous marriages, and she and circumstances combined to foil her companion's plans for arranging an introduction. It was partly that she had met an old acquaintance of her father's, George Granville Harcourt, a short staid widower of sixty-one, whose bland, pompous manner left him rather friendless. Frances was sorry for him. He was lonely and unhappy, and grateful for the interest she showed in him. His beautiful, extravagant wife had died nine years before, three years after their only child, Lavinia, had married Lord Norreys. Lavinia was neurotic, and the marriage was a constant trouble to her father. Peelite Member of Parliament for Oxfordshire, he was greatly pleased by Frances's ardent enthusiasm for Sir Robert.

He was extremely well read, widely travelled, and knew everybody. His father, the Archbishop of York, a younger son of Lord

Vernon, had changed his name in 1831 after inheriting the Harcourt estates from his maternal uncle. His mother, Lady Anne
Leveson-Gower, had produced thirteen children of whom George
Granville was the eldest, and he, therefore, had occupied Nuneham Park since the archbishop had inherited it. The fact that his
father was Archbishop of York was his greatest virtue in Frances's
eyes. A number of staunch Anglicans were still prepared to take
exception to her marriages to two brothers, but if an archbishop's
eldest son was her most constant visitor, it must show that there
was nothing exceptionable in them.

Mr. Harcourt lived for society and was charmed when this
lovely young savage told him how ill at ease she felt, and how
she longed to acquire the calm and poise of a woman like his
cousin's wife, the Duchess of Sutherland. Harcourt had never
been able to teach his Irish wife anything. The archbishop had
adored and spoiled her and quite undermined his son's authority,
until her infidelities had become so flagrant that he had withdrawn
his affection. Lavinia too had always gone contrary to his wishes,
but, at last, he had found a pupil. He was a shrewd business man
into the bargain, and was glad to advise her about her scattered
estates and the coal mines that were proving very profitable. Poetry,
prose, painting, sculpture, architecture, politics, anything, he
would painstakingly explain to her. In France or in Italy it would
have been simple to explain, with the wonderful galleries and
buildings at hand. If only he could show her them personally. It
was tragic that some young man would probably appear, marry
her and undo all the good his tuition had done. The idea came to
him with none of the frantic fervour of high romance, but with
his usual placid worldliness.

The Nuneham estate was entailed and it had been difficult to
make provision for Lavinia on her marriage. On paper it was
worth about £12,000 a year, but it was an expensive place to run,
and by the time he had paid for the upkeep of a town house
maintained in the style he felt his position demanded, there was
little hope of saving anything from the income. Lady Waldegrave's property was nominally worth nearly £20,000 a year, and
with judicious administration for a few years it would certainly
bring in at least that much. Their combined incomes would make
it possible for him to entertain in almost the same princely way as

his cousin Sutherland, and he would have the pleasure of having an admiring disciple drinking in his words.

The first step was to present Lavinia and Lord Norreys to Lady Waldegrave. Norreys was at once infatuated, but his wife was too accustomed to the vagaries of his restless heart for that to influence her either way. They had met John Braham at the York Festival in '35 so Lavinia went to Dover Street expecting to meet a plump little Jewess. The tall slender figure in black that met her, with a wealth of fair hair gleaming under the widow's cap, which sat so strangely on what appeared to be a girl of eighteen, betrayed not the least vestige of Hebraic blood. Possibly the wonderful vitality, that neither her deep mourning nor her shyness could disguise, was due to the Jewish forbears, but Lavinia, in her relief, could only see a lovely child playing at widowhood. The Queen had described Lady Norreys herself as 'extremely pretty' and Frances, who all her life appreciated other lovely women, was delighted with her. Lavinia, five years the other's senior, looked, thanks to ill health and the worry Norreys had caused her, every day of her thirty-one years, whereas Frances's glorious health and colouring, her diffident manner, and fair beauty were absurdly childlike in the gloom of her black clothes.

Within a few days it was a question which of the Norreyses called more frequently at Dover Street, and Harcourt was thankful when they left to stay with Lord Norreys's father, Lord Abingdon, at Wytham Abbey. He found it easier to write his plans than to discuss them and Lavinia was little surprised to read:

'If I consulted my own ease alone, no opportunity would induce me to change my present existence and abode but there are various circumstances affecting you and others, which press heavily on my mind and might induce me to make more effort and incur more risk than I could contemplate as agreeable or prudent for myself alone. I could more safely trust for future comfort to your affection and the attention of Mrs. Bowne but if a more strange and improbable chance should offer me a different alternative, I have no want of moral courage to encounter the ridicule of some and the disapprobation of others if I see the prospect of giving you not a mother-in-law but a useful sister.'

Mr. Harcourt's pompous stolidity appealed to Frances quite as much as it displeased most of his acquaintance. Since that May in

1835 when the site in King Street was 'bought, there had been nothing solid or stolid in her world. The Brahams were quite as irresponsible as the Waldegraves, and now all expected Frances to provide for them. It was particularly unfortunate that the only coolness that happened during her twenty years of close friendship with her lawyer, Pearson, should have arisen at this time. It was simply a misunderstanding on both sides and was forgotten in a few weeks, but in those few weeks Cutler had produced Madame de Bruntière, who, however remarkable her degree of culture, had not a grain of common sense, and whose advice on practical matters was invariably lamentable. Harcourt had for years been Chancellor and commissary of the archdiocese of York —by no means a sinecure—and his long administration of the Nuneham estates had given him the experience to deal with Frances's problems out of hand. She came to depend on him in so many ways that she was one of the few people in London who felt he was fully justified in proposing to her.

Having proposed, his tactics were subtle. Frances could not make up her mind, so each day he assured her that she must consider the claims of other and younger men before she decided. The tactical retreat succeeded. Frances was frightened of losing his advice and his knowledge of the world. A number of people openly said that she had married the dying John Waldegrave for his money, and had then made an incestuous marriage to gain a coronet. Then the daughter of Braham's old friend, Sir Francis Burdett, aired her disapproval and refused to drive Mr. Harcourt's sister to Dover Street. Angela Burdett-Coutts's philanthropy rarely began at home, and while she was prepared to finance homes for repentant prostitutes, she expected her acquaintance to be above the slightest suspicion, always excepting her bosom friend, Mr. Dickens, possibly because his seduction of Ellen Ternan was to provide yet another repentant fallen woman. He, of course, helped her admirably in the administration of the homes, lamenting the immorality of such social evils.

The attitude of a jaundiced critic would scarcely have influenced the most attractive widow in London, but the gossip there had been about both Waldegrave brothers, about their mother, and about the Braham finances, made Frances yearn for utter respectability. Her marriage to Mr. Harcourt might astonish the world, but no one could say it was for wealth or rank or insatiable physical passion. She knew he had no sense of humour. Madame de Bruntière, to whom the English laws of succession were a mystery, had assured her that Harcourt would inherit the archbishopric. Frances had repeated this to him as a joke that he found completely unfunny. He was pompous, prosy and intolerant, yet these very faults would, she felt sure, be a protection against the bigotry and spitefulness she had had to contend with for the past eight years. It would mean the possibility of friendship with people to whom her wealth and rank would be no obstacle. At the moment most of her acquaintance were anxious either to pursue her for the sake of her money, or to avoid her in case she might suspect them of such an intention.

Harcourt was completely frank about their financial positions. The settlements on his first marriage involved him in endless disputes with his brother-in-law, Lord Lucan, whose Irish estates, though considerable in extent, were rarely able to meet the charges on them, and Lavinia was still waiting for the money that should have come to her on her mother's death.

'I am too glad to do such small matters as I can for your comfort and I know that those weekly inconveniences often occasion more annoyance than more serious matters and for that end only I sometimes wish I was richer instead of being possibly less so by Ld. L.'s [Lord Lucan's] difficulties. Should I survive the Archbishop I should not have more disposable income unless I let Nuneham go to waste in my absence, or took the wise course of letting it. Either of these decisions would give me great annoyance, and I am therefore thankful to have been spared the necessity of making one.'

By Easter 1847, Frances had accepted him. The Norreyses were delighted, the archbishop furious. He had never quite forgiven Braham the amusement he had shown when the archbishop had so thoughtfully tried to teach him how to sing. Braham was himself too accustomed to adulation to show any for the prelate who was only benign if he could condescend and patronize. Lady Elizabeth had been dead long enough for her father-in-law to forget her frailties, and it maddened him to think that all the improvements he had made for her at Nuneham should be enjoyed by 'the little Jewess' whom he had never seen. Mr. Harcourt's brothers and sisters were at first indifferent. As the wealthy heir, his patronizing manner to them as poor relations, and his first wife's undisguised dislike of them all, had caused so long an estrangement that they took little interest, although the brother next in succession worried lest Frances should produce an heir.

Ward was still his sister's constant companion, and his odd appearance, weird ideas and fantastic capacity for mischief soon won him the friendship of Lord Norreys. Mr. Harcourt rightly considered that he had been too spoilt ever to make a clergyman, but for the time being he was benevolent. In July Lady Waldegrave went out of mourning just as the Brahams went into it for her uncle, Doctor George Bolton, whose death only affected her in so far as she had then to provide for her grandmother and greataunt. The following month she entertained Mr. Harcourt and the Norreyses at Harptree where Ward and Norreys infuriated everybody, particularly Madame de Bruntière, with their practical jokes.

Frances insisted upon waiting a full twelve months before she remarried and it was therefore arranged for Thursday, September 30. Sir Thomas Barrett-Lennard of Belhus, Essex, was an old friend of John Braham's, and had been on neighbourly terms with both Waldegraves. He and his wife asked Frances to be married from their house at the church of Aveley. The Norreyses accompanied Mr. Harcourt. The bride's relations, the Augustus Brahams always excepted, came from Dudbrook, and Spencer, the officiating clergyman, from Canterbury, where he was now rector of St. George the Martyr.

With her maid, her aunt Seph, her sister Josephine and Madame de Bruntière all anxious to help, the bride was dressed too early for the wedding. It was a fine autumn day, and she stood by her window watching the guests strolling on the lawns below. It was the first time she had seen Mr. Harcourt from that angle. His tubby little figure strutted to and fro. Frances's heart went cold. She thought of Mrs. Mildmay, a Radstock connection of Waldegrave's, who had besought her not to marry 'the old humbug'. She caught at her sister's hand. 'Oh, Trotty, can't I cut it and be off?'

The first days of the honeymoon were spent in Yorkshire. The 'sumptuous prelate' was ninety and had not been in a state of either health or temper to attend the wedding. A number of his children lived in or around York, and though the visit to Bishopthorpe was uncomfortable, some of the other visits were the beginning of very great friendships. The youngest sister, Georgie, recently married to Colonel Malcolm, became the staunchest woman friend Frances ever had, and two of the brothers, Granville and Charles, were from the first her devoted slaves for life. With the single exception of the archbishop, all the meetings were successful and in most cases the brothers and sisters infinitely preferred her to her husband. Mr. Harcourt, though relieved that his family had accepted his bride sympathetically, was not over enthusiastic about the warm affection some of them showed for her. He had always kept the family in what he considered was their place, and had discouraged any visits to Nuneham, but Frances in a few days was on such excellent terms with them that it was as though they were *her* brothers and sisters. He had dreadful visions of his elderly relations making fools of themselves, through the corridors of Nuneham, at childish nonsense like hide-and-seek or follow-my-leader. It was painful that his wife's presence made people lose all sense of dignity as if some of her excess of vitality had passed into them.

An incident, one day at York, to him typified his bride's frivolous attitude. During a meal they were having at an inn, the waiter serving them was clumsy. Mr. Harcourt reproved him sharply, only to find it was Ward Braham in disguise. That was bad enough, but the lovely sound of Frances's whole-hearted unaffected laughter infuriated him as much as it delighted the rest of the room. He found Ward's behaviour intolerable. Whenever he gave a penny to a crossing sweeper, it was Ward; if a groom or a postillion was troublesome, it was Ward. In a divinity student it was outrageous.

The rest of the honeymoon was a long continental tour which lasted seven months. With Lord Waldegrave she had travelled fairly extensively, but his interest had always been in the hunting, shooting or coaching. Dresden had meant a boar hunt, Munich was the place his dogs had killed an enormous rat, Hamburg and Genoa had provided boating. Everywhere Frances had been sadly conscious of the picture galleries, churches and museums to which Waldegrave could not be dragged. She wanted to spend hours in them all, to miss no building, no view, no historical scene that was worth while. This husband knew exactly what she should see wherever they went, and encouraged her interest in painting, sculpture, and architecture, while his knowledge of European politics was encyclopaedic. He was prepared to explain anything she wanted to know, but at such length that she had usually forgotten what they were discussing long before he had finished.

Harcourt was a little disappointed that his wife had not his view of history. He saw it as a meticulously detailed mathematical diagram, whereas she saw it entirely three-dimensionally. One vivid personality explained a whole period to her, and it became at once alive and exciting. To him a biographical dictionary chronologically arranged would take neither politics nor economics into account, and he loftily scorned her attitude.

Soon after they left England the archbishop died, but the news reached them too late for there to be any question of returning for the funeral. Harcourt inherited the Nuneham estate which he had administered since 1831. As the change was purely nominal, it could be handled by lawyers. In the late autumn Hamilton Braham, partly financed by his sister, had gone to Leipzig to have his voice trained according to the German method. A visit would have unsettled him at the commencement of his studies, and Frances had never forgotten the trouble he had caused while her parents were in America. Neither bride nor groom saw any reason to interrupt their honeymoon for her family or his. Most of the time they were very happy and had few quarrels. Their first was at Munich when Harcourt lectured her rather tediously on her extravagance. 'To pay him out', Frances immediately ordered an immense quantity of glass for Nuneham which his pride would not allow him to countermand.

After Easter at Rome, when the newly formed civic guard startled Mr. Harcourt by giving their muskets a baptism of fire in honour of the Resurrection, Frances and her husband made their way to Florence, where she was able, thanks to the lack of visitors and consequent shortage of money, to buy pictures and sculpture very reasonably. Thence to Genoa and Boisrond which made it simple for them to return by the Rhine, thus avoiding Paris where the elections were expected to cause trouble.

They arrived at their house in St. James's Place at the end of

May, in time for Frances to be presented on her remarriage at one of the last Drawing Rooms. Harcourt felt assured that the intensive training he had given her for the past fifteen months must have submerged the gay savage of the Waldegrave era, and that she was at last fitted to be the gracious hostess of Nuneham or of the town house. At the same time it was essential for a young married woman to have the advice and example of an older woman, and for him in all London there was only one shining example.

Brought up in the splendour of Castle Howard, remarkably handsome, one of the Queen's few intimate friends, and with her husband's fabulous wealth, it was not surprising that the Duchess of Sutherland was one of the great ladies of the period. She was an intelligent, good-hearted woman, but had never had occasion to question the credo of her own way of life, and was nonplussed by anyone who had a different sense of values. She was attracted by Frances, interested in her and anxious to be kind, but Frances had no bump of veneration for the people and things the duchess venerated unquestioningly, which included her Grace the Duchess of Sutherland. To a lesser degree the other women, whom Harcourt forced upon his wife, were of the same type.

If Frances showed enthusiasm about anything, they smiled indulgently, but made it obvious that they were overlooking her gaffe for her husband's sake. Her youth, her spontaneous gaiety, her amazing vitality, even her splendid health were treated as errors of taste. If in the privacy of her dressing-room she danced from sheer exuberance because the sky was blue, Mr. Harcourt was terrified the servants might see her.

It was a great relief to get away to Nuneham at the end of July. The house, though almost as pompous as Mr. Harcourt himself, was inconvenient and shabby, but the park of about twelve hundred acres, the magnificent woods and the gardens laid out by Capability Brown were a delight to her. It was an attractive reach of the Thames, and at least on the river she could escape from formality. It was pleasant to have the Norreyses there, as he was always cheerful, and Lavinia was her ally when Mr. Harcourt was irritating. An even greater happiness than the solitude of the woods or idling on the river was the presence of the foremost of Frances's idols. Sir Robert Peel had come with his wife to meet his greatest disciple, Gladstone, old Lord Lansdowne, the future Speaker and Lady Charlotte Denison, and Lord Harry Vane. The political discussions among this group entranced their hostess whose worship of Sir Robert would have astonished her Grace of Sutherland, but which won her the friendship of the Peels.

Other guests were Lord and Lady Villiers, Peel's elder daughter and son-in-law. Frances was considerably shocked at the increasing intimacy between Lady Villiers and Lord Norreys, and was astounded at the placid way all the others ignored the situation, but when she mentioned something that had happened in the Queen's Bench, that, to her husband, was unpardonably vulgar. Despite his disapproval, she was convinced that the invitations they received to Drayton and Bowood were because the Peels and the Lansdownes wanted to see more of her, and not because her husband was of the same political colouring. Charles Greville, too, who had come to inspect the new chatelaine and collect political titbits for his diary, seemed to enjoy her society.

In September came the excitement of Josephine's wedding. Lady Waldegrave had arrived back in England to find her sister engaged to an attractive young solicitor, Charles Wilson. Josephine and Charles were very much in love, his prospects were good and she had an allowance of £200 a year from her sister.

Charles Braham was to make his operatic début in October, but Harcourt and Frances were not so sanguine about it as his father. They both felt that a few years' study in Italy was essential before his voice would gain him any position on the stage. Charles was as great a problem as Ward. He was very good-looking, had the most affectionate nature, but was as pugnacious as he was affectionate, and as he was prouder of his chest measurements and his biceps than of his voice, he was a dangerous antagonist. All his life he was as guileless as a child and was swindled with unfailing regularity. Ward, to whom he was devoted, had a short allowance of front teeth thanks to a youthful argument with him, yet Ward's debts and troubles worried him infinitely more than his own. He had inherited all his mother's optimism and trusted as unreservedly in Providence as he did in every chance acquaintance.

Flotow's *Leoline* was produced at the Princess on October 16 with Charles as the count.

The success of *Leoline*—this was its first English performance—

meant further engagements for Charles, and the following month he was still at the Princess.

Chorley's criticism, in the *Athenaeum*, of his performance contained excellent advice.

'Mr. C. Braham's Hawkthorn [in *Love in a Village*] was virtually sung twice through—every song getting its encore. When the reward is so easily won and so signal, Criticism must prepare to abide Cassandra's fate. Aware of this, we cannot but emphatically protest against the propensity shown by our young tenor towards perpetuating the vicious traditions of Mr. Braham the elder. We had his tricks of tempo—his shout on some rich high note, his flourish, hurried to give the appearance of animation, but in reality to conceal careless execution—in capital fac-simile. Far preferable would have been some transmission of *the* Braham's temperate and finely felt musical style, when he sang not to "split the ears of the groundlings", but to charm the cognoscenti. With those of the present generation who deliberately choose what is inferior in art no terms are to be kept—and Mr. C. Braham is too richly gifted to be allowed to keep back public taste, and injure his own excellent powers, without earnest reproof.'

Lady Waldegrave could not get away from Nuneham for her brother's début, but was naturally anxious about it. Two days before it, she had written to Aunt Seph that 'I hope if he meets with the success which I expect, in his début, that *this* will only stimulate him to further *severe* study and sober habits'. She goes on to describe the visit to the Peels at Drayton and was 'delighted with his Gallery, which contains fifty portraits of the most eminent men, Statesmen and Poets of our own times. We met there Lord and Lady Shrewsbury, Lord and Lady Lyndhurst (the younger sister of the Miss Goldsmid who used to be our Horror at the Grange, but who is quite as disagreeable and as ugly as our former acquaintance), Miss Copley, Lord Lincoln, and Sir William and Lady Middleton'—an oddly inadequate account.

The whole atmosphere of Drayton Manor was taut with embarrassment. The most important guest was Peel's devoted disciple and friend, the thirty-seven-year-old Lord Lincoln. At twenty-one he had married the Duke of Hamilton's daughter, a grandchild of Beckford of Fonthill. It was possibly from the author of *Vathek* that she inherited the peculiar character that had

GEORGE, 7TH EARL WALDEGRAVE, 1842
Artist unknown

NUNEHAM

From an engraving by W. Angus

made the marriage a disaster from the first. They had five children, the youngest only three years old, but Lady Lincoln claimed that her indifferent health prevented her from taking any interest in them. At the beginning of August she had gone to Germany, ostensibly to consult a doctor. A few days before the Drayton party began, it had become generally known that she had met Lord Walpole, the Lord Tom Noddy of the *Ingoldsby Legends*, at Bad Ems, and that they were travelling about Europe as 'Mr. and Mrs. Lawrence'.

No one was surprised. Ill fortune had dogged Lincoln all his life to such an extent that his acquaintances were chary of associating with him in case they got involved in his troubles. His father, the Duke of Newcastle, was so rabid a Tory that the mob had burnt down his castle at Nottingham during the Reform Riots of 1831. The following year he had forced his tenants to elect Lincoln and his Oxford friend Gladstone as members for South Notts and Newark respectively. In 1839 he had been dismissed from the Lord-Lieutenancy of Nottinghamshire, for refusing to appoint the Lord Chancellor's candidates to the Commission of the Peace on religious and political grounds. He bought the vast Worksop estate simply to have more tenants whom he could force to vote in the Tory interest. When Lincoln supported his great leader during the Repeal of the Corn Laws, his father practically disowned him, and at the next election put up another candidate for South Notts who, with the ducal backing, defeated Lincoln. Two months later the Duke of Hamilton had him elected for Falkirk, but his father's enmity continued.

Lord Blachford described Lincoln as 'an honest and honourable man, a thorough gentleman in all his feelings and ways, and considerate of all about him. He respected other people's position, but was sensible of his own; and his familiarity, friendly enough, was not such as invited response. It was said of him that he did not remember his rank unless you forgot it. In political administration he was painstaking, clear headed and just.' Unfortunately for himself he was too honest and honourable. His uncompromising integrity made him an uncomfortable colleague for those who considered that political expediency justified any double dealing.

His absolute probity had earned him the friendship of Prince Albert and Sir Robert Peel, but most people, although they sympathized with Walpole's wife, felt that Lincoln's lofty idealism partly excused Lady Lincoln's behaviour. It was doubtful if there would ever be a divorce. A vow taken in church was doubly sacred to him, and he was prepared to have her back and help her to live down the scandal.

The other guests at Drayton were considerate and kind to Lincoln, but a certain amount of gossip was inevitable. Lord Lyndhurst was enchanted to meet Lady Waldegrave. He remembered all the details of the Wright case when he had defended Braham, and therefore had a slightly scabrous curiosity about Frances's private life. His morals were on a par with those of Lord Palmerston and, though his admiration was rarely carried to so vigorous a conclusion, he too could never resist a pretty woman. He had a bawdy mind, and was anxious to give her chapter and verse of the Lincoln scandal.

Frances, for all her outspoken good humour, had an underlying primness that often surprised herself. In a moment, aflame with indignation more on Lincoln's behalf than at any offence to herself, she became his zealous champion. The sly pleasure that so many people felt at seeing him cuckolded because they resented his integrity, disgusted her. With her usual straightforward friendliness she devoted herself to him for the rest of her stay with the Peels. She was passionately interested in everything that concerned her friends, and for the first time since his mother's death Lincoln found someone who actually wanted to hear him talk about himself.

The Peels were greatly relieved that Frances had had the courage to take their unhappy guest in hand. It pleased both of them to see her so gay and confident under their roof, listening to and sifting the political talk, and then making some shrewd comment that proved she had seen right to the heart of the question. It amazed Sir Robert that she, whose matter-of-fact humorous conversation was so worth while, should be nervous and silent with the great ladies and their polite chatter. He mentioned it and was told all about the misery of the dinner parties at St. James's Place. Peel's quiet comment did more for her morale than any of the adulation she was to receive for the rest of her life. 'One of these days you'll find you're a remarkable woman.'

VI. VAUDEVILLE À LA LOUIS XV 1849–1851

IT WAS at a party at Lady Granville's that Frances finally over-came her shyness. Granville, a prominent Whig, was one of Mr. Harcourt's relations with whom she was never entirely friendly. He appreciated her intelligence and fascination, and in later years freely acknowledged her tremendous influence in affairs of state, but he took a feline pleasure in watching for any slip she might make. His slightly condescending manner and the aloof civility of some of his women guests irritated Frances, after the friendli-ness of Drayton. Mr. Harcourt's everlasting lectures on the indis-cretion of her frankness and spontaneity usually made her too nervous to say a word, yet if she forgot all about him and spoke unreservedly, her success was immediate. For over a year she had tried unsuccessfully to be a pale copy of the Duchess of Suther-land, but on this occasion, aware that Granville's malicious eyes were watching her, she suddenly decided to be Frances Walde-grave or nothing. It might fail with society but at least she would be herself and happy whereas the other attempt had already com-pletely failed, and had bored and cramped her to despair.

At first Frances's changed attitude did her some harm. The realization that she could attract both men and women intoxicated her, and she set out to fascinate everyone she could. She gave her animation too free a rein and made herself a little conspicuous. A beautiful dancer, she spoilt the effect by dancing too well, although her love for dancing was genuine and her pleasure in her own ability held little conceit. Dancing was an outlet for her pent up vitality, and she was always trying to persuade her guests to dance anywhere and at any time. It had led to a quarrel with Harcourt. Nuneham had become shabby since the death of his first wife, and Frances wanted a new carpet for the drawing-room. He would only agree if she promised never to allow dancing on it. She refused to promise, and had to make do with the old threadbare one.

Grandmamma Bolton died on 25 January 1849, at the cottage

at Starch Green where she had been living with her widowed sister, Mrs. Carshore, and old Mrs. Wilson, all on Lady Waldegrave's bounty. Four days before, Frances had written to her from Nuneham:

Jan 21st 1849

'My dear Grandmamma,

We shall send you tomorrow a brace of pheasants, which will be forwarded to you by Josephine, as I am sending her some game at the same time. Are you not surprised at my Father being able to electrify his hearers again at Exeter Hall. He certainly is the marvel of his age and must be almost as much a subject of wonder to himself as he is to others.

'I am delighted that Charlie is going on so well, both in public and private, and hope some day he will make as great a fortune, as these bad theatrical times will allow. I suppose you know that dearest Ward is intending soon to enter at Cambridge. I do not doubt that dear Saffy has told you of our movements lately, and how much pleased I was with my Woburn visit. We were invited to meet a Cabinet party and I liked much what I saw of Lord John Russell, but Sir Robert Peel is still my favourite. We have taken a charming house in Carlton Terrace for three years, belonging to Lord Caledon, but as Lady C. is to be confined there we cannot get into it until May. How are sweet Polly's love affairs proceeding? Give my most affectionate love to her and Aunt Carshore. With the same to your dear self, believe me, dearest Grandmamma,

Your most affectionate,
Frances Waldegrave'

February and March Mr. Harcourt and his wife spent at St. James's Place, and then, while the removal to 5 Carlton House Terrace was taking place, they went over to Paris for a few weeks. She was able there to compare her husband with Madame de Bruntière's candidate as on April 21 they went to 'a grand ball at the President's. He was exceedingly polite, as he is in a marked manner to the English. The best dressed person there was Lady Ailesbury.'

The new house was delightful, but had involved a great deal of expense. The Waldegrave estates were gradually being nursed back to health, but Frances had still little ready money. It was therefore a bad moment for her to learn that, despite the money she had already paid out, her father's debts were still so serious that unless he settled them at once, he would go to a debtor's prison. In any case Mr. Harcourt would not allow his wife to give money, so Braham was obliged to leave the country and let his solicitors try for some settlement. Ward took him over to Brussels in July, where Seph, a little shocked at the equivocal position it put her in, joined him a few weeks later. On £600 a year life in Belgium could be quite pleasant and all his children could easily visit him.

Apart from the anxiety about her father, it was a pleasant season for Lady Waldegrave. She saw a good deal of the Peels with whose younger daughter she had become very friendly. No. 5 Carlton House Terrace was admirably suited to the entertainments she liked to give, and her invitations were coveted. By the end of July they were back at Nuneham with a succession of guests until September when Ward, Charles, and Trotty, with her husband and baby son, came to meet Hamilton on a visit from Leipzig with news of Braham and Seph whom he had seen on the journey. Frances had at last persuaded Charles to give up his English engagements and go, at her expense, to Italy to have his voice thoroughly trained. She was delighted with the progress Hamilton had made. Ward left Nuneham in October for Cambridge. With the exception of Augustus whom she allowed £100 a year, but refused to meet, the family were causing her no trouble for once, though apart from the expense of Hamilton and Charles, they were costing her £1,280 a year in allowances.

Lady Waldegrave and Mr. Harcourt were again at Woburn in January 1850, for the New Year's party the Duke of Bedford invariably gave for his none too wealthy brother, the Prime Minister; then—Mr. Harcourt always found a ducal invitation irresistible— they moved north to stay with the Sutherlands at Trentham. When they arrived back at Carlton House Terrace for the season, Frances found that London was seized with a mania for amateur theatricals. The only quality she had inherited from her mother was a passion for the theatre. One of several reasons for John Braham's being so much greater in oratorio than in opera was that he was an execrable actor. Hamilton, Augustus and Charles, despite their fine voices, were to fail in opera for the same reason.

71

Frances and Ward, on the other hand, were brilliant mimics and their dramatic ability was outstanding. She immediately set about getting together a company of amateurs for the August parties at Nuneham. Monckton Milnes promised to write a play, and there were almost daily rehearsals at Carlton House Terrace.

It was an endless succession of dinners and balls. In April Thackeray wrote to Mrs. Brookfield that he was going to a ball at Lady Waldegrave's after the Garrick Club Shakespeare dinner: 'She gives the finest balls in London and I've never seen one yet.'

On June 29 Sir Robert Peel was thrown by his horse in Hyde Park. For three days his condition was critical, and in the evening of July 2 he died. To Frances it was a personal loss. For years he had been her ideal statesman and had become an intimate friend and counsellor. The effect his death would have on the political world was incalculable.

Though, since his defeat in 1846, he had been nominally leader of the opposition, he and his handful of followers, Aberdeen, Gladstone, Lincoln, Cardwell, Sidney Herbert, Harcourt and a few others, had more often than not supported the motions brought in by Lord John Russell's government, though they had disagreed bitterly with Palmerston's foreign policy. The real opposition had been Lord Stanley and Disraeli who had seceded from Peel to form the Young England party. The Liberal Government, with the Duke of Bedford as a benevolent duenna, had been flirting with the Peelites for some time, and now that Peel's death left his followers to the leadership of Lord Aberdeen, Bedford felt that his brother should woo them twice as fervently.

The Peels had been invited again to Nuneham for the theatricals in July, though as Mr. Harcourt assured Dicky Milnes, 'It is somewhat imprudent of me to ask Peel to Nuneham, for he is as much hated in the country as the Pope—not but that the Pope would come to Nuneham if he visited England'. Despite the general sorrow over Peel's death, the Nuneham party was a success; Lady Waldegrave was delightful as the duchess, with Milnes as the earl, in the play he had written for her, and which he had printed with a dedication to her. The Norreyses of course were there, he disconsolate that the bereaved Lady Villiers was unable to attend. The Granvilles came and the Belgian Minister, Van de Weyer, who was to become one of Frances's most intimate friends. Young

72

Lord Dufferin was another guest, for whom the match-making hostess was trying to find a wife, though to Dufferin none of the candidates was so fascinating as Lady Waldegrave. Other dramatic amateurs were Georgina Lygon, Lord Beauchamp's beautiful niece, and the stiff, languid but extremely handsome Irish M.P., Chichester Fortescue.

The cottage at Starch Green had become the distributing centre for Braham information, since all the family either visited or wrote to the two old ladies. Great-Aunt Carshore was an industrious correspondent and the activities of her great-nephews and nieces were her only interest, as her sister-in-law, Mrs. Wilson, was by 1850 too senile to be any company for her. Since Mr. Wilson's death she had grown more and more miserly and even refused to receive guests on the score of expense. On September 2 she died at the age of ninety-three. Trotty and her husband were staying with Spencer at Canterbury, Frances was at Nuneham, Hamilton at Leipzig, and Charles in Italy, but Augustus and his wife came to help Aunt Carshore. The only possessions were in a tin box and included an old pair of stays most suspiciously heavy. When they were cut open, hundreds of pounds in coin and notes were found. Frances, on whose charity the old woman had been living for years, was at last disillusioned.

Through Aunt Carshore she learnt that Augustus, not to be outdone by Hamilton or Charles, had decided to make his operatic début in Carlisle in the middle of the month before a winter season in Glasgow and Edinburgh. He had had very little training, and his sister had no confidence in his success. She however took little interest in it as her husband was taking her to Paris for the winter 'having been tempted to do so by the offer of Lord Holland's apartments in the Place de la Madeleine, which are newly and comfortably furnished'.

Mr. Harcourt was anxious that she should improve her always uncertain French, and meet a number of his Parisian friends. He also wanted to take her away from the endless discussions with Charles Wilson and Ward about her father's debts. Paris, however, proved no refuge.

Within a month of their arrival, Ward, despite the £500 a year his sister allowed him, was chased to Boulogne by his creditors. By the end of October Braham and Seph were writing anxiously from Brussels to complain about young Wilson's handling of the money Lady Waldegrave sent her father through him. It was sufficiently serious for her to summon Charles Wilson to Paris. He succeeded in reassuring her, paid the money into Braham's account, swore that he had pacified the old man's creditors, and invited him and Seph to live with Trotty and himself at their new establishment in Bloomsbury Square. While Wilson was in Paris, Charles Braham suddenly appeared from Milan on his way to London for a week on St. James's Theatre business. Mr. Harcourt began to yearn for the comparative privacy of Nuneham.

By the beginning of December Charles had re-let the theatre, John Braham was comfortably settled in Bloomsbury Square with his younger daughter and, except for Ward, there was calm in the Braham affairs. Lady Waldegrave's season in Paris was socially immensely successful. Princess Lieven took her up and it was also the beginning of a long friendship with Lady Sandwich whose elder daughter was the first wife of the President's cousin, Count Walewski. The President himself was affable and on December 6 Frances informed her father that 'we were at a large ball at the President's last night. To the honour of England her women were the prettiest and best dressed. He does the honours of his house with good taste and without affectation.' Early in January 1851, Thackeray met them at a ball Lady Sandwich gave, almost the last of the British festivities in Paris before they all moved back to London for the season. Before Frances left, however, she went to see the fashionable clairvoyant, Henri, who assured her that 'she would marry a Prince of the blood and govern France, or should have it in her powers to do so, if she chose', a prophecy that amused Mr. Harcourt not at all.

At the end of April Charles Wilson's handling of his clients' money was found to be so unconventional that, with his wife, he had to take the first ship to America, leaving their small son in the care of a nurse, and by the middle of May they had sailed.

Lady Waldegrave behaved superbly, paying the passage money, arranging for her sister's allowance to be paid in New York, and appearing in public as gay and as charming as ever. The relief of having avoided any prosecution, and the probability that the young Wilsons could fashion a respectable future for themselves, caused the Brahams to await the first news from America with quite benevolent interest. The news of their safe arrival in New York was, however, brought by Trotty herself. Her husband had behaved so shockingly to her on the voyage and on their arrival, that she had accepted the protection of a married man and returned by the next ship. She optimistically imagined that divorces could be arranged all round, and that she could marry her new friend.

Frances was disgusted, refused to see her, and announced that the allowance would be stopped unless Trotty returned to America at once. On July 10 Spencer changed his name by deed poll to Meadows on account of the scandal and Frances could not bring herself to blame him, though old Braham was furiously indignant.

Meanwhile Catherine Hayes, the Irish singer, had asked Augustus to join her in an American tour which was to open in New York in September. Lady Waldegrave had of course again to pay the passage money for him and his wife. The only moderately bright aspect of the Braham fortunes was that Hamilton was singing with some success in Vienna, and that Charles appeared to be studying hard in Florence. It was not till the end of September that Josephine was prevailed upon to leave again for America.

In view of the amount of worry they caused his wife, Mr. Harcourt was most forbearing with her relatives, but when he was feeling querulous he liked to remind her of his great magnanimity in having married so very far beneath him. The fact that the Charles Wilsons had often stayed at Nuneham and were therefore well known to all his servants angered him more than their odd morals. Old Braham's financial troubles and Ward's bumbailiff dodging were notorious, and though Frances sailed through the London season as radiantly as ever, her husband felt that everyone was gossiping. He mournfully assured her that Nuneham had never harboured refugees from justice in the archbishop's day, when even the Queen herself had come with Prince Albert on a visit.

Frances acidly pointed out that the Queen had visited the Archbishop of York and not his eldest son, but she determined to silence his complaints. George III's daughter, Princess Mary, had married 'Silly Billy', Duke of Gloucester, her first cousin, and great-uncle of John and George Waldegrave. The Duchess of Gloucester had always taken an interest in Frances and had admired her devoted care of her two Waldegrave husbands. She was therefore delighted to be tactfully approached about the possibility of a visit to Nuneham.

Lady Waldegrave planned her summer visitors carefully. The gayer, younger set were invited for the end of July, the more pompous were asked for August 15, the day before the old duchess arrived. Mr. Harcourt was enraptured, even though the royalty was graciously pleased to refer to her visit to her great-niece. As usual Frances managed with a minimum of protocol and a maximum of charm, and the visit was a great success. Harcourt wrote to his brothers who, he had felt, were not grand enough to be invited, that Lady Waldegrave 'had surpassed herself, when the Duchess of Gloucester was with us, in all respects'.

The success of the royal visit pleased Frances in that it more than consoled her husband for the Wilson scandal. For herself she really only enjoyed the young parties at Nuneham when every attic was occupied, and there was acting, dancing and gaiety all the time. Her parties had already the reputation of producing several engagements a year, for she was a notorious matchmaker. She had an unlimited supply of eligible young men who were delighted to be asked to meet attractive girls, but unfortunately their greatest attachment was usually to their hostess.

Julian Fane, the baby of the Burghersh family in the Grange days, had grown into one of the handsomest young men in the kingdom, and, as a friend of long standing, felt he was entitled to some degree of priority at her parties. He was charming to all the girls she produced as possible brides, but his allegiance was unswervingly to her. Just before the Gloucester visit, he wrote a poem *Nuneham* to her, which was published in the small volume he brought out the following year.

Another of the young men who formed her court was young Lord Dufferin who, not to be outdone by Julian Fane, promptly wrote a song for her, *The Moon Shines Bright on Nuneham's Walls*. A young nephew of Mr. Harcourt's, William Vernon Harcourt, was a particular protégé of Lady Waldegrave's. Like Julian Fane, of whom he had been a fellow 'apostle' at Cambridge, he was twenty-four, very tall and remarkably handsome. This summer he wrote to his mother that 'I am under a permanent engagement to go there [Nuneham] every Saturday, and Uncle G. has ordered a carriage to meet me always on that day. She [Lady

W.] recounted to me the other day the whole of her history. I assure you no romance could be more extraordinary, and considering the incredibly difficult position in which she has all her life been placed, I am more surprised at the good points than at the foibles of her character.'

He was one of the most self-satisfied and opinionated men Frances ever knew. For the rest of her life they quarrelled violently and often, yet a deep affection bound them to the end. In politics he flouted her advice and contradicted her more often than not, but the regularly increasing importance of the offices he held was very largely due to her influence and interest.

Robert Morier, a young diplomatist, who stayed at Nuneham in 1851, graphically described the party he found there. After listing the guests he refers to his host and hostess:

'The latter two personages were far the most interesting of the whole lot. I can only describe them, their ways and their entourage, by saying that they seem to have been intended by nature as the principal characters in a Vaudeville à la Louis XV; he, the old Marquis, heir to palaces and broad acres, a genealogy "as long as my tail" and an ungovernable temper, who has all his life ruled supreme over an obedient household of former wives and younger brothers, all drilled to watch and administer to his every whim, and at last in his old age, with all his despotic habits and selfishness ingrained into him like dirt into the mechanic's palm, marrying a wife with a wit and a will a thousand times stronger than his own, and no disinclination to use both to the best advantage. She, the young wife aforesaid, a widowed "Duchess" with immense fortune, beauty, accomplishments, whims without end, gigantic animal spirits, the world-spoiled child, with every denomination of admirer flitting about her, really fond of the old "Marquis" but determined to stand no humbug and possessed of a laudable ambition to prove to him that his temper is not so bad as it appears. Place your scene in a splendid château surrounded by magnificent gardens with terraces sentinelled by grand flower vases overlooking a majestic river, throw in a handful of subordinate characters, admirers, cowed younger brothers taking courage since the advent of Madame, wits, a poet, a fat philosopher, some agreeable and espiègle women of various ages. Now imagine the thousand and one freaks which, with such an entourage, would suggest themselves to Madame la Duchesse, and the way in which they would be received by Monsieur le Marquis, and you will really have some idea of the *plaisanteries* of Nuneham during the last week.'

Another good-looking and eligible bachelor, in whose matrimonial and political future she took a considerable interest, was the Liberal member for Co. Louth, Chichester Fortescue.

With the death of William Charles Fortescue, second Viscount Clermont, in 1829, the title had become extinct. In 1833 the estates passed to a youth of eighteen, Thomas Fortescue, whose father had been Whig member for Co. Louth until his death in 1826. Thomas considered his health far too delicate to combine parliamentary duties with the care of his large estates, but he decided that his younger brother, Chichester, should one day occupy his father's old seat.

Chichester, too, had indifferent health and his shyness caused a slight stutter that made public speaking an ordeal for him. His Oxford career was brilliant. In 1843 he was given a studentship at Christ Church, and in 1846 won the Chancellor's Prize Medal for the English Essay. In 1845 he passed six months in Italy where his considerable good looks gained him the friendship of Edward Lear, who was addicted to handsome young men.

The winter of '46–'47 he spent in Greece, but was recalled by the illness of an uncle by marriage who was to leave him a small estate at Ardee. A general election was imminent and Thomas, on whom he was still partly dependent, insisted on his standing as Liberal candidate for Co. Louth.

In 1840 Thomas had married the Marquis of Ormonde's daughter, Lady Louisa Butler, but Chichester was still his heir-presumptive, and so he felt it would be in Chichester's own interests to enter Parliament for the express purpose of having the Clermont title revived in his elder brother's favour. The rent roll of the Clermont estates was over £16,000 which Thomas thought more than justified a peerage.

The election cost him over £5,000, but he had the satisfaction of having his brother returned. Chichester made his maiden speech the following May in support of Lord John Russell's Bill for the removal of Jewish disabilities. Despite his nervousness his speech was well received as was the pamphlet he published a few weeks later, *Christian Profession not the Test of Citizenship*. He found rooms at 45 St. James's Place and settled down to the usual town life of a good-looking young bachelor. He retained his fellowship and his contacts with Oxford, his clubs were Brooks and the Alfred, and his position as heir to his wealthy but unphiloprogenitive brother ensured his popularity. He was in no hurry to marry, as he had made the acquaintance of Miss Polly Fleming, one of the two equestrian sisters from Astley's Amphitheatre, neither of whom had yet realized that they might demand marriage as the price of their kind services.

Despite the air of languid reserve that his shyness and indifferent health combined to give him, he was invited everywhere. He refused a good many invitations to the grander functions where he was inclined to become stiff and frigid from sheer nerves, preferring the company of his Oxford friends, or of such mildly Bohemian people as the Duff-Gordons, the painters Phillips and Watts, or Edward Lear, with all of whom he was completely at ease and could then be the charming, amusing companion that his aloof manner and almost dandified appearance concealed.

Possibly on account of his own diffidence, he enjoyed the company of strong-minded women. His unmarried younger sister, Harriet, was an intense, untidy young woman, full of political fervour and social welfare, and a disciple of Ruskin's, to whom she introduced Chichester who was, however, only interested in the 'pretty little Mrs. Ruskin'. Another strong-minded woman friend was Lady Stanley of Alderley, who preferred intellectual to fashionable society, though she forced her daughter Blanche to forget the charming artist, Richard Doyle, and to marry the dull but rich Lord Airlie. It was at the Stanleys that Chichester met Thackeray at the time when the town was flocking to his lectures on the English Humourists. Chichester had spoken of Swift as an Irishman, but Thackeray would not allow that and said, 'No. He called a poker a poker, no blarney in him.'

The great change in his life is best described in his own words. 'I had first seen and known her in the Spring of 1850, when she was 29, and I was 27. I saw her for the first time in an open carriage in Piccadilly,—Mr. Harcourt was with her, and they were sitting with their backs to the horses to avoid the wind. After this my old friend, Lady Hislop, was anxious to introduce me to her. . . One evening at old Lady Grey's, Lady Hislop was running about

looking for me to present me to her. Eastnor [the future Lord
Somers and husband of Watts's beloved Virginia Pattle] was sitting by her. He said, "Don't take the trouble of knowing Fortescue. I know him, he doesn't deserve to know you now—he's an
ass. He ought to have found you out before you married again—
he is the very man who would have suited you." After one or more
failures, it was settled that I should go to a party she gave at
5 Carlton House Terrace. I went. Lady Hislop had not arrived and
I introduced myself. She was standing by a statue in the ante-
room. When Lady Hislop came up to her she said, "You are too
late, we have done it ourselves without you." Soon after I was
taken into the Nuneham theatrical company, partly through poor
Granville E. Vernon. I dined and rehearsed at Carlton Terrace
and then went to Nuneham and acted an old man's part, her father
in the play. There I met Georgy Lygon and fancied myself in love
with her—a handsome girl.'

Georgina Lygon was the daughter of General Lygon, later
Lord Beauchamp, and was being chaperoned by her aunt, Lady
St. Germans. Lord St. Germans was a first cousin of Mr. Harcourt's, and so Miss Lygon was frequently at Lady Waldegrave's.
The amateur theatricals at Nuneham made flirtation easy, and the
matchmaking Frances was delighted when Chichester and Georgy
appeared as Ivanhoe and Rebecca at the fancy dress ball she gave.
During the autumn and winter they had little opportunity of
meeting, and by the beginning of 1851 Chichester felt that a coolness had grown up. Lady Waldegrave, however, was encouraging
and got up a number of her friends to work on his behalf. His own
approach to romance must have been a little odd, for writing of
'Georgy' on March 2, he simply puts it, 'I left it in Lady W's.
hands'. He scarcely saw Miss Lygon this season, and it is possible
that she did not much appreciate a courtship that necessitated his
spending ten times as much time with Frances Waldegrave as
with herself.

In April he was very indignant with the new Lord Waldegrave's
son, George, of the House of Commons library, who was 'bitter
about his father's ancient inheritance being left away. He allowed
she was good hearted and had been a good wife to Lord W.' In
May he went to the Academy to see Swinton's portrait of Georgy
where he found the face had 'a certain pinched look'. Four days

later he did meet her at Miss Coutts's ball, and was surprised that she refused to be Rebecca to his Ivanhoe again 'at Lady W's fancy ball if she had one'. However, the next day he went to Lady W's 'to report progress and get consolation'. A few days later Georgy 'either could not or would not dance with me' at Lady Londonderry's ball, and the day after that at Lady Ashburton's 'she all but cut me'.

The entry in his diary next day begins 'I have just come back from Lady Waldegrave's ball—a memorable night in my life—I am awakening from a dream'. He goes on to the events of the day. In the morning he 'went to have a talk with Lady W.—she allowed my prospects were uncertain'. Various other visits, and the House of Commons where he paired to get away to 'Lady W.'s ball—a very good one'. Georgy Lygon would not dance with him. 'Lady W. with her usual kindness made me dance the Lancers with her.' Then Lady St. Germans tells him it is quite hopeless. The next day he remembered his role enough to write 'I must expect to feel many a pang of disappointment', and now, of course, in his profound grief he felt entitled to a little talk with Lady Waldegrave every day. 'I had a most interesting and consolatory talk—she showed great womanly tact and feeling.' Then exactly four days after the shattering of his romance he 'told Lady Waldegrave I only regretted I should have no such good reason in future for coming to see *her*', which at least was honest. 'How unjust many people would be to this gay, handsome woman of the world with her good heart.'

Within a fortnight Lady Waldegrave was suggesting new loves for him. 'Her way of viewing me and my position is pleasant and gives me confidence. I told her something of my self tormentings —curious how much more I confess to her than to any friend or relation.' He must have been the only person in London by this time to find it curious.

The enthusiasm Fortescue developed for theatricals threw them a lot together until the first Nuneham party of 1851 which began on July 23, when he could ask for more matrimonial advice. 'She as usual most encouraging—I am so fond of being with her, she is indeed charming. Somehow everyone seems dull to me after talking to her.'

On August 5 he had to go to Ireland, bitterly envious of Duf-

ferin and Julian Fane whom he left at Nuneham. He spent most
of his time telling his sister Harriet all about Frances, and finding
resemblances to her in everything he read, even Portia in the
Merchant of Venice. 'Her character, quickness, wit, spirit, joined
with that outspoken frankness and warm heart reminds me of
Lady W. Portia shall be my favourite Shakespeare heroine.' Then
'a letter from Lady W. delightful, it brightened up the day—asks
me to Nuneham for 7th. October'.

When he got back to Nuneham he found the usual vast party,
including his friend Henry Grenfell who said of their hostess that
'she is the only really remarkable woman of our day, sometimes
she looks like an enchantress'. Two days after his arrival he was
greatly impressed because 'an illegitimate brother and his son
who have taken the name of Meadows, came for the day—he a
Minor Canon of Canterbury—she kissed him in the middle of the
room'. After a little more than a fortnight he had to return to
Ireland, but in the middle of November was consoled by a 'note
from Lady W. to say she was going to Woburn and I am asked for
the same party'. Miss Lygon was quite forgotten, and he had,
some months since, renounced the kind services of Miss Polly
Fleming. For the next eleven years he led a life of the most scrupu-
lous chastity, a change that startled his friends as much as the incessant boils and nervous headaches, from which he suffered for
the next eleven years, appeared to amuse them.

THE BRITISH, with a misplaced sense of humour, had found Louis Philippe, the Citizen King of the French, too undignified a figure to fear. The endless caricatures of his pear-shaped head amused them, and the many years the Orleans family had spent in exile in England made their one-time hosts benevolently patronizing. One of the daughters had married the King of the Belgians, and the Duc de Nemours had married a Princess of Saxe-Cobourg, which established them all in Queen Victoria's affection. The fact that the whole Orleans family was rabidly Anglophobe seems to have struck few British politicians.

Louis Napoleon, on the other hand, despite his affection for England and untiring efforts the whole of his reign to win this country's goodwill, was a Bonaparte and therefore a menace. Britain's distrust of him was so obsessive that it enabled Prussia, almost unnoticed, to become master of continental Europe.

In most things Lord Palmerston's foreign policy—if he ever possessed one—was indefensible, but he was one of the few British statesmen who was reasonable in his attitude to the Prince President. Although Lord John Russell and Palmerston were so frequently Cabinet colleagues, they were never at ease together. Russell, a decorous little man with a violently Whig background, never trusted the amorous, blustering giant who had begun life as a Tory. The British, however, adored the older man and, apparently for no better reason than that he was their ideal of a bluff, full-blooded, hard-riding, hard-living English nobleman, insisted upon his being Foreign Minister.

After a long liaison with Lady Cowper, Lord Melbourne's sister, her husband's death had enabled Palmerston to marry her in 1839, and her great social influence was invaluable to him. She was so extremely well liked that the very strong resemblance most of her children bore to their step-father was little discussed, and her Saturdays at Cambridge House were crowded season after season.

Lady John, on the other hand, though kind and simple mannered, never succeeded in putting her guests at their ease, and was embarrassingly indiscreet in her political gossip. Though the Duke of Bedford was prepared to entertain for his brother either at Woburn or at his house in Regent's Park, he was not generous in the allowance he made him, with the result that Lord and Lady John could do little entertaining of their own either at Pembroke Lodge in Richmond Park or at their town house at Chesham Place.

When the Russell ministry was formed in 1846, Lord Palmerston, who had already been Foreign Secretary in the Grey and Melbourne Cabinets, was again given that office, despite the antipathy both of the Premier and the Queen. His independent handling of foreign affairs increasingly irritated his chief, until his unfortunate private conversation with the French Ambassador, Count Walewski, expressing his approval of Louis Napoleon's *coup d'état* on 2 December 1851, gave Russell the opportunity to dismiss him.

There was the usual Christmas party at Woburn in 1851. By December 15 most of the guests had arrived there. Frances and her husband, Fortescue direct from Ireland, partly for the bliss of being in her company and partly to pester the Prime Minister about Thomas's peerage, the Cowleys, the Barringtons, the Mitfords, the Bulteels—mostly a young party. Three days later they acted *The Honeymoon* with Lady Waldegrave as the heroine 'magnificent in white, orange flowers, myrtle and diamonds'. Fortescue was Lopez, and his friend Robert Morier 'did not know his part or had too much sherry in him', but Fortescue forgave him when he said that he found Frances 'the most attractive woman he ever saw'. Another friend, Henry Grenfell, who was later to write the account of her in the Dictionary of National Biography, 'took the *warning* line' about Fortescue's devotion, but the latter was too enraptured with 'the picture she was today in her black velvet and white waistcoat' to pay any heed. The next night Frances took the lead in *Love and Law* and on the 23rd they did Augustus Stafford's *Fairy Extravaganza*.

'There had been great whispering and mystery in the house for days', and after the *Extravaganza* the 'great news was divulged. Palmerston out of office—Granville succeeds him'. Russell and the Queen were both delighted that Palmerston had made such a gaffe, though his comments to Walewski had been indiscreet rather than unreasonable. Even Carlyle, no friend of Louis Napoleon, assured Monckton Milnes at that time that he was pleased and 'thinks Louis Napoleon a heaven sent man to govern for the good of the people and keep his parliament in its proper subordinate position'.

The French President's *coup d'état* had aroused the old Napoleonic bogey of invasion, and Lord John hastily formulated a new Militia Bill which he explained to the House on February 16. It gave Palmerston the opportunity he was praying for. On the 20th he proposed an amendment which was carried by 135 votes to 126 against the Government which at once resigned, and on the 22nd the Queen sent for the Earl of Derby. The position of the new ministry was hopeless from the start. The Peelites would certainly never vote with the Derby-Disraeli Conservatives, some of whom had pledged themselves to the re-enactment of the Corn Laws. There was bound to be a dissolution and the Liberals were determined to win over the Peelites.

Despite Lord John's many political worries during the month, he found time to consider Chichester Fortescue's petition, and on the 11th Thomas was granted the Irish barony of Clermont with special remainder to Chichester. Thomas and his wife were enchanted, but, a little ungratefully, became more insistent than ever that Chichester should marry and save them the fatigue of begetting an heir.

The Clermonts probably never realized how much they owed their title to the affection Lord and Lady John felt for Chichester. He was always welcome at Pembroke Lodge, and most enjoyed those visits when he was alone with his host and hostess whose political confidences and reminiscences were an invaluable education to the budding politician.

Chichester was however still regular in his attendance at Lady Palmerston's Saturdays, though that was possibly because he was certain to meet Lady Waldegrave there. Her allegiance was to Lord Palmerston, and she emphasized it by giving a dinner for Madame Walewski and the Palmerstons nine days before the Russell ministry fell. Despite this, her intimacy with the Bedfords was steadily increasing, and the Duke would freely discuss his brother's shortcomings with her. Within a month of Lord John's resignation, Bedford was telling her about 'the combination with the Peelites now in course of arrangement,—Duke of Newcastle to go to India—puzzled what to do with Normanby who wants India himself'. Frances suggested making him Lord Chamberlain, 'which the Duke liked, he said it had puzzled him, Lord John and Graham that morning—she also made some suggestion about getting Gladstone—she advised the little duke to give political dinners—he said he would, if he could get over his shyness'. As Fortescue prophetically wrote, 'With her power of winning confidence, her fidelity in observing it and the flashing intuition into men and things, which must often make her advice so valuable, she will become more and more influential'. It was a few days after this that at dinner at the Palmerstons' Chichester overheard Sir Henry Bulwer telling Frances, 'No one treats the world as well as you do. You despise it, you rule it, you do what you wish—but at the same time you make it respect you.'

Newcastle, Dufferin, William Vernon Harcourt and Chichester were among the many who came to visit her almost daily, all rather sour about the others. Chichester resented Newcastle's 'making her all kinds of family and personal confidences', considered W. V. Harcourt 'sententious and pugnacious' and was desolate when Lady Waldegrave said she thought him 'magnificent, the handsomest man she knew except Julian Fane—like the Penseroso in the Medici Chapel—like a hawk ready to pounce on his prey'.

In May Fortescue dined alone with her and Mr. Harcourt before they saw *Mind Your Own Business* at the Haymarket. The following day at Morier's newly founded Cosmopolitan Club, Monckton Milnes said to him, 'You're out of spirits—I suppose you haven't seen Lady Waldegrave lately.'

Chichester replied, 'I was with her and Mr. Harcourt at the play last night.'

'What play?' enquired Milnes.

'*Mind Your Own Business*', Fortescue was delighted to inform him.

The day after that the slightly feline Milnes, laughing over the reply with Frances, told her 'how admirably she managed to carry on her friendships without scandal'.

86

Lord Lincoln had done all in his power to persuade his wife to
return to him. Henry Edward Manning, the very Anglo-Catholic
Archdeacon of Chichester, was an old friend who did his best to
prevent a final break and had intended to visit Lady Lincoln himself in Italy, but was unable to get away. Gladstone, whose wife's
family was intimate with the Douglases, and who was himself indebted to Lincoln for his political début, offered to go, and finally
on the last day of July '49, reached Como where 'Mr. and Mrs.
Lawrence' were living at the Villa Mancini. 'Mrs. Lawrence' refused to see him and left the next day for Verona. A few days
later she gave birth to Horatio Walpole. Gladstone, who had been
half round Italy in his attempts to track her, had to admit defeat.

At last Lincoln was persuaded to have a Bill of Divorce brought
in which came up before the House of Lords in May '50. Gladstone was obliged to give evidence, and was made a guardian and
trustee to the children when the Bill was passed on August 14.
The old duke died in January 1852 and it was generally assumed
that the new duke would marry again.

He had, in 1848, acquired control of the *Morning Chronicle* of
which he appointed J. D. Cook to be editor. The paper was, of
course, Peelite in policy, but attracted a number of young men,
such as Fortescue and W. V. Harcourt, who were not themselves
Peelite. As the Duke of Bedford was the prime mover in the pro-
jected Liberal-Peelite coalition, it was unfortunate that the
Chronicle should so frequently have attacked him in the early
months of '52. Although its circulation was not large, the *Chronicle*
was of some importance as Cook had gathered quite a clever team
of contributors.

Frances was much in favour of the coalition and used her very
great influence with the two dukes to compose their differences.
In February she had them together to dine, and spent the rest of
the year breaking down Newcastle's obstinacy. Although at this
period her attendance at court was limited to drawing-rooms and
balls, she was peculiarly well-informed about the opinions of the
Queen and the Prince. Lady Churchill, whose death was so to
affect the Queen that it hastened her own end, was one of Frances's truest friends. The Van de Weyers, intimate friends of both
the Queen and the Prince, were also greatly attached to her, as was
Lord Torrington on whose amusing gossip the royal couple relied

for their knowledge of contemporary society. From all three sources she gathered that such was the Prince's estimation of Newcastle that any government in which he had a prominent part would meet with little opposition from Windsor.

There was a very gay party at Nuneham for Whitsun, mostly 'regulars'. The Bulteel family of whom mother, son and daughters were equally devoted to their hostess, Lady Hislop, Lady Morley, who was posthumously to acquire fame as Lady Isobel's successor in *East Lynne*, and—to Chichester's annoyance—young W. V. Harcourt and the Duke of Newcastle. The season had come to an abrupt end with the preparations for the general election which took place in July, leaving the Derby Government in a hopeless minority.

Poor Chichester Fortescue was by now entirely obsessed. He spent most of his spare time wandering about the places where Frances's youth had been spent. He gazed entranced at the semi-derelict Colosseum in Regent's Park; at Brompton, though the Grange had been demolished and the grounds built over, he walked up and down Yeomans Row and Michael's Grove, picturing the years she had spent there. He went down several times to Strawberry Hill, and in September with her almost equally besotted brother-in-law Charles Harcourt, he went out to Switzerland to explore Boisrond and Dombresson. Old John Braham had had his farewell season at Exeter Hall in the spring when Fortescue had gone twice to hear him, on the second occasion seeking him out in his dressing-room and introducing himself.

Notwithstanding the results of the election the Liberals were in no hurry to force Lord Derby to resign. It was essential for them to gain the support of the Peelites and that was by no means easy. When, in 1850, the Pope had re-established the Roman Catholic hierarchy in England, Lord John Russell had written a letter to the Bishop of Durham which reads as though he contemplated an armed invasion of the United Kingdom by papal forces. In February '51 he brought in his Ecclesiastical Titles Bill which, though supported by the usual British no-Popery hysteria, nauseated such rational beings as Lord Aberdeen, Newcastle, Sir James Graham, Gladstone, Sidney Herbert, and, to some extent, Lord Lansdowne. During the ministerial crisis at the end of February '51, Lord Aberdeen had refused Lord John the support of the Peelites on account of his attitude to the Catholic Church. The Bill, of course, passed triumphantly through both Houses, causing, as the Peelites had foreseen, irreparable damage in Ireland.

The well-informed Charles Greville, in October '52, assured Lord Clarendon that 'Sidney Herbert is wedded to Newcastle, who equally hates Derby and Lord John and dreams of a Newcastle administration'. It was none the less fairly certain that all the Peelites would follow Aberdeen's lead, but that they would not be prepared to take a position subordinate to the Liberals. At the beginning of December young William Vernon Harcourt published a pamphlet, *The Morality of Public Men*, attacking Lord Derby. Even the Queen was considerably influenced by it and, of course, Frances found it 'splendid'.

Writing to her father in December from Woburn, Lady Waldegrave informed him that 'we have been staying here since the 15th and intend to return to Nuneham on Monday for a few days, before proceeding to Lord Lansdowne's. . . . The Duke of Bedford is in good spirits about the new Government. . . . We travelled down with Lord John Russell, Lord Aberdeen and the Duke of Newcastle and found Lord Clarendon already arrived. Lord Lansdowne was also to have come with us, but he was at that time ill with the gout.' There was the usual gathering of dramatic amateurs but Fortescue was, to his misery, not invited, though W. V. Harcourt, 'gorged with praise and vanity', as Lady Norreys described him, with the success of his pamphlet, was there.

Disraeli had introduced his budget on December 3. The debate on it was adjourned till the 14th and then continued till the 16th. It was impossible for the Opposition to force the issue until the coalition had been arranged. Although Lord John and Palmerston were on such bad terms, they would both have to be in any new Cabinet. As Foreign Secretary, Palmerston was now totally unacceptable both to Windsor and to Lord John, yet it was doubtful if Palmerston would accept a seat in a Cabinet where Russell was at the Foreign Office. The Duke of Bedford dashed backwards and forwards between Woburn and London, struggling to pacify everybody.

Disraeli's speech on the 16th in defence of his budget was brilliant and witty. Gladstone closed the debate with one of the most sanctimonious speeches his righteous smugness ever produced. It proved, however, more effective than Disraeli's wit. There was a division on the house tax, and the Government was defeated by nineteen votes. The following day Lord Derby went to Osborne, and on the 20th the Queen sent for Lord Aberdeen.

The new ministry—another 'ministry of all the talents'—was predominantly Peelite. Lord John was certainly Foreign Secretary but his hands were well tied. Palmerston could do little damage at the Home Office. Lansdowne was in the Cabinet but without office, the Lords Chancellor, President and Privy Seal were Liberals, yet with Gladstone as Chancellor of the Exchequer, Graham at the Admiralty, Herbert Secretary at War, Newcastle at the Colonial Office, Cardwell at the Board of Trade, Canning as Postmaster-General and St. Germans Lord-Lieutenant of Ireland, it was a Peelite victory.

Even the formation of the new ministry and the rumour that he would be one of the Lords of the Treasury could not console poor Chichester Fortescue for his absence from Woburn. The day after Lord Aberdeen had undertaken to form a Cabinet, the Duke of Bedford, in excellent spirits now that his struggles had succeeded, sent a note up to Fortescue asking him there. Within an hour he was in the train. The house was so full that he was obliged to dine with two other bachelors in the tea room, but then he had the joy of dancing with Lady Waldegrave, and later Henry Grenfell discussed her 'noble character' with him at great length but assured him 'she wanted a great deal of care and protection—so utterly different from the cautious corrupt women of the world'. This advice Chichester took with profound solemnity, and as 'she was nervous, but perfectly charming' the next evening when they acted together in *Toads and Diamonds*, he 'took great care of her'.

Frances advised him to apply for a Lordship of the Treasury, which he did, first showing the little duke his letter of application. Clermont wrote protesting that, if the application was successful it would necessitate a by-election of which Clermont would have to bear the expense. Since he had his title he had no further interest in his brother's political career, who rather bitterly notes 'I never had any encouragement to distinguish myself, from my family'. Two days later Clermont wrote desiring him to withdraw his application which he refused to do. On New Year's Day Bedford regretfully told him that the Irishman, John Sadleir, had been appointed. It was a ghastly choice since Sadleir was a thorough-going rogue who, a few years later, poisoned himself to escape the consequence of his colossal frauds.

Nothing, however, could depress Chichester as long as Lady Waldegrave was under the same roof. Though she left Woburn two days before him, he fortunately had to go to Oxford to vote for Gladstone which made an excellent excuse for spending the night at Nuneham. Gladstone was not finding Oxford too respon-sive a constituency, and Mr. Harcourt's nephew, G. E. Vernon, who was on Gladstone's committee, wrote to Frances beseeching her to get Spencer Meadows to go to Oxford and vote. Canon Meadows was in process of moving to the living of Peldon which he had persuaded his sister to give him, since it was all too obvi-ous that Ward would never make a parson. Ward was at that time living at Cambridge, apparently on the assumption that there was something in the atmosphere that would in time make a scholar of him.

During the spring of 1853 Mr. Harcourt was freed from any contact with the Brahams. Hamilton in Germany and Charles in southern Italy were singing with considerable success. Augustus and his wife were in New York where Catherine Hayes had left them stranded over a year before. He had managed to find a few engagements, but in May Frances had to pay their passages back to England. Old Mr. Braham, after yet another sale to satisfy creditors, had left with Aunt Seph and Ward for Boulogne until they could raise the money to settle the remaining debts.

By the end of June Frances's patience was exhausted, as she explained to Aunt Seph.

'My dearest Seff,

I am really quite beset by begging letters. I shall not answer these people, but, I wish, that you would again inform them that I can and will do no more for the various members of my greedy family—Augustus and Spencer are as voracious as ever—I can promise you, that I am sick, disgusted and weary of the rapacity of these cormorants—Why is the Waldegrave property to be ex-pected to be devoured and destroyed by this curse of locusts? You know how I have crippled my means for those of my family who are more or less dear to me, and must be aware, that I have done for them more than they have any right to expect—

'I have heard lately from dear old Charley, he was disappointed (in the money way) at Corfu, but had much success at other places —he has returned to Messina—

'Give my best and most affectionate love to my Father and tell him that I wish he had never married and then I might not have been born to whet the appetites of all the Bolton and Braham pigs.

Best love to Ward.

Yours dearest Seff—in spite of your relations,
Most lovingly,
F. W.'

Although her Waldegrave husbands' disposal of their estates had caused some bitterness, Frances was on quite good terms with the eighth earl's two elder sons, Lord Chewton and the Reverend Samuel Waldegrave. In August the previous year her mother-in-law, Annette, Lady Waldegrave, had died at Sutton Place, near Woking, the home of the daughter Horatia, whose husband Captain Webbe-Weston, had died at the siege of Comern in Hungary in September '49. Doctor Hicks had made his relationship to Webbe-Weston his excuse for settling at Sutton Place with Annette and her unmarried daughter, Lady Ida. Frances and Lady Laura Money had always been on very affectionate terms, but the Moneys had for some years been living quietly on the East Coast with their two daughters and their visits to London were rare. General Money was now seventy-six, and his wife's health had deteriorated seriously.

Annette's death freed them all from the incubus of Algernon Hicks, as Laura wrote in answer to Frances's enquiry about mourning.

Crown Point
Sunday

'My dearest Fanny,

By this time you must have received my former note. I have answered your very affecte. letter as soon as possible, it was indeed a shock the death of my poor Mother for she was only ill 14 or 15 days a Billious Fever carried her off she is to be Buried to-morrow at the village next to Sutton, the name is Woking. Mr.

Hicks wrote to ask the General to attend which he declined. Now dearest you ask my opinion about mourning. I would certainly advise you for a few weeks to go into a slight one, not out of regard to her, but for the sake of your poor husbands, and especially as I have received two or three notes from our Relations, but none from Harley Street, with Black Seals etc. etc. Thank God we have no more to do with Mr. Hicks. On Wedn. or Thursday I will write and tell you any particulars I may hear. I have a great deal to communicate to you dearest. The General joins with me in kindest love.

In haste

My dearest Fanny

Your sincerely affecte. sister

Laura Money'

Most of her Harcourt in-laws were very fond of Lady Waldegrave. Three of the brothers, Egerton, Charles and Granville Vernon (the only brother who had not changed his name to Harcourt) adored her, as did their sister Mrs. Malcolm, but their affection for her seemed only to irritate Mr. Harcourt. He had wanted his wife to become a great society hostess, but she had succeeded too well, and she was invariably surrounded by a court of devotees, old and young, male and female, who consulted her on every possible occasion, attaching the greatest importance to her advice. It was no longer the shy Frances who would do nothing without Mr. Harcourt's advice, but a Frances who received adulation from everybody but himself.

He particularly disapproved of her affection for his nephew, W. V. Harcourt, who had become quite insufferable since the success of his pamphlet. He was a boorish young man who contradicted his uncle at his own dinner table, and yet Frances encouraged him to express his immature and intolerant ideas. The fact that all the Harcourts and the Norreyses sympathized with Frances in her quarrels with her husband naturally aggravated the trouble. Again the gaiety her high spirits infused into any party was to him undignified, and made him retire to his study with a book.

It was in trifling ways that he avenged himself. By some slight criticism he knew how to dash the radiant happiness that was making her the centre of attraction. He would wreck her amusing and witty account of some incident by correcting her on some totally unimportant detail, and could crush her enthusiasm for any project with a word.

By the beginning of May '53 his perversity and ill temper drove Frances to send for her old friend and solicitor Pearson, who frankly told Mr. Harcourt that his behaviour would certainly lead to a separation. At first it seemed to have had some effect. Towards the end of May they moved into No. 7 Carlton Gardens of which they had taken a ten year's lease. The excitement of decorating and furnishing it kept them both too busy to squabble, and a few days they spent alone at Harptree revived their earlier affection for each other.

VIII. THE BULTEEL QUARREL 1853–1854

OF ONE of his wife's friends Mr. Harcourt did approve. Early in the year she had met Lord Chelsea, a man in his early forties who found that his duties as Tory M.P. for Dover conveniently necessitated his leaving his deeply religious wife to her devotions in Durham. Frances's circle was horrified by the new friend. George Byng, for years an intimate of hers, called Chelsea 'the serpent who is more subtle than the beasts of the field', and Mary Bulteel, the closest of her women friends, exhausted herself with warnings. The one person who approved was Mr. Harcourt. He was as blind as was, at first, Frances herself to the oddly sinister suavity that made Chelsea so disliked.

Although her admirers did not noticeably admire each other, Lady Waldegrave insisted on their being mutually helpful. In March Edwin Arnold, who was later to write *The Light of Asia*, had produced a volume of poems dedicated to her. These she made Chichester Fortescue review, his notice appearing in the *Examiner*. As he was so nervous of speaking, he felt that he would probably be better writing political articles and found that J. W. Parker was glad to take them for *Frazer's*. Chichester tried to see Frances daily, but was also becoming rather involved with John Ruskin's socially ambitious wife, Effie. In the elegant house she had made her husband take in Charles Street she enjoyed confiding her woes to the sympathetic and handsome Fortescue. To leave his wife alone with good-looking, virile young men apparently provided Ruskin with a strange mental stimulus in his solitary pleasures, and thus he rarely interrupted their tête-à-tête. Fortescue's sister Harriet had switched her allegiance to Effie, though young Mrs. Ruskin shared none of John's or Harriet's passion for social welfare.

In June Harriet came over from Ireland to stay with the Ruskins, which led to her brother seeing almost as much of Effie as he did of Frances who, however, was always relieved to have her crush of admirers a little reduced. Soon after Harriet's arrival Chichester was at a Drawing Room with his sister-in-law, Lady

Clermont, and took the opportunity of introducing her to Lady Waldegrave. Lady Clermont, a timorous, retiring character, was petrified at meeting the dazzling, exquisitely dressed, brilliant leader of society whom she resented as the only obstacle to Chichester's marrying. It was very unjust as at that moment Frances was doing her utmost to marry him off to Dosia Vyner with whom she had done such propaganda that poor Miss Vyner was hopelessly in love with him. With the exception of Chelsea, none of the men in almost daily attendance at Carlton Gardens was singled out for particular attention, and if they all insisted on visiting her, Frances expected them to be affable to each other in her presence.

Although she had no premonition that she would ever again live at her Twickenham house, this summer, in a fit of nostalgia for the Bohemian Waldegrave days, Frances asked some of her most intimate friends to a champagne luncheon at Strawberry Hill. Chelsea, Chichester Fortescue, old Charles Harcourt, young W. V. Harcourt and the inseparable friends George Byng and Pucky Glyn, equally fervent in their friendship for their hostess, were there with Lady Norreys, Lady Poltimore—the daughter-in-law of Charles Braham's godfather, Sir Charles Bampfylde, herself Frances's devoted ally—Lady Ely, Lady Johnstone—Mr. Harcourt's sister whose children adored their young aunt, and the Lucans. His second wife's friendship with the Lucans Mr. Harcourt could never understand. Though Lord Lucan was his first wife's brother, he had mostly succeeded in avoiding him during Lady Elizabeth's lifetime. Since her death there had been endless trouble about the marriage settlements with which the feckless Lucan seemed unable to cope, yet Lady Elizabeth's successor forced his company on her husband.

It was a gay party, as light-hearted as in the summer of '39. They all went over the semi-derelict house with its 'rotting old walls', and then over Little Strawberry Hill, lunched in the garden and then played 'Friar's Ground' on the lawn. As the weather was perfect, they ended up rehearsing by the river-side the play they would be doing at Nuneham in July. At dinner that night Monckton Milnes delighted Fortescue by telling him that old Samuel Rogers still talked of Frances's first visit to Strawberry Hill, and remembered her as she was then, 'a very beautiful girl'.

As the season drew to a close Lady Waldegrave's increasing social success brought her little but unhappiness. Her husband was infuriated when Lady Ailesbury told him that 'Soapy' Wilberforce, Bishop of Oxford, whom she had been teasing about the frequency of his visits to Frances, had said, 'She's a first-rate creature, a noble character and the world sees the worst of her.' He was even angrier on hearing his cousin, Lord Granville, aptly nicknamed 'Puss', telling her one night at the Palmerston's, 'You ought to be a Prime Minister's wife, if you had been Lord John's you would have kept the Whig party together.'

An invitation from the Duchess of Sutherland to Dunrobin in September enthralled Mr. Harcourt, but Frances was furious as she had had a very exhausting season, and had been greatly looking forward to a few quiet weeks in Germany. The stiff formality of Trentham, Stafford House and Dunrobin depressed her, and she knew that her husband would expect her to shine the whole time. The fact that Chelsea would be there was an added embarrassment. Although there was something about him that fascinated her, she was also a little frightened of him, and it was largely only because her own friends so disparaged him that she continued to see him. Her husband's affection for him was to her incomprehensible, but if Mr. Harcourt forced her to go to Dunrobin, and forced Chelsea's company upon her, he could take the consequences.

The gaieties of the summer were considerably overcast for her by the old man's querulousness and his endless interference with her arrangements for the Nuneham parties. His passion for detail, the complacent pleasure with which he proved her wrong in front of her guests, and the wearisome prosiness of his lectures on her misdeeds drove her to desperation. There were times when she utterly understood the feelings of the first Napoleon who had terminated a boring, pointless discussion with Mr. Harcourt on Elba 'by making water against a wall'.

The visit to Dunrobin was not a success. Chelsea was the whole time in ardent attendance and Frances, thoroughly bored, flirted outrageously with him and with the Sutherlands' son, Lord Stafford, whose attentions had embarrassed Frances for some time since she was fond of his young wife. At the same time she was grimly determined that, if Mr. Harcourt would force her to be with men notoriously fascinated by her, he should learn his lesson. Her guest's flirtations in no way worried the Duchess of Sutherland, but she was scandalized by a different misdemeanour of Lady Waldegrave's. With the very late hours Frances kept during the London season and at Nuneham, she was too exhausted to face Mr. Harcourt's ill humour at the breakfast table, and had for some time made it her custom not to appear before luncheon. At Dunrobin breakfast in bed was only excusable on the grounds of illness, and the Duchess never completely forgave her for introducing so dissolute a habit into society.

The great excitement of January '53 had been Louis Napoleon's marriage to the Comtesse de Teba whom Fortescue had met at Lady Antrobus's ball eighteen months before, 'a pretty, fair, fascinating foreigner, sitting with her feet on the rung of a chair showing her ankles, *très entourée*'. Morier was delighted with the latest story from the Paris embassy.

Louis Napoleon had told his old Uncle Jerome, '*J'ai les pieds froids.*'

The cynical old man had replied: '*Eh bien, il faut coucher avec tes bas.*'

Frances was intrigued by the marriage, partly because of Madame de Bruntière's abortive plans in '47 and partly because Eugénie was reported to be the daughter of Lord Clarendon, despite Madame de Montijo's assurance, more honest than discreet, '*que les dates ne correspondent pas*'.

The last week of October and the first week of November, Mr. Harcourt, his wife, Canon Harcourt and Chichester were together in Paris. A number of their friends were there, the Poltimores, the Elys, the Barringtons and Thackeray among others, and it would have been a very pleasant fortnight had Mr. Harcourt not been disagreeable the whole time. On their return to London they all dined at the Norreyses'. Charles Braham, a great friend of Lady Norreys, was there on a visit from Italy.

Fortescue notes in his diary that 'Mr. H. made no attempt to introduce us. I shook hands with him—liked his looks—short man with enormous chest and arms—good looking, frank openhearted unaffected face with plenty of fire in it—speaking confidently but simply and without a grain of affectation of his singing, his successes, etc.—he often reminded me of his sister. When

she asked him, in spite of the objections of Mr. H., to sing after
dinner he stood up and sang in the most natural way and with a
voice and force and feeling which electrified me. I said it was like
expecting an accordeon and finding an organ, she was delighted.
C.B. made a simple apology to Mr. H. for not having pleased him
once at Nuneham—it was a scene in which Mr. H. had been very
rude to him—tonight he was civil, but inconceivably hard and
unsympathizing, without a shadow of the manner one would
expect towards the favourite brother of his wife—on the contrary
patronizing and full of that covert insolence which says "You
are an inferior being, you minister to the amusement of my class."
He seemed to say to *her*, "You, I admit, are an exception to all
rules, but your brother is nothing to me."' For Chichester the
evening was spoiled when Chelsea appeared after dinner.

Fortescue was invited to the cottage at Starch Green where old
Braham and Seph were staying with Aunt Carshore. He writes, 'The
party was Mr. B., C.B., Ward B., Miss Bolton or Aunt Seff, Mrs.
Braham's sister, Mrs. Carshore, a very old lady née Wilson, sister
of "Wom" and aunt of Mrs. B., whose husband was a merchant
in the South of Ireland, Chelsea and myself. What an evening this
was! Wonderful to look at Lady W. and then at the others, and
think of all her strange history, of the contrast between her life
and theirs, between the gilded mansion I had seen in the morning
where all the highest society in England would flock as soon as
its doors should be opened to them, and the little suburban
cottage, where these people are supported by her. We sat down
to table, Chelsea on one side of her, I on the other—she at the
head of the table, her father opposite to her, looking as fresh as a
rose under his wig. We had a great dish of macaroni, because it
was her favourite dish at the Grange. . . . Ward is a pleasant
looking, cheery little fellow with a short allowance of teeth. . .
Mr. Braham did not say much—he is shy and brusque, remarkably
independent in manner, as one used to hold his own with the
highest, he must always have been quite free from any obsequious-
ness. "Aunt Seph" is a nice creature, very much pleased at having
us, thanking Lady W. for coming. . . . To complete the party, a
little dog and a monkey must not be left out. We went for a few
minutes to Ward B's. room upstairs and then back to the dining
room, where Ganz was at the piano and Charles sang—his father

sat in a corner and listened—presently, with very little pressing, he went to the piano and gave us his old "Death of Nelson", accompanying himself, and singing with wonderful voice and force and spirit. I thought and so did she of her favourite Nelson and what we did for his memory last spring. Mr. Braham is very fond of whist and Lady W. proposed a rubber, she and I, Miss Bolton and Mr. B.—C.B. startled us by stepping out into the middle of the roon and singing some fine thing. Near 12 we broke up.'

Charles Braham was to leave again for Italy where he had an engagement at Vercelli. As Ward's presence in England seemed to serve no useful purpose, and as Charles had had a number of illnesses, their sister decided to send Ward out with him, an arrangement that delighted Mr. Harcourt. Hamilton arrived in London at the beginning of December from Germany where for the last year he had been unlucky with his engagements. Lord Chelsea, who had considerable influence in the musical world, at once took a great interest in him, to advance himself in Lady Waldegrave's good graces.

At the end of November Chichester Fortescue had Mr. Harcourt's nephew, Granville Edward Vernon, staying with him at the Red House, Ardee. Frances had decided that he would make an ideal husband for Fortescue's strong-minded sister, Harriet. Though twenty-eight, she showed no signs of marrying and was daily becoming more peculiar in her political outlook. Another woman to whom she was as devoted as she was to Effie Ruskin, was a neighbour, Mrs. Ross of Bladensburg, who together with her husband was a staunch follower of the frantic Russophobe, David Urquhart.

Urquhart, a great favourite of William IV, had been attached to Sir Stratford Canning's mission to Constantinople in 1831. He had become passionately devoted to Turkey and everything Turkish, and was by 1836 Secretary of the Embassy in Constantinople. In 1833 he had published a brilliant book, *Turkey and its Resources*, and two years later had begun to issue *The Portfolio*, as hostile to Russia as it was favourable to the Turks. In 1837 his independent attitude and virulence about Russia had obliged Lord Palmerston, as Foreign Minister, to recall him. This completely convinced Urquhart that Palmerston was a Russian agent, and his hatred for Russia was henceforth only equalled by his hatred of Palmerston. In 1847 he was elected M.P. for Stafford and immediately set about trying to have Palmerston impeached. In February the next year his follower, Chisholm Anstey, brought a motion to impeach Palmerston for 'subserviency to Russian designs' in his foreign policy. Thanks to the Rosses of Bladensburg, Urquhart's *Portfolio* had become Harriet Fortescue's political Bible.

Although the House of Commons had only been amused by the attempt to impeach Palmerston, the relentless perseverance of Urquhart's campaign caused its victim very considerable annoyance and though he endeavoured to ignore it, it may have been partly responsible for his misguided belligerence towards Russia in 1853.

By the end of September '53 the strained situation between Russia and Turkey had led to the British and French fleets being sent to the Bosphorus. Louis Napoleon felt that a war might take his subjects' mind off internal affairs, but Aberdeen was determined not to involve England in war over a matter that concerned her almost not at all. Palmerston was violently anti-Russian. On that point, though on that point alone, Lord John Russell was one of his few allies in the Cabinet. Aberdeen and Gladstone thoroughly distrusted the Turks, and could not see that Britain's interests were in any way involved in the Russo-Turkish quarrel. Sidney Herbert, Granville and the Dukes of Newcastle and Argyll were for peace, firmly supported by the Queen who was disgusted at the way Aberdeen had already been blackmailed into an unfriendly attitude to Russia by Palmerston's and Russell's threats to leave the Government.

Lord Aberdeen's difficulties increased daily. At the outset it had not been easy to persuade Lord John to join his administration. Aberdeen himself brought only some fifty supporters to the Government, whereas Lord John brought five times that number. Lady John therefore felt that he should accept the premiership or nothing. He, himself, if he joined, was determined to be Leader of the House of Commons, but was unwilling also to accept the duties of the Foreign Office. Lord Clarendon, the other candidate, managed to persuade Lady John to agree to her husband's becoming Foreign Secretary only on condition that Clarendon would take over immediately should Lord John find his double duties too onerous. Thus, early in February, Clarendon found himself at the Foreign Office.

Some idea of the clash of personalities within the Cabinet is given by the Duke of Newcastle's description of a scene there. 'One day in Cabinet, Lord Aberdeen was sitting between Lord John Russell and the Duke himself. Lord John made some captious and fretful criticism as usual. Lord Aberdeen, seized with a sudden impulse, said to him, "Lord John, the trouble is that your object is to get me out of my place and seize it yourself—but if you succeed in the former, don't be so sure that you'll be my successor. I should not wonder if it were the Duke", pointing to him. After the Cabinet the Duke said to Lord Aberdeen, "What makes you say that? You have ruined me. Lord John will never rest until he has ruined me. You have roused his jealousy." '

The Government was pledged to support the Reform Bill Lord John intended to bring in, but on December 15 Palmerston resigned, ostensibly to mark his disapproval of the Bill. He well knew it was almost impossible for the Government to carry on without his support, and he proposed to make the disagreement about Reform his excuse rather than disagreement about Aberdeen's, to him, dilatory war policy. Having successfully shaken the country's confidence in the Aberdeen Cabinet, and having forced Aberdeen himself to realize the weakness of the Peelite position, Palmerston graciously consented to withdraw his resignation within less than a fortnight.

During this winter Lady Waldegrave was too preoccupied with the alterations and redecoration of 7 Carlton Gardens and with the splendid London début she was planning for her brother Hamilton to have much time for politics. When Fortescue arrived at Nuneham for a short visit after Christmas, she was full of her plans both for the London house and for her brother, but was again insistent that he should apply for a Lordship of the Treasury should one fall vacant. Things were still very difficult at Nuneham, as Chichester's diary for the last day of '53 shows.

'Dec. 31. One of my strange conversations with Mr. H., invited, as usual, by himself after a great quarrel with her. I wd. not enter into the merits of the small question at issue, in wh. he may have been in reality reasonable & sensible, but said all I cd. about the way of dealing with her—told him how provoking his manner was—admitted that she was hot & impatient, but tried to make him feel that he must keep his own temper in order for her sake & his own. I hope to God I made some impression—certainly I struck him at the time—for I was very earnest & strained every nerve to say the right thing. I implored him to believe that any sacrifice of pride, of the love of being in the right, etc. was worth making for the sake of harmony between them . . . her brother John [Hamilton] came after we had sat down to dinner —a large featured, broadchested, thick limbed fellow, with jet black eyes and hair, & a rich complexion—striking looking but very showy—quite at his ease—not so taking as "Charley" but talked better—he sang after dinner a beautiful German thing "Eine Perle nenn' ich mein" etc, Lady Norreys played. Lady W. was delighted, and sang something herself in that sweet voice— she looked delightful in her crimson shawl.'

The next day at dinner Hamilton 'rattled away à tort et à travers—bad jokes, bad puns—exuberant spirits—very likeable fellow—she says,—so like her—"I'm afraid he'll never make a gentleman".' After Hamilton's six years alone in Germany, 'a loose stage life' he had become 'an utter man of the stage' and Frances persuaded the embarrassed Chichester to give him 'some hints about manner and dress, to be quieter, less loud etc. which he took beautifully, poor Hamilton!'.

When Fortescue got back to Ardee, early in January '54, he found that Harriet had filled the house with David Urquhart's publications. It led to a number of quarrels with her brother, especially after the news that Sadleir (Dickens's 'Mr. Merdle'), had resigned his Lordship of the Treasury. Chichester decided that he would accept it, if it were offered to him, and on January 23 he had the offer from the Premier.

His acceptance of course meant a by-election for Co. Louth, and it was a difficult contest. The Irish could not be made to see that it was to their advantage to have Irish members in the Government. The moment one of their members accepted office, he was considered a traitor—to have sold himself for English gold.

The new Lord of the Treasury worried less about the election than about the headway Lord Chelsea was making. Old Braham and Seph had taken rooms in Great Ormond Street where Chelsea became a constant visitor. He had persuaded Frances that he could be of 'immense value' to her brothers, and was pulling all manner of strings for Hamilton. It was decided that the latter should have a course of lessons from Garcia before his English début, and it all meant daily meetings between Lord Chelsea and Lady Waldegrave. Chichester followed his rival's example and was assiduous in his calls at Great Ormond Street where the astonished Seph soon found herself acting hostess to half her niece's admirers. Young William Vernon Harcourt, whose own great affection for his aunt caused some comment, was another who resented Chelsea intensely, and he made common cause with Mary Bulteel in protesting about it. By the end of March Mr. Harcourt himself had swelled the number of those who detested Lord Chelsea, with the result that the rows at Carlton Gardens increased in quantity and intensity.

Having changed his mind about one man, Harcourt now decided that Chichester was the good influence and was pressing in his invitations. He took Frances to Harptree for Easter, and asked the young Irishman to join them. Chichester had been there on a short visit the previous year, and was delighted to see her in a setting of which she had told him so much. Harptree Court was, at the time, occupied by the man who was Frances's manager at the lead mines which had not been worked since Roman times. Since their reopening the locals swore that even by daylight legionaries could be seen marching along the hill-tops. She had some idea of enlarging the house, and this visit was to see what could be arranged. Mr. Harcourt was good humoured all the six days, and Fortescue was enchanted by the reception the villagers and tenants gave their beloved countess.

A fortnight later Hamilton made his operatic début at Drury Lane as the Duke in *Lucrezia Borgia*. His sister bought tickets by the score, and had Lady Norreys, Georgie Malcolm, Fortescue and, of course, her husband in her box. Old Braham and Seph were in the pit box, the Cutlers and the Pearsons in the stalls, with Chelsea everywhere at once, behaving as though he not only owned the theatre, but had written music and libretto into the bargain. The notices were quite favourable, but Hamilton's audience always experienced a vague feeling of disappointment.

Although during the season of '54 Lady Waldegrave had been

entertaining on a considerable scale, the decorations at Carlton Gardens were not completed until June, which together with her preoccupation with Hamilton's affairs had prevented her from taking the usual interest in the political situation. Palmerston and Russell had prevailed upon Aberdeen to declare war on Russia at the end of March, but the national optimism was such that it had had little effect on the gaieties of the season. In May Madame Walewski had given a superb *bal costumé* at the French embassy, at which the whole Royal Family was present. Lady Waldegrave's quadrille was dressed in the period of Henri Quatre, the costumes designed by the sculptor Marochetti. Frances was La Reine Margot. In dancing Prince Albert complimented her on her quadrille, adding, 'But can anything be more beautiful than yourself.'

A week later at the Queen's ball, Mr. Harcourt was apparently taking no chances with a second royal compliment, for he 'made a horrible fool of himself, insisting on her going away early, following her about, etc.'. She was not, however, to forego a second royal compliment since the same week at a Drawing Room as she made her curtsy, the Duchess of Cambridge was overheard saying to the Queen, '*wunderschön*'.

Towards the end of the month Lady Waldegrave gave her most magnificent reception of the season. The greatest singers then in London were engaged, Ronconi, Bosio, Didier, Gordoni—and Hamilton Braham. Fortunately Hamilton was at the top of his form and the whole occasion was spendid enough to dazzle any adverse critic. Old Braham was there with Ward who was on a visit from Italy. Frances had told Chichester to bring the Clermonts with him. She sat with Louisa and had a few words with Lord Clermont, who was unfortunately far too canny about money to be anything but aghast at the princely scale on which his hostess entertained.

Clermont felt he had reason enough to be depressed. At the beginning of the month Harriet had announced her engagement to David Urquhart. He was twenty years her senior, and hopelessly impractical—it was doubtful if his whole income amounted to £500 a year. His morals were probably as Turkish as his politics, and apparently he expected Harriet to spend the rest of her life in the steam bath which he considered hygienically essential. The only one of the family who sympathized with her was the one whose career would probably be most adversely affected—Chichester. He had already realized that his sister was too eccentric a character to make a possible wife for a conventional man. He had told Frances the day he heard the news, and she was equally pleased at Harriet's courage.

Chelsea had used Hamilton as a stepping-stone to Lady Waldegrave's favour, and Chichester was determined to level things up by turning Ward's visit to account. He suggested a little excursion to Paris to which Ward gladly agreed. Most unexpectedly it was the beginning of the greatest friendship of their lives. Frances, delighted that their trip had been a success, welcomed them back with news of her latest scheme. Dudbrook was within easy distance of London, and with a little alteration would make a charming place for Saturday to Monday parties during the season. Harptree was too far off and would be too difficult to alter, and for her was full of memories of Lord Waldegrave's last ghastly illness. Mr. Harcourt and she took Lady Norreys and Chichester to inspect Navestock and Dudbrook. Mr. Harcourt was in an excellent mood, Frances was as excited as a child, and Chichester as usual enraptured when a little more of her past life was revealed.

Mr. Harcourt's good moods were becoming increasingly rare. Lady Norreys herself told Frances to treat his temper as a disease, yet his behaviour was totally unpredictable. One day he came into the room to find Frances admiring a sketch of Chewton Church Fortescue had given her. He promptly wrapped it up and carried it away, telling her it was foolish to pass the day looking at drawings. A few weeks later he took Frances to Kew Gardens for the day. When they got back she assured Chichester 'he was in the best possible humour, he beats you all when he is like that, so agreeable'. Two days after that Chichester was telling him, 'I fear no human counsellor can make any impression on that fatal self-satisfaction of yours'. It is scarcely surprising that Mr. Harcourt had spoken to him ten days earlier 'of the position which circumstances, he hardly knew how, had brought me into . . . that conversations took place between us which he never thought of with his own brothers'. There had been a tremendous quarrel because Harcourt had flatly refused to allow her to buy a billiard table for Dudbrook. When they next went to Nuneham, Frances was enraptured to find a billiard table in the Octagon room there. She stared at it in amazement, as she said 'as a cow does at her calf and wonders how the devil it got there'.

For once the July party at Nuneham was disastrous. As usual, Chelsea, Mary Bulteel and Chichester were among the guests, each of the three busily warning their hostess against the other. All three of them had protested about her affection for young William Harcourt who Miss Bulteel was convinced had no principles, but since William had joined her in the attack on Chelsea she was more friendly to him. The Bulteels all liked Chichester, yet it was only just to point out to Frances that if her intimacy with Chelsea was causing a great deal of talk, the fact that Chichester saw her as many times a day as he possibly could was also eagerly discussed. The war was keeping Newcastle too occupied for his attentions to cause much comment and Frances had found brides for another two of her slaves, G. E. Vernon and George Byng.

The Nuneham parties were so popular that every attic was requisitioned, and there had usually to be an early and a late dinner. The younger guests were generally happy to be at the early dinner as it was a gayer affair. One evening, for some reason, Mary Bulteel refused to join the early dinner. Frances, always impatient and quick tempered, exhausted by the constant scenes with her husband, lost her temper completely and told Mary it was utter treachery. It was all trivial and absurd, but neither would apologize and everybody enjoyed making further mischief. When, towards the end of July, Lady Waldegrave and Mr. Harcourt left for Carlsbad, it seemed that the devoted friendship of six years had come to an end.

AT LAST Mr. Harcourt was happy. He had realized that the visit to Dunrobin the previous year had been a mistake, and that Frances then, as now, had wanted to get away from all the men who surrounded her. In a letter on their arrival at Calais she describes Mr. Harcourt's reactions.

'We had a delightful passage. I did not feel in the least ill but was more surprised than I can tell you to see Mr. Harcourt in such a state of happiness that he did nothing but sing at the top of his voice, love and drinking songs all the way. Imagine his singing to me 'Drink to me only with thine eyes'. On landing we found we had been travelling in company with Lord Robert Clinton so he got into our fly and we supped together at 3 o'clock in the morning. . . . He remarked to me that he had never seen Mr. Harcourt with such a happy expression of countenance. Soon afterwards he said "I wish that I had known that you were on board" and then rather grunted at having been kept awake by a happy careless dog, who would insist upon singing a lot of old fashioned songs. You should have seen his face when I told him that the noisy dog was G. G. Harcourt. I never in my life saw any human being happier, and when he told me it was owing to his being alone with me, I could not help being a little *attendrie*. I was also very much pleased at his telling me on our way to the station that he had kept a bit of good news for me as he expected that I should be low at leaving all my friends. He then read a letter from Mr. Barwell announcing the agreeable news that they had lighted upon a fine vein of lead. The consequence of this to me and to Mr. Barwell will be particularly pleasant.'

Mr. Harcourt's good humour lasted spendidly through the summer. After a restful month at Carlsbad they made their way via Prague, Dresden, Berlin and Frankfurt to Lucerne, where Charles and Ward met them. By the end of October they had all reached Florence, where on the 27th they were joined by Chichester Fortescue. He had been over to Ireland for Harriet's wedding to David Urquhart, but had also been supervising the alterations at Dudbrook. There was a great deal to discuss. A fortnight earlier Mary Bulteel had accepted William Vernon Harcourt's proposal of marriage, and naturally the fiancés repeated everything unfavourable that Frances had said about the other. Everyone was astonished at the engagement and few of their friends believed the marriage would come off. On the 16th, Norreys's father had died so Lavinia was now Countess of Abingdon, and the same week they heard of the death of Lord Chewton of wounds he had received at the Battle of the Alma, leaving a young widow and a small son who presumably would become Frances's heir.

In the middle of November Charles and Ward left for Naples, and a few days later the other three began their homeward journey, travelling together as far as Susa, at that time the railway terminus. Chichester described the journey over the Mont Cenis. 'Nov. 28. Lady W. and Mr. H. went off this morning early to cross the Cenis. I left Susa by the Courier at 11-30, beautiful day, blue sky without a cloud, but I saw the snow blowing like steam or dust from the edges of the mountains, showing wind. As we went up, a traveller, who met us, stopped the Courier, and I heard something said of a private carriage having been overturned higher up. I was frightened but relieved by being told that no harm had happened to the travellers. I kept on the look out and begged the courier to stop when we came up to them. One could scarcely look out of the sledge window from the violence of the wind driving the fine snow before it. At last the traineau stopped at one of the Refuges, Casa di Recovero No. 2. Shall I ever forget it? I fought my way in, being hardly able to make a few steps from the sledge to the door of the Refuge against the *tourmente*, and found Lady W. sitting on a table in the wild looking room, unlike herself, her hair blown about, scarcely able to speak, nervous and almost breathless. Mr. H. anxious and frightened. It relieved her to see me come in and she said, "Stay". So of course I let the Courier go to the devil, carrying off all my luggage. They had been blown over on the road, had been got out and carried into the Refuge, and, just as I came, had attempted to return to the carriage, in order to go on, but my Lady, who had been quite cool when the accident happened, could not endure the furious wind, lost her nerve and made the men who were carrying her bring her back. There was nothing for it but to pass the night in the Refuge and we did. We got some rough, eatable food, were smoked out of an inner room where there was a quantity of beech leaves in a corner for beds and where the servants passed the night, and Lady W. settled herself in her travelling chair near the stove in the kitchen, well wrapped up. I lay on the carriage cushions on the floor, wild looking but cheerful and civil cantonniers and guides round us who crouched round the fire and slept as best they could. . . . Mr. H. slept on a dirty bed in an inner room. There was a poor penniless Piedmontese confectioner there, making his way to Chambéry. We found out his story, he had not a sou to buy bread. She and I gave him his supper and money to buy shoes, etc. He made the journey to Chambéry on the step of the carriage behind, without Mr. H. knowing anything about it. I shall never forget that delightful night in that miserable place.'

After a week in Paris with them, Chichester preceded them to London. Within a week, however, he was again able to pay his daily visits to Carlton Gardens. Lady Waldegrave at once set about plans for the widowed Lady Chewton, and, less agreeable, trying to explain away to young William Harcourt the criticisms of him that she had made to Miss Bulteel. He acidly assured her that her position in society would greatly deteriorate without the support of the Bulteels, a remark scarcely calculated to promote the revival of that friendship, but a remark that considerably changed Frances's attitude to the world.

The year 1855 began in an atmosphere of political tension. After decades of peace, the Duke of Newcastle had found the War Office hopelessly antiquated, and the Crimean War began before there had been time to make any considerable reforms. On January 23 J. A. Roebuck gave notice of his intention to move for the appointment of a Select Committee 'to enquire into the condition of our army before Sebastopol'. Lord John Russell seized the opportunity to spite all his Cabinet colleagues, and promptly resigned. It was a death blow to the Aberdeen adminis-tration which was forced to resign on February 1. The Queen sent for Lord Derby, but neither he nor Lord John were able to form a Government, and finally the task had to be entrusted to Lord Palmerston.

The Peelites were naturally disgusted with Russell, but were prepared to support Palmerston who had taken a strong line with Lord John about his conduct. Frances, as the Peelite hostess and as a close friend of Newcastle, showed her sympathies by appearing in the gallery of the House of Lords to hear the speech Newcastle made in his own defence. Fortescue, on the other hand, stung by her warm support of the duke, was one of Russell's few adherents. Lord and Lady John's affectionate interest in him somewhat blinded him to their political misconduct. The previous autumn Lady John had written warning him of the dangers of his intimacy with Lady Waldegrave. Chichester had not chosen to reply to that, but soon after the fall of the Aberdeen Cabinet, he told Lady John some of the unfavourable comment he had heard on her influence and advice to her husband. Lord John wrote, asking Chichester to call on him next day, and claimed that he was much obliged for the information. He denied the truth of the gossip but admitted that his wife possibly talked unwisely, 'but how Lady Palmerston talks'. Fortescue pointed out that Lady Palmerston was a very worldly woman whereas Lady John was a very unworldly one. Lord John said, 'Yes, that's very true and I am afraid I shall never cure her of saying things of that kind.' The danger lay not in what she said to others, but what she said to him.

The quarrel with the Bulteels and her determination to break with Lord Chelsea had led Frances once again into the political arena. Strangely enough it was Mary Bulteel's uncle, the third Earl Grey, who had supplanted Chelsea. A son of the great Lord Grey, he had held various political offices and had been Colonial Secretary in the Russell administration, but could not bear Lord John, whom his father had called 'a mean, impertinent little fellow'. Like Lady Waldegrave's two other old friends, Bedford and Lansdowne, Grey seemed to have more political influence when he was out of office than when he was a minister.

Whenever her political heroes were making speeches Frances usually appeared in the gallery, a fascinating distraction for the listening peers who envied the orator joining her at the end of his speech. On one occasion the Lord President of the Council so far forgot the dignity of his office as to send up a note congratulating her on her bonnet.

After less than three weeks in Palmerston's Cabinet, Graham, Herbert and Gladstone resigned, thus making it a purely Liberal

Government. In the consequent reshuffle Lord John was offered and accepted the Colonial Office, which delighted Chichester as much as it disgusted Frances. It was while Gladstone was explaining his secession that Harriet Urquhart was introduced to her in the Strangers' Gallery. Urquhart's fanatical denunciations of Palmerston considerably embarrassed Chichester now that he was serving under him. The new Premier was invariably cordial, yet Fortescue, a little disappointed that the formation of this Government and the later rearrangement had still left him as a Lord of the Treasury, feared that his relationship to Urquhart was telling against him. The Queen had few illusions about the sagacity of her cousin, the Duke of Cambridge, and it was probably only during these years that she paid much attention to any of his political observations. On his journeys both out to and back from the Crimea, where he commanded a division, Cambridge had seen Louis Napoleon who had discussed the whole Crimean situation frankly with him for the Queen's information. Again, Cambridge was able to give her first-hand information about the mismanagement at the front. It was at this time that a curious intimacy grew up between the Duke of Cambridge and David Urquhart, that would have caused Palmerston no uneasiness had not Cambridge been temporarily in favour at Windsor. Whatever the Premier's reactions really were, Chichester found the whole position too awkward, and in March resigned his Lordship of the Treasury.

Lord Lucan had by then returned to England to defend his conduct over the Charge of the Light Brigade and Frances, of course, was his vehement partisan. 'Looking lovely, pale and excited, in a brown silk dress and straw bonnet', she was in the gallery of the House of Lords to hear his speech, taking with her Lady Palmerston and her latest friend, Madame Bernstorff, the gay young wife of the new Prussian ambassador. Chichester was ordered to take Mr. Braham, who was delighted to see Lord Lucan join Lady Waldegrave the moment he had finished his speech.

Two days later Frances called on old Lord Lyndhurst to get him to assist Lord Lucan in his case and pamphlet. The old man received her in his library with 'What a love you are', and refused her nothing. The Duke of Bedford had just been to consult her about his will. His own son, though far more generous than the duke, was an eccentric character, a recluse whose only interest was the mistress for whom he later built a small palace facing the Broad Walk at Kensington. As it was unlikely that the son would ever marry, the dukedom would eventually pass to his nephew, Hastings, son of the witty and caustic Lady William Russell, 'a half concealed Roman Catholic'—later she admitted her conversion—and Hastings was much influenced by his mother. Frances, although on excellent terms with Lady William who addressed her as 'Fairest of the Fair', and although she politically distrusted Lord John, advised the little duke to enable Lord John to accept a peerage by providing him with sufficient property 'so as to make sure of at least one Protestant Lord Russell'.

She was even called in to settle diplomatic disputes. Van de Weyer, the Belgian Minister, as doyen of the Diplomatic Corps in London, was worried about a quarrel as to precedence between Madame Usedom, the wife of a Prussian diplomat, and the newly arrived Madame Bernstorff, and so came to Carlton Gardens to beseech her to reason with her new friend, which she did with complete success.

At the beginning of April Dudbrook was ready for its first party. Frances was enchanted with her little house, and decided to lend it to Lady Chewton who was looking for a house in the country. She was preoccupied with plans for others of her family at the same time, as Charles had decided that he had had enough of Italy and with Ward arrived on the 18th in London. This decision was partly due to a very just paragraph H. F. Chorley had written in the *Athenaeum* the previous autumn. 'Mr. Charles Braham—say the Italian journals—has been singing with the utmost success . . . at Bari. The place and the praise taken in context with the number of years which have elapsed since Mr. C. Braham's *début* form a sadly illustrative commentary on the wanton waste of gifts which English singers consent to make, owing to their impatience of study. We have heard no such voices in France—there are few such in Italy—as the three owned by this gentleman and his brothers; but of what value are they either to their possessors or to the World of Music?'

Abingdon, who had succeeded his father as Lord-Lieutenant of Berkshire, was now in a position to arrange a commission for Ward in the Royal Berkshire Militia. Stationed at Reading he would be conveniently near Nuneham, and it would at least provide him with some form of occupation. His activities as Mentor to Charles had scarcely been crowned with success as Charles had the previous winter secretly married a charming Neapolitan girl, Maddalena Cippoletti, who looked like a startled fawn in the cold, grey northern capital to which her husband had brought her. She was expecting a baby in August, and Frances could only pray that marriage and paternity would have a stabilizing influence on Charles. Meanwhile there was all the excitement of making plans for his London concerts and operatic opening which gave the insidious Chelsea his chance to creep back again into her favour. Hamilton was somewhat in disgrace. In the autumn of '54 he had moved into the living quarters of the St. James's Theatre and in October Frances was writing to Seph from Venice: 'I am sorry to say that I have lately heard from London that he is living in a disgraceful way at the St. James's Theatre. I understand that a low slut of a woman, who lives in the house with him, he is beast enough to live with improperly. I do not like to write to him upon such a disgraceful subject, but you can tell him from me that if he does not alter his mode of life, he will seriously offend me.'

Chelsea, by helping Hamilton with engagements and by continual attentions to old Braham and Seph, had contrived to make Frances feel unpleasantly indebted to him, but her greatest annoyance was to find that Mr. Harcourt with his usual perversity, seeing that his wife was proud of her break with Chelsea, suddenly turned and did all he could to encourage him. However, because he could be useful to her beloved Charles, Lady Waldegrave was pleasant to him, and he was at a magnificent concert at Carlton Gardens where Charles was one of the singers. Lady Palmerston and her daughter, Lady Shaftesbury, had asked him to sing *Di quella pira*, and later Lady Palmerston remarked to Chichester that his voice lacked flexibility. Chichester saw fit to repeat this to his hostess who, always vehement and impulsive in defence of her idols, flared out at poor Lady Palmerston and at Lady Shaftesbury who had for years been a great friend. Fortunately her two guests understood her extremely well, and it was all soon forgotten, but to the end of her life Frances was unable completely to control her impulsive temper.

Even Charles and Ward at times suffered from her sudden tempers. Every string had been pulled to ensure Ward's success in the

Berkshire Militia. Colonel Malcolm and Fortescue had accompanied him on his first visit to Reading to introduce him to such of the officers as they knew, while both Abingdon and Lavinia helped him in every way. Charles had gone to Paris to arrange for his winter engagements, which was to result in a financially disastrous seven months in Lisbon. To Frances's annoyance he made Ward bring Maddalena over from London, with the result that her baby, Constance, was born amongst strangers in Paris with only the irresponsible Ward and the incurably vague Charles to tend her.

The season of 1855 was brightened for Frances by a number of little intimate parties at Dudbrook, but the usual great July and August parties were at Nuneham. She had had a more successful year than ever matchmaking, and in July a crowd of marriageable girls were asked, among them Maria Theresa Villiers, a niece of Lord Clarendon's. She herself described an embarrassing gaffe she made there that summer. 'Her parties at Nuneham were large and very amusing for young people. We danced and played games of an evening, and were out all day. These parties lasted for a week instead of only from Friday to Monday as they do now. I remember on one occasion the company which was young and gay were chaffing about a ridiculous old saying that turns on the most lucky day for marriage.

> *Monday for health, Tuesday for wealth,*
> *Wednesday the best day of all,*
> *Thursday for losses, Friday for crosses,*
> *Saturday no luck at all.*

I foolishly . . . turned to Lady Waldegrave and said, "Which day were you married?" meaning of course to Mr. Harcourt. She answered "Oh my dear, I have been married nearly every day in the week." '

One of the matches Frances had arranged took place this autumn, Francis Stonor, Lord Camoys's son, to Eliza Peel, old Sir Robert's younger daughter. Lady Peel had refused to countenance any suggestion of an engagement, principally because the Stonors were Catholics, and had sent Lady Waldegrave a copy of the letter she had written to the young man.

Frances had, at length, arranged things and the young couple

I

became her lifelong friends, despite the difficult situation that the bride's sister's affair with Lord Abingdon caused. Lavinia's children sympathized with their mother, as did Frances, which won her the devotion of her step-grandson, young Norreys. That was enough to make Fortescue immediately invite Norreys to spend the winter at Ardee and Ravensdale, the Clermont's place. Another marriage, that Lady Waldegrave very definitely had not arranged, did not take place. W. V. Harcourt's cantankerous but sincere affection for his uncle's wife made it very difficult for Mary Bulteel, whose friends were all alienated by her fiancé's insufferable manners. In October, to no one's surprise, she broke off the engagement.

His attachment to Frances was the cause gossip chose to give. It had become obvious even to her enemies that she genuinely preferred the company of the older men such as Lansdowne, Grey, the Bishop of Oxford, Macaulay or Bedford who surrounded her at every party, and her prowess as a matchmaker was too notorious for any real scandal to be caused by the adoration of her younger men friends. Thanks to Mr. Harcourt and the exigencies of Charles's career, Chelsea had quite re-established his position. The Duke of Newcastle had been constantly with her until the end of May, when he had gone to the Crimea to study conditions there for himself. His affection for her was widely discussed as Edward Lear tactlessly assured Fortescue. Even Lear himself, whose emotions usually took a very different direction, found her fascination so 'incredible' that 'I find when I look at her myself sometimes, I can't speak'. In view of Chelsea's apparently predominant position, her other slaves, to their fury, were known in society as the 'Chelsea Pensioners'.

It was as Frances and Mr. Harcourt were setting out for Harptree in October that she heard of Mary's decision. She was so pleased with her efforts at Dudbrook that she wanted to do the same for Harptree Court, but as usual when she arrived there she could come to no decision about it. It was not until the end of November that she made up her mind. She would restore Strawberry Hill.

On her first visit to Drayton, Sir Robert Peel's portrait gallery of contemporary celebrities had pleased her. Horace Walpole had had a similar idea at Strawberry Hill, and she at once decided to commission portraits of a number of her friends. The first was to be of her father, and the old man agreed to sit with great joy. In the autumn of '54 he had had a serious illness, and on his recovery had become 'softened and improved by finding out that he was not immortal upon earth'. The following autumn he spent, with Seph, at Brighton, returning to the cottage at Starch Green for Christmas. He found himself much in demand. There was his portrait to sit for, Hamilton had launched a season of Italian opera at the St. James's which he hoped his father would patronize, and Ward, who had achieved considerable popularity in his mess by organizing theatricals and redecorating the Reading theatre at his own—or rather at Frances's—expense, wanted him to come to the opening night.

Old Braham was not well enough to go to Reading, but Ward's venture into production was a great success, and his sister took a large party over from Nuneham. Even Mr. Harcourt was delighted that the weirdly eccentric, incoherent Ward could make a success of something at last. As Frances described it, 'Mr. Harcourt has not ceased turning up his eyes in astonishment how Ward can be so clever, against all the rules of education and the *convenances*.'

An intimate dinner for Newcastle, back from the Crimea, and more assiduous in his attention to Frances than ever, began the season '56 at Carlton Gardens. John Braham and Seph were again at Great Ormond Street, and as usual Chelsea and Chichester were regular callers. On the 12th Frances had a note from Seph to say that old Braham was ill.

The next day she and Chichester each called at Great Ormond Street. The old man had been in pain for some considerable time, but, as he hated to admit to any weakness, he had taken too large a dose of morphine to dull the pain. Doctor Cutler was summoned, and Chichester sent off to find more convenient lodgings to which the old man and Seph moved the following day.

Despite Braham's age, Cutler was fairly optimistic and the old man enjoyed having Frances and Chichester continually beside him, though when Chelsea called on the 15th, he said to his daughter, to Chichester's delight, 'Do you often see him now? He is a most disagreeable man.' To increase Frances's anxieties, Mr. Harcourt chose these days to be thoroughly perverse, and insisted on his wife carrying out her social engagements. On the night of the 16th Lady Palmerston had invited herself to dinner and, as old Braham was so much better, Frances got up a little party for her. Lady Shaftesbury came, too, so it was an opportunity to efface the little scene about Charles's singing. None the less it was a trying evening, and it was a relief when the other guests went, and the faithful Chichester could be sent off to Conduit Street for news. The old man was sleeping peacefully, his hand gently held by the devoted Seph who insisted that there was no reason for Lady Waldegrave to come round. The fact that it was the anniversary of Mrs. Braham's death increased the anxiety.

At one o'clock the following morning the great singer died. Frances was magnificent and ignored her own sorrow to comfort poor Seph. Mr. Harcourt, with an old man's distaste for the subject of death, did nothing but nag at her because she had invited some guests to dinner without consulting him. She was reminded of Doctor Parr's saying of him early in the century, 'If that young man were in Abraham's bosom he'd kick his guts out.' Luckily Chichester was there to support her, and saw to all the formalities. Until the funeral he was with Seph and her niece every day at the new lodgings in Conduit Street, and found himself admitted to an intimacy that hitherto only Charles and Ward had enjoyed.

Charles, in Lisbon, could not come for the funeral, but Hamilton and Augustus, who were singing at Liverpool, appeared. Chichester had already met Augustus at Great Ormond Street, but Lady Waldegrave had not met him for eight years. She shook hands with him and he apologized 'for the brutal language he had written to her'. There was another reconciliation. Spencer Meadows had exchanged the living of Peldon, which his sister had given him, for that of Chigwell without her authority. That, too, was forgiven, and on the day of the funeral Frances at last met Augustus's wife, 'a nice-looking Jewess, modest and simple', at the cottage at Starch Green.

Five days after the funeral another death occurred that was considerably to affect Frances's future. Lady Laura Money had been desperately ill for months, and had made the sister-in-law she adored guardian of her two children in the event of their elderly father's death. Lady Laura's death brought Lady Waldegrave into closer contact with the two other Waldegrave sisters. Lady

Horatia had remarried at the end of '54 and, with her husband, John Wardlaw, and her unmarried sister, Lady Ida, was living in Princes Gardens. In view of the precarious state of General Money's own health, Frances and Horatia had to set about planning the children's future.

X. 'YOUNG OLD STRAWBERRY'   1856–1857

THREE MONTHS after her father's death, Frances gave her first big dinner party, when the Gladstones among others were asked to meet the Duke of Newcastle. She 'stood up to Gladstone about the Lucan case and he did not half like the want of *reverence* with which she treated him'. G. E. Vernon 'got on the treatment of the Peelites at the Carlton, the Duke complained bitterly, and wished he had the opportunity of trying the hardness of his fist on some of their faces. Gladstone did not say one word about it, he goes there now and is very civilly received. Lady Waldegrave, talking of the advantages of *party*, appealed to Mr. Gladstone and asked him what should be done to revive parties. He said he saw no other remedy but to treat certain individuals as she proposed to treat Colonel Tulloch. She had just said that she would hang Tulloch and then abolish capital punishment. Gladstone meant no doubt imprimis D'Israeli, with a thought perhaps of Lord John.'

Frances's support of Lord Lucan was vehement. She was almost daily at Chelsea Hospital where the case was being heard, and would proudly walk away with him in full uniform and medals. She announced that she found him very handsome and was very fond of him, but 'it's an odd thing—he never could fall in love with me nor I with him'. That was perhaps as well, since his utterly feather-brained wife had infuriated Lady Waldegrave at Nuneham the previous summer by a relentless pursuit of that startlingly handsome, incurable philanderer, Julian Fane.

At the beginning of June, to his sister's delight, Charles arrived from Lisbon. For weeks she had been using all her fascination on the impresario Lumley, a distant cousin of her father's, and lessee of Her Majesty's Theatre. She had persuaded him to give Charles a trial during the operatic season of that year, and her excitement at that prospect almost overshadowed the excitement of her first party at the restored Strawberry Hill.

Two days before the party began Chichester rode down 'to her young old Strawberry. I saw her at the window of the Holbein

Chamber. There she was in her working dress, plain black dress tucked up, Seph and the Pearsons there too. I was taken round to every room beginning with the dining room. She was as proud as possible and happy as a child, delighted to show everything and make me admire everything. I was surprised and delighted, she has made it the prettiest, freshest, gayest place I ever saw.'

For the next six weeks there were the regular Friday to Monday parties at Strawberry Hill that for the next twenty years were to be such a dominant feature of the London season. Most of Frances's most intimate friends managed to appear there before she left for Nuneham in the middle of July—Lady William Russell, Monckton Milnes, Lady Ailesbury, the Clanricardes, Lord Lansdowne, Lady Molesworth, Lady Morley, the Bernstorffs, Lady Churchill, Lady Sandwich, the George Byngs, the Frank Stonors, Lady Shaftesbury, Newcastle and his daughter Lady Susan, Bidwell, Grenfell, Beauchamp Seymour, Willie Harcourt and Chichester Fortescue—almost all names to be found at Strawberry Hill on any Sunday in June for the next twenty odd years.

Lady Waldegrave had always found the drive out to Starch Green troublesome, and finally decided to take a more central house for Seph, Aunt Carshore and Ward, where Charles and Augustus could go when they wanted to escape the cares of domesticity. No. 6 Bolton Row, Mayfair, was inspected and, but for the slight drawback that its neighbour was the notorious brothel 'Mother Cotton's', seemed ideal. Charles was to appear on July 12 as Gennaro in *Lucrezia Borgia* at Her Majesty's with Mlle. Wagner, and his sister determined to have Bolton Row ready for a supper of celebration after the performance.

Charles's first appearance at Her Majesty's was on a Saturday, but his sister deserted her guests to hear him. Mr. Harcourt had met the Duc and Duchesse d'Aumale whom Frances, remembering the clairvoyant's prediction in Paris, had refused to meet at both the Monckton Milnes's and Holland House. They were more insistent than ever about meeting his wife now that she was their neighbour at Twickenham. It had been arranged that she was to take her older guests to Orleans House to dinner that night, but she sent excuses 'as she would not give up Charles for the Queen'. Chelsea, Fortescue, G. E. Vernon, old Charles Harcourt, the Pearsons, Seph and Ward were all at the theatre. It was a disastrous night. Charles, who was always ready to waste his superb voice at any friend's house, had a violent attack of nerves, made a fiasco of the dying duet with Lucrezia, and completely lost his head and his voice.

Lumley, however, was impressed by his voice, and continued his engagement. In August he was singing in *Traviata* with Piccolomini, and during the autumn and winter made a successful provincial tour with Catherine Hayes, the singer who had left Augustus stranded in New York four years earlier.

Among the guests whom Frances had deserted were Newcastle and his seventeen-year-old daughter Lady Susan Pelham-Clinton. The Duke was anxious for his children to know and like Lady Waldegrave, and Lady Susan was soon a devoted friend. The endless misfortunes of his domestic and political life had seriously affected the duke's health and character. Terrified that his children might inherit their mother's morals, his treatment of them was disastrously bigoted, and his eldest son, Lord Lincoln, had already reacted, spending most of his time and all his money on racing.

The Nuneham parties began at the end of July. Mr. Harcourt had settled the Aumale question for Frances by inviting them on August 12 for a few days. The Van de Weyers, Chelsea, Lady Ailesbury, Lady Shaftesbury, Monckton Milnes and Chichester were among the guests who were there to meet them. The visit was an immense success. Frances, whom her husband's endless lectures on the correct formalities had exhausted, was fascinated by Aumale's remarkable good looks and the eager friendliness of his little Neapolitan duchess. As usual protocol went by the board and by the following evening, to Mr. Harcourt's horror, the royalties were being made to play the usual absurd Nuneham games. The Duchesse d'Aumale, who had never been treated so informally in her life, was enraptured.

Everyone at Nuneham was pleased and relieved that the royal visit was passing off so easily. If Frances remembered her premonitions at all, she probably thought they were caused by her dread of formality. The duchesse was a dear little woman, Mr. Harcourt would be in a good mood for weeks, and she herself was glad that the whole question of their introduction had been taken out of her hands.

Early in September Lady Waldegrave insisted on going to

Dudbrook. It was mostly a family party, though Chelsea, Fortescue and one or two other men were there as Frances was reviving
the Tenants' Ball at the Green Man, Navestock, after seventeen
years. It was a great success. Lady Waldegrave 'was received with
"God save the Queen" and looked like one but was most charming and kind and natural. She was in grey and coral.' Some of her
Somerset tenants were there and 'said they were jealous of Essex'.
She and Mr. Harcourt had planned a little autumn tour of the
châteaux of the Loire. Old Charles Harcourt and Chichester
Fortescue, by a strange coincidence, also made similar plans.

Mr. Harcourt was beginning to find these coincidences a little
too strange, and was yet more annoyed on their arrival in Paris to
find that his nephew W. V. Harcourt had decided that a sudden
visit to the French capital was essential. Frances, herself like some
gallant medieval page in her cloak and feathered hat, with her
walk that was an enchantment to watch, brought centuries of
French history vividly to life for her companions. Even Mr. Harcourt was 'in a most benign state all this time', though that was
largely because he knew how very hard his wife was trying to
find a wife for Chichester. Lady Waldegrave was very fond of
him and valued his friendship, yet his obsessive devotion to her
was embarrassing.

Frances was determined to keep him at a healthy distance until
the opening of Parliament and, after he had left them to visit his
old aunt at Ardee, wrote long letters twice a week exhorting him
to consider nothing but Mrs. Ruxton's happiness, blandly ignor-
ing his pathetically shameless angling for invitations to Strawberry Hill or Nuneham. He found a little solace by going to hear
Augustus sing in Dublin, and in December by having Charles to
visit him at the Red House, Ardee.

The work that had been done at Strawberry Hill in the spring
had been only provisional. Horace Walpole's 'little play thing
house' was totally inadequate for parties on the Nuneham scale.
An immense amount of building would have to be done and
Frances, who had all her mother's financial optimism, heard that
her Radstock coals were 'doing capitally' just at the time her level-
headed, practical husband was advising a little prudence and
economy in the grandiose plans she was making.

Mr. Harcourt's perversity over trivial things was disastrous in its effect. It was partly for his shrewd business ability that Frances had married him, yet after eight years she could no longer realize that, if his advice was contrary to her wishes, he was not simply once again being perverse. He was naturally hurt that she preferred her own houses to Nuneham, of which he had learnt her opinion in numerous squabbles. While the discussions about the new work at Strawberry Hill were in progress, she wrote to a friend from Nuneham, 'I cannot say how shabby and uncosy I find this house after old Strawberry. Positively my *own* armchair is the only comfortable looking thing I see here. I suppose it is very wrong to dislike so handsome and respectable a place as Nuneham, but I do most cordially.'

At the same time he realized that, as on his death Nuneham Park would go to his eldest brother, she must provide herself with a home for her widowhood, and was therefore genuinely ready to help her with the restoration of Strawberry Hill. It was when he tried to explain that almost no estate could meet the sudden call on it for the fortune she wanted to spend at Twickenham, that she at once suspected him of spite.

Till the end of her life Frances would every now and then settle down to calculate how much she had spent on Strawberry Hill, but each time that £100,000 loomed up unpleasantly near, she decided that she must somehow have miscalculated, and the subject would be dropped for another year or so. Despite her habitual courage she never dared face up to the total it had actually cost her.

By insisting on how much his old aunt enjoyed having him at Ardee, Lady Waldegrave had managed to keep Chichester Fortescue in Ireland until Parliament reassembled at the beginning of Febuary '57. After the tremendous self-sacrifice his Irish exile of three months had been to him, he felt he deserved some reward. In the next three weeks he contrived to dine exactly eleven times at Carlton Gardens, twice at Bolton Row and once with her at the Palmerstons'. Apart from meals there were almost daily calls, and a day spent with her and Mr. Harcourt at Strawberry Hill. He was by no means the only one whose everlasting presence irritated Frances's husband, but he was the only one who had established himself on a truly intimate footing with the Bolton Row household. Again since his lady's happiness was his one preoccupation, he was always prepared to reason with her about her squabbles with Mr. Harcourt, a fact that the old man fully appreciated.

Chelsea, Dufferin, John Bidwell, Henry Grenfell and Beauchamp Seymour were almost as assiduous, but the nephew Willy —W. V. Harcourt—used his relationship to be as much in her company as was Chichester. His early promise at the Bar had not been fulfilled as his sarcastic manner annoyed jurymen and judges equally. He had become an ardent Radical, and it was obvious that he was considering a parliamentary career. The uneasy affection between his young aunt and himself steadily increased—and also their violent quarrels. His rivals loathed him, but occasionally were consoled by her reaction to his rudeness. One evening, dining at Carlton Gardens, young Harcourt 'being put out about something, was doing tremendous tragic business, folding his arms and looking like Hamlet'. Lady Waldegrave, hoping to cheer him up, asked what he was thinking about. Looking up from his plate with usual mixture of hauteur and insolence, he said, 'Beef'.

Her reply flashed back, 'Overdone!'

The dinners at Number 7 were increasingly political. The Gladstones were frequent visitors, although his flirtation with the Conservatives was causing considerable talk. Lord John was another who was anxious to cause trouble for the Government, and at the beginning of March they both had their opportunity. The previous autumn Sir John Bowring had ordered the bombardment of Canton in reprisal for a Chinese attack on the Lorcha *Arrow*. Cobden brought in a resolution censuring the Government, which was supported by Lord John, Milner Gibson and Gladstone, whose oratory caused the defeat of the Government. Palmerston announced the dissolution two days later and, in the subsequent election, found that the country fully supported his policy whatever the opinion of the Commons.

Chichester, whose shyness made him dislike the endless interviewing and speeches of an election, and the weeks of absence from Lady Waldegrave that it entailed, was depressed at having to return to his exile after less than six weeks. The election was, however, greatly to affect him. The Under-Secretary for the Colonies lost his seat, and on April 20, Henry Grenfell wrote to Frances:

'Dear Lady Waldegrave,

Ball, the Under Secy. for the Colonies is going to resign. I think this would suit C. Fortescue to a turn. I have written to him to put in his claim. But I don't know if he will—it would not require another election.

Pray back me up,

Yours ever

H. R. Grenfell'

Frances, who had already written part of his address to the electors of Louth, soon arranged it, and his appointment was announced by *The Times* on May 11, giving Mr. Harcourt the chance of telling him on that morning when he came downstairs late at Strawberry Hill, '*The Times* says this is the last time you will be late in the morning.'

Even the dispersal caused by the election could not lessen Frances's delight in her alterations at Strawberry Hill. In the middle of his Irish canvassing Chichester was overjoyed to hear from her.

Strawberry Hill

Twickenham

April 5th

'Dear Mr. Fortescue,

Here I am settled in this most enchanting of all charming places. *I am certain* that you have not the faintest idea of its *now* wonderful beauty. Altho' it poured all day yesterday, old Granville, Jessie, etc. of the family thought it the most intoxicating place they had ever seen. They said they had heard so much of it from those who had been here that they expected it to be lovely but that *no* imagination could come up to the perfection of its beauty.

'I believe that I am the only person *not* surprised. Mr. Harcourt was *enchanted* with it. I said, "Have I ever said a *word* too much in its praise?"

'He answered, "No, it *would be impossible* to do so!"

'After this burst of good feeling he became rapidly more cross than I have ever seen him, so I suppose jealousy about Nuneham has set in.

'I cannot doubt this as Mr. Matthews and B. were overheard by him, saying "No one will ever bear Nuneham after this place."

126

I am delighted to hear that you are getting on so well and I hope
and trust that you will be at the head of the poll. I must not forget
to say that the cannon fired all the afternoon yesterday in my
honor and that the field near the river was decked out with flags.

'As I looked at the curling smoke and the flags from my
Drawing room window I felt sadly happy at being reminded of
my coming of age here, the last time I had seen these manifesta-
tions of joy. How much has happened since and how I still feel
that I have been loved as no other woman ever was loved.

'I like feeling that I owe everything to that love, and that
nothing has been *really* done for me except from that feeling. I am
sure you understand what I mean, tho' I am expressing myself in
a mystified way.

'Charles is here in Beauty room, which is my favourite room
next to Walpole's which I love with all my heart. Lizzy Perry
looks quite happy here, in fact the only bother of this place is
that no one can bear to go away.

'The Vernons and Malcolms have positively refused to go
away to-morrow. Mr. Harcourt is furious about it and says that
it is most impertinent, that the Duchess of Sutherland would not
allow such a liberty to be taken at Trentham, nor Lord Lansdowne
at Bowood, nor the late Duke of Beaufort at Badminton, etc. etc.

'What day do you expect to be in town? I suppose you may
engage yourself here for the 1st Saturday to Tuesday in May.

Yours most truly,

F. W.'

Her excitement about Strawberry Hill was justified, since her
Saturday to Monday parties were the talk of the town and every
other hostess envied her her brilliant assemblage of guests. During
the week her hospitality at Carlton Gardens was on her usual
magnificent scale, but an invitation to her beloved Strawberry
was the coveted honour. Newcastle and his daughter Lady Susan
appeared regularly both at No. 7 and at Twickenham, the girl's
devotion to her hostess almost equalling her father's. The French
ambassador Persigny, with his pretty little wife, so amorous that
she used to drag her ambassador behind screens at other people's
parties, the Belgian, Prussian and Sardinian ministers, the Clarendons, the Greys, the Grosvenors, the Staffords, the Duchesses of

Sutherland and Somerset, and the faithful Bishop of Oxford, were a few of the more notable.

The strain of so much social activity and of her husband's querulous jealousy at the success of what were her own parties made Bolton Row a very pleasant refuge for Lady Waldegrave. Seph's conception of bliss was to entertain her niece and she, herself, would prepare the dishes Frances had adored since childhood. No one could dress a crab like Seph, her macaroni à la Grange was superb, and she had a recipe for coco-nut pie that was so good that Lady Waldegrave, inviting her once down to Strawberry, added 'and if there is any of the cocoanut pie left you might bring it with you'. The 'boys' (Charles and Ward), found their sister's visits a double pleasure as there was always a special meal. One day Seph roasted a capon whose appearance at table Charles greeted with 'Cock-a-doodle-doo', whereupon his sister indelicately remarked, 'That's adding insult to injury.'

She particularly liked dining there before any specially pompous event, to have a few hours complete freedom from ceremony. It was before she dressed for the Queen's ball that a Bolton Row dinner was enlivened by a Punch and Judy show in the street below. The next day the most fashionable event of the season took place. There was a vast 'breakfast' on the lawns of Strawberry Hill. The Ducs d'Aumale and de Montpensier were the guests of honour, there was a large Saturday to Monday party, which of course included Newcastle and his daughter, and the rest of London, who had not managed an invitation to stay, returned to town in the late afternoon. It was a perfect day, but the success of the party was the Punch and Judy man from Bolton Row.

Frances had modified her original idea about a portrait gallery of celebrities, and instead was collecting portraits of the more beautiful of her women friends. She was completely lacking in jealousy about other women's beauty, although she realized that the beauty generally attributed to her was due rather to her radiant vitality, her superb figure and carriage, her lovely colouring and, above all, to her personality than to any perfection of feature. She delighted in the beauty of others and was greatly excited when Louis Napoleon's beautiful mistress, the Countess of Castiglione, accepted an invitation to the concert she gave at Carlton Gardens at the beginning of July.

Three days later, at a ball at Spencer House, the Duke of Cambridge, after telling her that her dress was the most beautiful he had ever seen, said that Madame Castiglione was nothing to her. 'You were determined to bring us all to your feet and you have done it.' Van de Weyer, watching the little scene, said he 'saw her growing prouder and prouder, and taller and taller as she sat with the Duke, being on the defensive'.

Before the season ended Mr. Harcourt's increasing jealousy exploded. Frances's staunch support of Lord Lucan during the Crimean Commission had led Fortescue to do all he could to reconcile Mr. Harcourt with his brother-in-law. He had long interviews with each of the men, and, if anything, would have given Mr. Harcourt the rights of the case, but as usual the old man's handling of it had been so absurd that Lucan won his sympathy. The day Lucan had sailed for the Crimea Mr. Harcourt had dunned him for arrears of the marriage settlement, and quite naturally Lucan insisted that as the other had gone to law about it, he himself would also keep exactly to the letter of the law.

All Fortescue's efforts were in vain, but at a moment when there seemed to be some hope of success, Lady Waldegrave had agreed to dine with the Lucans. Mr. Harcourt was livid. He told Chichester, 'If my Lady dines with Lord Lucan, I shall never forget or forgive it. It would be more offensive to me than if she made love to him. That would be, of course, wicked and immoral, but not so offensive to me.' In despair Frances cancelled her engagement.

The day before they left for Nuneham there was a fête at Orleans House, the Aumales's Twickenham home. The intimacy with the Aumales had been steadily growing, and as, with the exception of the old Queen of the French, the entire Orleans family were there, Frances now met them all. Except for the Prince de Joinville, she liked them, and did everything to make their party a success. Montpensier said, '*Sans Lady Waldegrave tout serait resté là—c'est elle qui a fait tout.*'

With a home of her own at last Frances had changed considerably. At Strawberry Hill she could behave as she chose to her guests without having to comply with her husband's idea of the perfect hostess. At Nuneham, for his sake, she had set out to fascinate his guests, but in her own house she determined that her guests should accept her when she was being completely herself.

The success of her parties had given her new confidence and poise and a calm that made her better able to contend with her husband's bad moods, almost to ignore them. She had made no effort to fascinate the Aumales, in fact, with the odd premonitions she had had about them, her reception of them had been a little too non-chalant. So many of the passionate devotions that embarrassed her, she felt, were largely due to her own fault in, from a lack of confidence, having tried to fascinate. In this case there could surely be no danger of another obsessive friendship.

AFTER the usual August parties at Nuneham on which the presence of the Aumales had laid a certain restraint, Mr. Harcourt took his wife on a visit to Clumber. Frances had a very high opinion of the Duke of Newcastle's political capabilities and fervently hoped to see him one day Premier of a Liberal administration into which he would bring his Peelite colleagues. Although at the recent election the country had shown its confidence in Palmerston, the House of Commons appeared to resent his personal popularity with the electorate, and he was having an astonishingly difficult time in Parliament. Even Prince Albert, who always disliked him, felt that he was being unfairly treated. He was seventy-three, and therefore it might be his last period of office.

Lord John Russell, despite his numerous followers in the Liberal Party itself, was not popular throughout the country, and was distrusted by the small but influential Peelite group. It seemed as though Gladstone had decided to rejoin the Conservatives, which would leave Newcastle as the likeliest successor to the present Prime Minister. At one of the Strawberry Hill parties, Lady Waldegrave had taken all her guests across the river to Pembroke Lodge to effect a reconciliation between Lord John and Newcastle who, with his daughter, was among her guests.

The duke and Lady Susan were again at Nuneham in August, when young Willie Harcourt had spitefully teased the girl about her father's devotion to their hostess. He had only succeeded in increasing her affection for Lady Waldegrave and she had thought it particularly unfair as she knew how hard Frances was trying to marry the duke to Miss 'J. L.', whose identity it is now impossible to ascertain.

At Clumber Frances found J. D. Cook, the former editor of the Duke's *Morning Chronicle*. In 1855 he had started the *Saturday Review* which had already become one of the most powerful periodicals. She at once determined that the *Saturday's* great influence should be exercised on behalf of her new protégés, the

Orleans family. So complete was her enslavement of Cook that within five weeks she could boast to Lady Clarendon that 'Lady Palmerston and I are two Delilahs. She has cut the hair of *The Times*, and I of the *Saturday*.'

Another guest was Abraham Hayward, who had been a contributor to the *Morning Chronicle* when it was the Peelite organ, and whose articles in the *Quarterly*, the *Edinburgh* and *Fraser's* had enormous influence. Politically he was probably the best informed man of his time, and from the Clumber meeting to the end of her life he shared every scrap of information he gleaned with Lady Waldegrave.

Even Frances herself had a journalistic début in the *Saturday Review*. The letting of the St. James's Theatre had been so monotonously unsuccessful that Charles had decided to go in for management himself, and in November introduced a season of *opera buffa* which was eventually to cost his sister hundreds of pounds. She had the editor of the *Saturday Review* in her box on the first night, and herself wrote the notice which appeared on November 21. Her husband 'was surprised and pleased at her article', but when she told Chichester her ideas for another, 'she complained that my way of receiving them discouraged her, which I certainly did not mean. She blew me up for tediousness and fear of failure —very just.'

Chichester, however, was in favour, as he had agreed to write a pro-Orleans article for the *Saturday*, and was endeavouring to sort out the ghastly tangle of Ward's debts. Ward's efforts at the Reading Theatre, and his intimacy with a young actress, Miss Wadham, had involved him in over £1,000 of debts. His sister complained that 'when she listened to his explanations, she felt she was going mad', and was grateful to Fortescue for trying to comprehend Ward's incoherent and fantastic account.

In December further family complications arose. Lady Abingdon had annoyed her stepmother by treating Carlton Gardens as though it were her own establishment, and when Frances protested, Mr. Harcourt informed her that Lavinia 'had lost a great deal by his marriage to her'. There was naturally a tremendous row, and Lady Waldegrave refused to go to Nuneham where her stepdaughter would be. Mr. Harcourt scarcely improved things by assuring her that he was going to tell the Duchess of Sutherland all about it, and that it was a great pity that God had not modelled all women on the duchess. 'God likes a variety,' Frances snapped back at him. He told her that the duchess always asked and took his advice, whereas Frances only took other people's. 'Ah, she's like me. She never takes her husband's advice.'

The situation became still more difficult when young Norreys announced that he was going to marry Caroline Towneley whose family were staunchly Roman Catholic. The Abingdon household was altogether an unhappy one. Lord Abingdon's liaison with Lady Villiers had undermined Lavinia's health and made her irritable in her dealings both with her children and with Frances. It had always a little amused her that she was her stepmother's senior and she was, from the first, despite her sincere affection, inclined good-humouredly to tease the younger woman, which Frances mistakenly felt was patronizing. Her relationship to Lavinia was one of the very few she was quite unable to handle successfully.

Lady Abingdon was as horrified by Norreys's engagement to a Catholic as Lady Peel had been by her younger daughter's. It widened the breach with Frances who had no sympathy with any form of religious intolerance. She was a religious woman, a regular churchgoer, and took great interest in the disposal of the various livings in her gift to suitable incumbents, but the religious controversies that tortured England during her lifetime left her indifferent.

During the autumn there had been parties at Dudbrook and Strawberry Hill where, before they left to spend Christmas at Nuneham—Frances having relented—Mr. Harcourt's cousin, Lord St. Germans, appeared. From 1852 to 1855 he had been in Ireland as Lord-Lieutenant, and his wife had died in 1856. They had therefore seen little of him for some years, and Frances was delighted to welcome the witty, polished man of the world to her circle. The party included Newcastle, the Van de Weyers, the Greys, Poodle Byng and Frances's old friend, Maria, Lady Ailesbury, whose own childhood home, Ham House, almost faced Strawberry Hill across the Thames. She was a good-humoured, worldly woman, whom everyone mercilessly teased, especially about her disastrous passion for the fascinating but dissolute Lord Wilton.

St. Germans amused his fellow-guests and embarrassed 'Maria, Marchioness' not at all, by speaking of her wedding at Ham House in 1833. As she and Ailesbury were driving off on their honeymoon, the then Duke of Cambridge, with his usual flair for expressing himself badly, assured the astonished bridegroom, 'You'll be at least seven hours about it,' referring naturally to the journey.

The Nuneham party in January 1858, included Newcastle and the Aumales who brought with them the Orleanist pretender, the young Comte de Paris, son of the widowed Duchesse d'Orléans. That, too, was the beginning of a lasting friendship for Lady Waldegrave. They arrived three days after Orsini's attempted assassination of the Emperor and Empress of the French.

The whole plot had undoubtedly been hatched in England and the French press was furious at the asylum this country afforded assassins. Their attacks were so virulent that the Emperor apologized, through his Foreign Minister, to Lord Clarendon. Parliament met on February 4, and five days later Lord Palmerston introduced his Conspiracy to Murder Bill. Doctor Bernard, living in Bayswater, had had the grenades made, and had arranged for their delivery in Paris. His complicity was obvious, but the Commons, already out of humour with Palmerston, were annoyed by the French attacks on England, and made up their minds to protect the man they knew to be one of the instigators of the attempted assassination of the ruler of a friendly neighbouring power.

On February 19, on the proposal for a second reading, Milner Gibson, who on the previous day had assured Fortescue that it would 'do the Government no harm', though 'he let out his hatred of Palmerston', had brought in an amendment which was carried against the Government by a majority of nineteen. Gladstone joined the Tories and the Radicals in bringing down Palmerston. On the 20th the Government resigned and the Queen sent for Lord Derby.

It was no easy task for Derby since the Conservatives were in a minority in Parliament. Gladstone, despite his behaviour to Palmerston, was not prepared to join a government in which Disraeli was Leader of the House of Commons, Lord Grey also refused, and Lord Derby was obliged to ask the Queen herself to try to persuade Newcastle to join him. On the 22nd she wrote to tell him she had been unsuccessful.

Frances was too distracted by family affairs to pay much attention to the change of ministry. Young Norreys had decided to become a Roman Catholic. The thought of his conversion was a terrible shock to the rather evangelical Lady Abingdon. Her health gave way completely, so completely that there seemed little hope of her recovery. It brought out the best in her husband's peculiar character. He was tender, charming and attentive to her, and entirely forsook Lady Villiers.

The friendship between young Lord Norreys and Chichester Fortescue had increased during the past two years and the young man confided the whole history to his older friend. Fortescue, however, had also his own family worries. He had returned from Ireland at the beginning of February to find his sister, Harriet Urquhart, in great trouble. The Urquharts had settled at Rickmansworth where they had promptly built a Turkish bath on to their house and, with their children and astonished visitors, spent most of the day in it. Urquhart, busy building Turkish baths throughout the kingdom and full of excitement about a ship he had chartered to seek buried treasure, had still time for the 'Foreign Affairs Committees' that he had organized in most large cities, and for his political publications, still violently Russophobe and anti-Palmerston.

At the beginning of the month their small son Willie, had, while in the steam room, had a fit, from which he had died. The neighbours, all scandalized at the odd way in which the Urquharts were bringing up their children, at once blamed them for the child's death. The inquest was adjourned and, when it was resumed, Chichester attended with a young barrister, Henry Hawkins. The evidence all proved that there had been no negligence, but the foreman and most of the jurors, incapable of grasping any new idea, brought in a verdict 'highly censuring Mr. Urquhart's treatment of his children'. The monstrous injustice of the verdict won Urquhart a great deal of sympathy, though Chichester found his sympathy sorely tried when at the funeral Urquhart announced that 'Lord Clarendon had got it done'. What interest the charming, good-natured Foreign Secretary had in the death of a small boy at Rickmansworth, only Urquhart's fantastic mind could imagine.

It was painfully embarrassing for Chichester since the Clarendons were among Lady Waldegrave's most intimate friends. Clarendon said of her, 'really there is no one like her—she is the most remarkable woman in society—so much imagination, and yet so much strong sense'. He would dance with no one but the Queen and Frances, whom he teasingly treated as royalty, always addressing his letters to her '*très chère cousine*'. His wife, who was equally fond of Lady Waldegrave, had once spoken of her fear of any marital infidelity. Frances pointed out that she had almost twenty years of successful married life to reassure her. 'Yes, but look at Henry VIII. After twenty years with Katherine of Aragon, along came Anne Boleyn.' For years afterwards Lady Waldegrave was known as Anne Boleyn.

Most of her greatest friends were by the spring of 1858 becoming wearied by the everlasting presence of the Aumales. The little Neapolitan duchesse could not bear to pass a day without seeing her 'very, very dearest Frances', for whom a suite of rooms at Orleans House was always reserved, though it practically adjoined Strawberry Hill. They dined once or twice a week at Carlton Gardens, came over for every Strawberry Hill party, and were at Nuneham several times every year. Queen Victoria, though anxious to be kind to the exiled royalties, was always a little nervous of asking them either to Windsor or Osborne in case it offended Louis Napoleon. She need not have worried since visits to Windsor meant to them the loss of their neighbour's society. The little duchesse proclaimed that she preferred exile with Frances to a regal life in France without her.

The Duchesse d'Orléans had come to England and they asked Lady Waldegrave to give a dinner and dance for her and the Comte de Paris at Carlton Gardens. Their hostess 'looking superb in green and gold, did the honours to perfection' and the Duchesse d'Orleans told her brother-in-law 'that she had never seen anyone receive so well'.

Those who were irritated by her new friends were partly consoled by the departure of another whom they all disliked. Chelsea had been offered the Secretaryship of Embassy at Paris, and had asked her advice. She advised against it as he was 'too old to begin'. That immediately decided him to accept it. She scarcely felt his loss as there were a great many new members of her circle. Old

Poodle Byng, a sort of amateur horse-coper and pimp to his friends —Lord Melbourne had said of him, 'There's nobody like Byng to get you a horse or a woman'—J. D. Cook, Hayward, Lord St. Germans, and the young Comte de Paris were constantly with her and even Lady Palmerston's slave, Fleming 'The Flea', shared his gossip with her.

By the middle of May it was clear that the Derby Cabinet could not last long and there was great discussion in the Liberal strongholds as to the distribution of offices in the next Cabinet. 'The Flea' assured Frances that at Cambridge House it had been decided that Chichester should again be Under-Secretary for the Colonies, but this time with the Secretary of State in the Lords, which would make Chichester the colonial authority in the Commons. Frances was still determined to bring harmony into the very divided Liberal ranks and set about reconciling Clarendon and Lord John. She had the Gladstones down to Twickenham in an attempt to stop his backsliding towards the Tories, and by July Lord Granville was writing to Lord Canning, the Governor-General of India, that 'Frank Waldegrave is the great political woman of the day, and intends to make Newcastle Prime Minister. In the meanwhile she accepts as admirers Clarendon and (you will be astonished) Grey.'

Half-way through the season of '58 Frances caused a considerable sensation in both England and France by inviting the new French ambassador, Pelissier, Duc de Malakoff to a dinner to meet the Aumales. She had attempted a similar thing at Nuneham the previous summer, but news had come of the death of Madame de Persigny's father, the Prince de la Moskowa, and they had left the day before the Aumales arrived. The French Embassy had always been a favoured establishment for Lady Waldegrave, Drouyn de Lhuys, the Walewskis and the Persignys had all been her friends, and as she saw no reason to except the new ambassador, her other intimates—the Aumales—must be prepared to meet him. Possibly she had not realized the consternation it would cause at the Tuileries, but since Malakoff and Aumale met as fellow officers and embraced as old friends, the meeting started any amount of conjecture.

She was, of course, vehemently pro-Orleans, and Willie Harcourt, Fortescue and others were kept busy writing articles in

their favour. The editor of the *Saturday Review* was always prepared to be reasonably helpful, but she was anxious to find a
weekly paper whose policy could be directed both to the Orleans
cause and the unification of the Liberal Party. Early in July Lord
Grey sent her Thomas Ballantyne, the editor and founder of the
Statesman. His paper financially was in a bad state and, as it had
already changed its formerly Radical tone to Liberal, Frances was
prepared partly to subsidize it. Fortescue was commissioned to
apply for subscriptions to those of their friends who were both
of their political colouring and trustworthy, since the whole
arrangement was to remain secret. Lord Clarendon was a willing
victim, Clermont gave £100, Sir Hamilton Seymour £300, and
within a month the prospects seemed so good that Lady Waldegrave was trying to change the *Statesman* into a daily.

By the time the Nuneham parties began, even Lady Waldegrave's superb vitality was feeling the strain of the last few months.
Apart from the *Statesman* and the daily contact with the Aumales,
she had been entertaining more lavishly than ever at Carlton
Gardens, and the brilliant Saturday to Monday gatherings at
Strawberry Hill had meant great organization on her part. She
rarely missed a night at the opera or a notable debate in Parliament. There were concerts, balls, Drawing Rooms at the palace to
be attended, and the endless visits from all the men who enjoyed
her advice. Her affectionate sympathy for young Norreys caused
trouble both with the Abingdons and Mr. Harcourt, but she managed to persuade the old man to attend the wedding. The day
after, Lavinia left London in a dying state.

Further trouble came from Newcastle. His son, Lincoln, had
besought Frances to use her influence with the duke to have his
racing debts settled, and it was principally at Carlton Gardens or
Twickenham that father and son met. Lady Susan had reached
London from Clumber in April, and Lady Waldegrave had chaperoned her for the rest of the season. That had involved her in still
greater trouble. Lady Susan had fallen in love with Lord Adolphus
(Dolly) Vane, Lady Londonderry's son. He was a complete
wastrel, and though Member of Parliament for North Durham,
was generally believed to be verging on insanity. For his mother's
sake, he was still accepted, but everyone avoided him as far as
possible.

At the end of August more worry appeared. General Money, Lady Laura's old husband, died, leaving his two daughters to Frances's care. She decided with their other aunt, Lady Horatia Wardlaw, that they should live at Little Strawberry Hill with their governess. The whole summer and autumn was a sad time, as there was no hope of poor Lavinia's recovery, and on October 16 her unhappy life came to an end.

Fortunately Lady Waldegrave had a new venture to distract her at the time. She had finally decided to sell Harptree Court, but as she required some *pied-à-terre* in Somerset, she had bought 'The Priory', an architectural nightmare at Chewton Mendip. Of course Fortescue had to see it, and towards the end of October, as 'the boys'—Charles and Ward—were spending a few days at the Waldegrave Arms in the village, that provided the excuse. He 'went to see the Priory—the situation, the ground, the trees very good—rather staggered by the house—so whimsical—bad architecturally and environment'. Frances had bought it, however, simply with the intention of providing herself with a lodging for her visits to her Somersetshire estates.

Mr. Harcourt was by no means pleased that his wife was acquiring yet another establishment, even though it was only for estate purposes. It had led to the usual row at Dudbrook, early in the month, when the Wardlaws, Georgie Malcolm and old Charles Harcourt had been unable to restore peace. The party had been ruined by Harcourt's vile temper and his brother Charles had said that 'his powers as a wet blanket were wonderful'. As usual the aggrieved husband sought out Fortescue to put things right, and there was another of their amazing conversations at the Irishman's rooms in St. James's Place.

Even Mr. Harcourt had come to consider Chichester as one of the family. The Bolton Row household treated him as one of themselves, almost all the Harcourt brothers and sisters were on intimate terms with him, the Abingdon family all confided in him, and the Wardlaws had at once become friends. Poor, lonely Maddalena was delighted whenever he called on her, and he was on excellent terms with the Augustus Brahams. He was one of the few who had accepted Frances's intimacy with the Aumales and was a great favourite with the little duchesse. After seven years, society no longer commented on his utter enslavement. With his diffidence about public speaking, his incurable unpunctuality, and the frequent attacks of depression and indifferent health the years of chastity had caused, it was unlikely that he would become a notable political figure. Though he was prepared to surmount any obstacle to further any wish of his lady's he was quite incapable of pushing himself forward in his own interest.

LADY WALDEGRAVE'S passionate anxiety to end the disunion in the Liberal Party was more than justified by the endless political crises during the eighteen-fifties. Palmerston, the ex-Tory, could rely on his great personal popularity, due partly to the staunch backing of *The Times* and—strangely enough—of *Punch*, but the Radicals considered him reactionary, most Liberals resented his forcing his own friends, such as Clanricarde or the young Sir Robert Peel, into office regardless of their capabilities, and he was disliked at Windsor. The Peelites, probably the best brains in Parliament, feared that the country, with its strange faculty for only appreciating a public figure when old age has decayed his powers, would keep him in office till his death.

Gladstone had justified the Liberals' suspicions by going to the Ionian Islands, then a British protectorate, on a special mission for the Conservatives in November 1858, and temporarily becoming High Commissioner there. Palmerston valued him for his oratory and his financial genius, but had suffered too much at his hands to have any confidence in him. Lord John Russell was unquestionably leader of the Whig core of the Liberals and had some influence with the Radicals, but the Peelites disliked him, Palmerston distrusted him, and he was no longer so popular at court.

At Windsor the favourites were Lord Granville, Lord Clarendon and Newcastle. Granville and Clarendon particularly were liked by the Queen, Clarendon admitting to his friends that 'it is ridiculous, but she treats me as if she were my sister'. Prince Albert, at last created Prince Consort, was on equally friendly terms with Newcastle, and even wept in sympathy at the duke's continual misfortunes, but it was largely Newcastle's notorious ill luck that made him rather a dreaded colleague.

Frances felt that a common interest in the *Statesman* as the Liberal organ might help to unify the party, but unfortunately her great sympathy for the Orleans cause divided her interests, and lessened public enthusiasm for the paper. In September '58, she wrote that she would 'like Mr. Ballantyne to point out the impropriety of our statesmen making the French alliance consist in friendship for the Emperor instead of for France. His personal influence seems to have a weight in the change of our Govts. which in a right state of things would be impossible. Lord M. [Lord Malmesbury, the Conservative Foreign Secretary] & Dizzy are his devoted humble servants and considering they got into office from the suspicion that the late Govt. was too friendly to him, this state of affairs should never be lost sight of. I should also like strong appeals to be made to the long dormant patriotic feelings of the Liberal Leaders rousing them out of their shamefully selfish motives as to who is to be first in the Govt.'

The subsidy to the *Statesman* worked out at about £50 a week and, thanks to Frances and her indefatigable slave Chichester, contributions flowed in for some time. In November '58 she thought of a new victim. 'I have an idea that Dicky [Monckton] Milnes might be useful as to money. He has just come into his Father's fortune and might like to have a finger in the pie. He must be told not to talk about it. I wonder whether he is a man to be trusted. I don't yet feel sure upon this point, but am rather in favour of his discretion than otherwise.' At the end of the following January she is 'very much amused at the bleeding of the Duke of B.'—the Duke of Bedford was notorious for his stinginess. Lord Lansdowne gave £100 in February, at the end of which month appeared the *Statesman's* last number as a weekly.

On 31 March '59, the Derby Government was defeated at the close of the debate on the second reading of their Reform Bill, despite a brilliant speech by Disraeli listing Lord John's political misdemeanours since 1835. Five days later a dissolution was announced. The Opposition seemed hopelessly divided, as Newcastle pointed out to Lady Waldegrave in a letter a few weeks later regretting his inability to join her Strawberry Hill party: 'I am sorry to miss the Duke of Bedford. I have not seen him for 3 or 4 years & I should have liked to hear his opinion of present affairs.

'My belief is there will be no motion to remove the Govt. which will succeed, because honest men (I do not mean the extreme men) feel that they have a right to know before they displace one Govt. whether a *stronger* can be formed, and even if

Palmerston and John Russell can come to any agreement (& this seems doubtful) they see on all sides amongst the *junior* Whigs so much selfishness and intrigue that they can place no reliance upon what is to come. C. Wood's after-dinner speech at Wakefield was disgraceful and meant nothing more or less than "Give *me* a place whatever you do"—& the two Articles in the Times of yesterday & Friday are obviously dictated by a *Feline* intriguer of small calibre for the purpose of supplanting *both* his Leaders.'

Derby thought an election might give the Conservatives the majority they so needed, but the country decided for the Liberals. The Queen opened Parliament on June 7, and young Lord Hartington at once moved an amendment of no-confidence to the Address. On the third evening of the debate the Government was defeated and the Queen sent for Lord Granville. It was scarcely possible to form a Liberal Cabinet without Palmerston and Lord John, but each having been Premier, either would probably be more willing to serve under another man. Granville, however, found the task impossible, and Palmerston became Prime Minister. The Queen had hoped to see Clarendon at the Foreign Office, as did Palmerston, but Lord John would only join the Government if he was given it. Lord Palmerston asked him outright, 'Do you claim the F.O. as a right?' The unabashed Lord John replied, 'I do'.

It was generally thought that through Lady Waldegrave's powerful influence Chichester Fortescue would be made Chief Secretary for Ireland, but it was again given to Cardwell, and Palmerston took a slightly malicious pleasure in sending Newcastle to the Colonial Office with Chichester again as Under-Secretary. As his chief was in the Lords, it was this time a considerably more important appointment, but, with their much discussed devotion to Frances, it was an amusing situation for everyone but the two most concerned.

The election had once again wrecked the season, but for the rest of June and July there were the usual brilliant Saturday to Monday parties at Strawberry Hill. It was almost an annexe to the Colonial Office since Fortescue and Newcastle were there as often as they could manage an invitation. Lady Susan was still determined to marry Dolly Vane, and her father was equally determined to prevent it. For him it was the excuse for innumerable consultations with Lady Waldegrave, to the fury of his rivals. Chichester, meanwhile, had acquired another ally. Braham's old friend, the Duke of Sussex, had had two children by his first wife, and the daughter, Mlle. d'Este, had married Lord Truro. Early in '59 she became very friendly with Frances, and won Chichester's heart when he overheard her saying that Lady Waldegrave 'wouldn't be beautiful if she wasn't herself, but as it is . . .'. After that, he was so invariably charming to her that, later in his life, her friendship was to prove invaluable.

The Strawberry parties lasted till the beginning of August in 1859 to Mr. Harcourt's great dissatisfaction, as Fortescue describes it on July 30. 'To Strawberry at 1. Found Lady W. in the Kitchen garden—said I might do good if I had a talk with Mr. H., which I took care to have. He complained of many things "too much company—too much D'Aumales—no rest—he was getting too old for it—she overdid it all". Some truth in this, I felt myself, but I put it all in the best light. The party came. . . . Dancing in tent. . . . Party at dinner Ly. A. [Ailesbury] Ly. Charlotte Denison, Sidney Herbert, B. of Oxford, Stratfords. Ld. St. Germans, Chelsea, Abingdon, W.H., Milnes & Sir Charles Macarthy. Went off to Orleans House. Danced with Lady W. she was lovely in a spotted muslin & scarlet flowers. To bed, quite *done*.'

At Nuneham poor Mr. Harcourt found he was entertaining all the people he had already had too much of at Strawberry Hill, the list as usual beginning with half the French royal family and the Duke of Newcastle. His only consolation was that his nephew Willie was again trying to marry, this time Thérèse Lister, a niece of Lord Clarendon's. Her family was at first very much against the match. Her mother wrote to Clarendon that 'if he could not hope to obtain your goodwill, which he had left in Lady Waldegrave's hands to try and obtain, he could not expect that I should allow him to speak to Thérèse'. A fortnight later she informed her brother that Lady Waldegrave was 'right in saying that his faults are on the surface, and they are far less apparent as you know him more'. The next day the engagement was announced, the evening before the whole party broke up. Frances was delighted with the match she had arranged, and even more pleased to find that it led to a reconciliation with the Bulteels.

Although Mr. Harcourt was happy at the prospect of a marriage which would mean a little less of Willie's society for him, the size of the gathering at Nuneham had decided him to retire to his bed with a rather nebulous complaint. He clung still more firmly to his bed at the end of the month when his wife went to Dudbrook, where she had been building on a few rooms. It was not the fresh plaster he dreaded, but that there was no longer the excuse that the house was too small, to keep the Aumales away. When Fortescue arrived at Dudbrook from Ireland, where he had nobly gone for one week after Nuneham, he was less dissatisfied to find the Aumales than he was to find Chelsea, whose everlasting presence had irritated all Frances's circle since his return from Paris six weeks before.

Mr. Harcourt, who always resented Dudbrook, was happy when Lady Waldegrave was again at Nuneham at the end of October, even though it meant the Aumales and the Comte de Paris. While they were there, the young Prince of Wales drove over from Oxford with General Bruce to lunch at Nuneham, which put Mr. Harcourt in a good mood for the rest of the year. In fact, when he took Frances on a visit to Trentham in December, he told her, 'I am proud of you—I am proud of you—there were three Duchesses here today and men like Gladstone, the Duke of Argyll etc. and there seemed to be no one there but yourself. You were the centre of everything.' As Frances laconically commented, 'Some people are always *talking* of vulgarity!'

She was genuinely fond of the Duchess of Sutherland, but Mr. Harcourt's tactlessness very nearly destroyed her affection for the older woman. She was devoted to the duchess's daughter, Lady Westminster, who, though herself one of the loveliest women in Britain, told Frances about this time, 'You look as though you fed upon roses.' It was a few days before this visit to Trentham that Corti, an Italian who worshipped Lady Waldegrave for years, told someone that she was so dazzlingly fascinating that he 'really couldn't look at her, he felt as if he should have a fit'.

Frances took all their admiration light-heartedly. When a few months later Lord Somers brought his wife, Virginia, to dine at Strawberry Hill, Chichester reports that Lady Somers 'was opposite to me next the Duke D'A., beautifully dressed and looking even more than usually beautiful. Lady W. was delicious in a fresh looking dress of muslin and blue ribbons, but she said to me afterwards—intense femme that she is—"I forgot that Ldy. S. was coming or I would have armed myself better"—but it was quite unnecessary.'

Poor Maddalena Braham did not share her sister-in-laws' glorious health. Sunshine one autumn day had tempted her to wear a thin dress. A cold had developed and by the end of the year she was desperately ill. Charles, always bewildered at any misfortune, was overcome with remorse for his vague, happy-go-lucky attitude to marriage, and suddenly devoted himself to her. Her mother and sister were fetched from Naples, but there was nothing to be done, and towards the end of February 1860, Chichester accompanied Seph in a sad little cortège to the Roman Catholic cemetery at Kensal Green.

Immediately after the funeral Charles had to leave for Edinburgh where he had an engagement for the next two months. His small daughter, Constance, went to stay with Seph at Bolton Row, but the Bohemian friends, whom Ward and Charles continually entertained there, scarcely made it a suitable home for a child of four and a half. Frances was very taken with her and realized that Charles was far too vague to be trusted with her education. While he was away it was impossible to come to any conclusion, but, when he returned towards the end of April, she made her decision.

Fortescue wrote in his diary on 24 April 1860: 'A long talk with Mr. H. on the same subject—all his grievances, as before. I gave him my mind and said whatever I thought might be useful. What a man he is! He said that she often asked him "whether he was very fond of her *indeed* etc", and then if answered that that would depend on her conduct towards him, she was very angry! He talked of the child, said it was "an attractive child", but complained of her making too much of it etc. It was a lovely day. I sat on the lawn and read for some time until he joined me much improved in temper, after a talk with her. At last Lady W. appeared, he went off and I sat on the lawn under the limes with her before and after luncheon—we had much quiet talk—she was very free and bright, because there was no one that day at O. House, and she was mistress of her time. This was one of my happiest days. Charley brought little Constance. We all drove to Bushey Park, to see the horse-chestnuts. The dear Lady was crying at first on account of something between him and her just before, on seeing which the little creature kissed her again and again.'

After that there was no hesitation. By the beginning of July Constance had been formally adopted, and her aunt had already settled her future. Uncle William, the eighth Earl Waldegrave, had died the previous October, and Lady Chewton's small son had succeeded. Frances and his mother were on very friendly terms, and both decided that in some fifteen years Constance should also become Lady Waldegrave.

Meanwhile two other marriages had taken place that caused Frances endless worry. On January 2, Susan, Lady Lincoln, Newcastle's divorced wife, had married her Belgian courier, Opdebeck, causing a sensation that seriously affected the duke's health. He could no longer bear even to discuss his daughter's infatuation for Lord Adolphus Vane, and the scenes between them were public knowledge. Lady Waldegrave and the girl's governess, who was a great friend of Edward Lear's, did everything to dissuade Lady Susan, but her father's intolerance and utter tactlessness had more effect than the advice of the two women. Newcastle was frantic as he was to accompany the Prince of Wales to Canada in July, and during his absence anything could happen.

On March 24 the Duke was 'in very bad health, one eye affected —in better spirits just now because Dolly Vane is mad & Ly. Susan can hardly marry him'. He naturally saw Lady Waldegrave on every possible occasion. On April 21 he sent her a note: 'Shall you be in Town tomorrow?—I am *very* anxious to see you. If you can let me come, pray name any hour that suits you tomorrow afternoon.' The next day he called 'to pour into her sympathising ear his complaints and griefs about Lady Susan'. Fortescue's sympathy for his chief had considerably diminished when Frances had told him that Newcastle 'is excessively fond of me & I like him better than ever'.

Two days later Lady Susan left her father's house in Portman Square and married Lord Adolphus. By May 4 Lady Selina Vernon was telling her friends that 'Adolphus Vane has gone mad again, and threw a decanter and knives and forks at her, yet she wrote to the Duchess of Marlborough that she had never had so happy a week in her life'. On the 20th Newcastle wrote to tell Frances 'I hear accounts of her behaviour—worthy of the Wife of such a Blackguard', and two days later that 'Ld. A. was on the verge of another attack yesterday! He is *probably* under restraint today, but I do not know it yet.'

The duke spent every moment he could at Carlton Gardens or Strawberry Hill until he left on July 8 with the Prince of Wales for Canada and the United States. Another fervent admirer of Lady Waldegrave accompanied him, Lord St. Germans, who was Lord Steward of the Household and the Queen's confidential adviser on family affairs, so Frances was kept well-informed of the progress of the royal tour.

The tour was a great success to everyone's astonishment. Even the King of the Belgians was surprised that the poor Duke of Newcastle got home without accident, and Emily Eden expressed the public opinion, 'I am so glad the Prince of Wales has arrived. I always thought they would have to put Jonah, Duke of Newcastle, overboard before the ship could make any way.' The 'evil genius' which Lord Selborne claimed 'followed him in all the relations of life' awaited him on his arrival. He found Lord Lincoln had left the country, having raised £28,000 to pay his racing debts, for which he had given post-obits amounting to £230,000.

Possibly the only anxiety the tour caused was that the ship on which they returned was nearly a fortnight overdue by the time it reached Plymouth on November 15. Ten days later Newcastle was again at Strawberry Hill to delight his hostess with news of the Garter the Queen had offered him two days after his arrival in London, although it meant creating an extra knight until a vacancy occurred.

The duke's absence had left Fortescue in charge of the Colonial Office and thus brought him into some political prominence. He was intensely interested in colonial affairs and hoped that the experience would lead to his some day becoming Colonial Secretary. He was forced to overcome his shyness to address the House on a number of occasions, and though his nervousness made him a dry, stilted public speaker, it was clear that he knew his subject intimately.

In another political field he was less fortunate. Garibaldi's successful campaign against the King of the Two Sicilies during 1860 had made him a popular hero in England, and Chichester was his ardent supporter. It led to serious quarrels with Lady Waldegrave whose sympathies had been listed for King 'Bomba' by the Aumales, both of them his first cousins since old Queen Marie Amelie was herself a Neapolitan princess.

Frances's sympathy with them over the Garibaldi campaign did not however mean that their political views usually influenced her. The Orleans family's pronounced dislike for England infuriated her in view of the hospitality they had all enjoyed in this country after the falls both of Louis XVI and of Louis Philippe. Once when Aumale had offended Lady Waldegrave by his comments on England, it had taken endless notes and visits from his little duchesse to persuade her to forgive him.

He was undoubtedly the most brilliant and best looking of Louis Philippe's sons, and had inherited the vast fortune of the old Prince de Condé, who had been found hanged in mysterious circumstances in 1830. Rumour claimed that, though suspicion fell heavily on Condé's English mistress, Louis Philippe had agreed to drop any charge if the Condé fortune went to his fourth son, the Duc d'Aumale.

Aumale's fine intellect, which led to his becoming a member of the Philobiblon Society and even taking the chair at the Literary Fund dinner, was politically disadvantageous to him. His standpoint was too detached and objective to give him the fire and enthusiasm he would have needed as a political leader. The various pamphlets he published certainly attracted a great deal of attention by their cool, logical reasoning, but that is a quality of little service to a demagogue. Frances herself admitted there was 'something arid' about him. 'I am not at all sentimental. I like them very much when I'm with them but I don't *want* them.' She said of herself after the reconciliation with Mary Bulteel, 'she was one of the very few who got down *here*, very deep, and then it's impossible to get them out again—Charley's another—old Pearson's another'.

The duc shared his wife's attraction to their Twickenham neighbour, and sought her advice on every occasion. She was even called in to settle family rows. The little duchesse was incurably extravagant and, when faced with the enormous bills she had not the courage to acknowledge to Aumale, would appeal to Frances to pacify him.

After the Duchesse d'Orléans's death, Aumale had taken charge of her two sons, the Comte de Paris and the Duc de Chartres, and brought them up with his own two boys, Condé and Guise. Young Condé was the single member of the Orleans family who was genuinely pro-English, and was therefore Frances's favourite. Most foreign royalties staying in London visited their kinsmen at Orleans House, and were immediately taken over to Strawberry Hill to meet 'very, very, dearest Frances', an honour her other guests found increasingly tiresome. As Ralph Sneyd, one of the earliest 'Nunehamites' said of Aumale, 'However agreeable he is, there is a certain gêne about it—at all events I should like to *try* it without them.'

It was possibly the difficulties of her life with Mr. Harcourt that induced Frances to allow the Aumales to absorb so much of her time and interest. In June '60, Lady Cremorne, who years before had been prejudiced against Lady Waldegrave, said 'that she had been thinking of her half the night with tears in her eyes—that she pitied her—such a loving nature as hers, no children and such a husband—such a want of fireside happiness—such perpetual brilliancy and admiration *abroad*, such a *manque* at home—so much restlessness. She felt a great admiration of her, a strange attraction towards her whenever she saw her—understood her wonderful influence over others.'

The Aumales, of course, arrived at Nuneham with the Clarendons, Chelsea, Lady Truro and the usual gathering of regulars, as soon as the summer parties began, but the death of Mr. Harcourt's eldest brother and heir, brought the gathering to a sudden end, and it was succeeded by the strange hotch-potch of in-laws and relations whose only link was their kinship to Frances, yet who had somehow been welded into a mutually devoted family group. Ward, however, had been causing her trouble since the beginning of the year. Once again he had spent the spring dodging bum-bailiffs, appearing only at night or on Sundays. To complicate matters, Miss Wadham had decided to marry, and wanted him to return the jewels she had lent him to pawn during an earlier crisis. Luckily Fortescue had settled everything, but Ward was still somewhat in disgrace. With his fellow officers at Reading his success was amazing, though he seemed to consider his militia duties theatrical rather than military. At some amateur theatricals at Aldershot he had even made Queen Victoria laugh till she cried.

Fortescue was one of the 'family' party, as was Edward Lear whom Frances had commissioned to paint two pictures of Nuneham. She had been delighted with two he had done for her of Jerusalem and Masada, and was always glad when he was her guest. With her passion for enlarging her houses every year, the question of their decoration occupied her considerably. In February there had been an exhibition at the French Gallery of the portraits Sant had been painting for Strawberry Hill, which included those of the Duchess of Sutherland, of her daughter-in-law the Marchioness of Stafford, her daughter Lady Constance Grosvenor, the Aumales and Frances herself. A few men had been painted—Clarendon, the Bishop of Oxford and old Lord Lyndhurst among them. The only portrait not by Sant was the painting of Lady Churchill by Grant.

Henry Phillips had been commissioned to do a series of paintings for one of the large new rooms, and at the Academy in May there was a full-length miniature of Lady Waldegrave by H. T. Wells, probably the best representation of her that exists. Sant's Strawberry Hill portraits were generally considered to be the best work he ever did, but they suffered the great disadvantage of being in the same building as the superb Reynolds' 'Three Ladies Waldegrave' and 'Maria, Lady Waldegrave', the Ramsay 'Charlotte and Laura Waldegrave', and the other masterpieces Frances had bought in at the sale in 1842.

Since the restoration of Strawberry Hill, she had occasionally asked her brother Charles to attend picture sales on her behalf. A few lucky purchases had persuaded him that he had a talent for picture dealing and, in the Bohemian world he frequented, so gullible a buyer found any number of people with Giottos and Botticellis for him to offer his wealthy and adoring sister. His various operatic engagements in Italy continued and provided him with the opportunity to discover masterpieces everywhere. Within a few years he had entirely forsaken the stage for this new career that was to involve him in thousands of pounds worth of debts.

She saw no reason why the mourning at Nuneham should affect Dudbrook, where she had built yet another suite of rooms, and 1 September 1860 found her in Essex receiving her Twickenham neighbours from Orleans House and Marble Hill. The latter, built by George II for his mistress Mrs. Howard, belonged to

General Peel, a brother of old Sir Robert. His two daughters were favourites of Frances's, who had great plans for the elder, Alice. Chichester's friend, Robert Morier, was on leave from Berlin and Lady Waldegrave decided that he needed a wife who should be Alice Peel. They had never seen each other until they arrived at Dudbrook, but they were each seized by their hostess and her coadjutor, Chichester, and made to listen to a detailed list of the others' virtues and qualifications.

At first Morier was so enchanted to see Frances again after so many years that he scarcely noticed Miss Peel. 'He talked with the greatest admiration of Lady W.—marvelling to find her so un-changed in friendship, so unspoilt by the world—so fresh *und herrlich wie am ersten Tag!*' In his German philosophizing way he applied to her the word *'unmittelbar'*, so fresh and first hand a nature.' She was, however, too accomplished a matchmaker to be daunted by such very accustomed behaviour, and before the party broke up, it was certain that Morier, on his next leave, would make his declaration.

THE FIRST MONTHS of 1861 were another period of anxiety for the unfortunate Duke of Newcastle. In Nice Lord Lincoln had fallen in love with an extremely pretty girl, Henrietta Hope, the illegitimate daughter of the immensely rich Henry Hope of Deepdene. Hope had married his French mistress some years after the birth of their child, but the fact of Henrietta's bastardy was no secret. She was very popular and it was rumoured would eventually have £50,000 a year, but Newcastle was aghast at the thought of such a marriage. The Hopes, on the other hand, determined that their daughter should be a duchess, settled £10,000 a year on her and persuaded Lincoln to marry, without his father's consent, in Paris on February 11. By the autumn the duke had so far accepted the situation that Lord Lincoln was present when the Prince of Wales stayed at Clumber in October.

For Lady Susan things had gone from bad to worse. In March Dolly Vane was arrested for creating a disturbance in Coventry Street, but, when charged at Marlborough Street, was remanded for medical examination. Ten days later it was announced that he had been removed to a lunatic asylum. His position as Member for North Durham and as Lady Londonderry's son enabled him discreetly to leave the asylum as soon as the question of any further charge had been dropped.

. It was unlucky for Josephine Wilson that she should have chosen just this moment to write to the duke complaining of Lady Waldegrave's treatment of her. Josephine, who had got herself into a position in America that not even she could brazen out, had come to England in an attempt to twist yet more money from her sister or from her son's trustees. Her stories proved to be such a tissue of lies that at last her easy-going brothers revolted, and Frances refused to meet her. In an attempt to force her sister's hand, Josephine had written to the duke whose devotion to Lady Waldegrave was public knowledge. If anything, her letter increased the duke's affection, and a few weeks later he assured Frances that 'he couldn't live without seeing her'.

With so much domestic trouble it was assumed that he would be tempted by the suggestion of succeeding Lord Canning as Governor-General of India. In April, however, Lord Granville wrote to Lord Canning to tell him that:

'Lady Waldegrave who is his principal confidant, says he does not wish it, that he means to be Prime Minister.'

A Cabinet reshuffle was imminent since Sidney Herbert, who had recently been made Lord Herbert of Lea, was seriously ill and could no longer carry out his duties at the War Office.

Palmerston was again harassed by the composition of his Cabinet, but for once the difficulties came from another source. Lady Palmerston could not overlook the way both Lord John and Gladstone had behaved to her husband so often in the past, and her fierce opposition to every measure either of them introduced considerably embarrassed the Premier. There were quite as many politicians among the regular visitors at Cambridge House who were prepared to follow her lead as were prepared to follow Lord Palmerston's.

The position was not improved by the death of the Duke of Bedford towards the end of May. At times Palmerston had tried to persuade Lord John to accept a peerage, but at that moment he considered that the Foreign Secretary's presence in the House of Commons was essential. Lord John had for years complained that he found his work in the Commons exhausting, and would probably have gone to the Lords sooner had he had the means to support his coronet. With the death of his parsimonious brother and with his generous, if eccentric, nephew as duke the financial obstacle was surmounted and Palmerston found himself held to his earlier offer.

In the course of the ministerial rearrangement Cardwell became Chancellor of the Duchy of Lancaster which meant that the Chief Secretaryship of Ireland was vacant. On July 12 Newcastle sent for Chichester to tell him that he, Chichester Fortescue, was to be Chief Secretary. It was worth £4,000 a year and would be a popular appointment with the Irish, but Chichester was horrified.

'I told the Duke how I disliked the Irish Office, & had always wished to keep out of it. He didn't wonder, but thought I couldn't refuse unless my seat were in danger. He said I might naturally look and was "fully entitled" to be head of the Colonial Office one of these days, but it was generally necessary to go through an intermediate office, and the Irish Secretaryship was next to the Cabinet etc. Nothing could be more friendly & confidential than he was, both as to my affairs and his own.'

Naturally Fortescue at once rushed down to Strawberry Hill to discuss it. He had not mentioned to the Duke of Newcastle his principal objection to the appointment. 'I was in a turmoil of feelings. How could I bear to be so much separated from *her*.' On the 17th he called on Lady Palmerston and 'took the opportunity of saying that I did not seek or desire the Irish Office, though I would not refuse anything Lord P. asked me to do. Her tone made me think that Lord P. had then changed his mind.'

On July 22 *The Times* announced Chichester's appointment as Chief Secretary. He immediately went to the duke and found that *The Times* was wrong. Palmerston had decided that Chichester's seat for Co. Louth was not safe enough to risk the by-election, and had decided on the young Sir Robert Peel. Possibly the Premier was right about Co. Louth, but it is almost certain that his reason was really Chichester's open sympathy with the Irish Catholics.

Despite the Court mourning for the Queen's mother who had died in March, Frances had found it a very exhausting season. The previous year some of her friends had persuaded her to take up amateur theatricals again, and at a big Nuneham party in January she had appeared with increased success in her old parts in *The Honeymoon* and *The Dowager*. Mr. Harcourt's nephew, G. E. Vernon, was too seriously ill to be stage manager again, but Ward was infinitely more successful.

Apart from stage management Ward—with considerable help from Chichester—had written an extravaganza *The Battle of the Houses* which, with *The Dowager*, was performed in honour of Chichester's thirty-eighth birthday. Lord Clarendon received an account of it from his sister. 'Very clever and *very* much to the taste of our hostess. Ward Braham, dressed as a fairy, comes on earth to visit country houses, and summons before him certain personated châteaux whose merits are freely discussed. Nuneham, Strawberry Hill, Little Strawberry, the Priory (where the coals come from) and Dudbrook, the object being to show that Nuneham is dull, stiff and inhospitable, except when cheered by Lady Waldegrave, and the preference given to *all her* places—

Strawberry Hill in particular. I was told that our *host particularly* enjoyed the piece (this being the second representation). His face gave no signs of delight; but this might be from the intensity of his pleasure. . . . The management was excellent, being by Mr. Braham—so different from Granville Vernon.'

The year 1861 was the last season in which Lady Waldegrave took part in amateur theatricals, but one of her last appearances was to mark the beginning of a new set of relationships.

At the time of Frances's wedding to Lord Waldegrave, the Duchess of Cambridge, in common with most of her acquaintance, had discussed the legality of the marriage. Unfortunately her words had been repeated to the quick-tempered Frances, and although the old Duchess of Gloucester had done all she could to smooth things out, the subject still rankled. As the Duchess of Cambridge and her daughter, Princess Mary, lived mostly at Kew, they were frequently at Orleans House, but it took the Aumales years to change Lady Waldegrave's aloof attitude to their royal guests. The situation was not improved by Frances's passion for mimicry which found the stout, high-spirited princess an irresistible butt.

When at last, in June, the Aumales prevailed upon her to give a dinner at Carlton Gardens for the Cambridges before a performance of *The Dowager*, Princess Mary's description of the party was slightly acid, though she admitted that her hostess 'acted to perfection'. However, the ice was broken and in time a considerable friendship came about.

The Duchesse d'Aumale scarcely left Twickenham during that spring. Her health was seriously affected by yet another of her continual pregnancies that resulted in a stillborn child at the end of the season. She expected Frances to spend as much time as possible with her, and even at Carlton Gardens her illness made itself felt by the daily presence there of either her husband or her nephews. Aumale consulted Lady Waldegrave constantly about the pamphlet he published attacking the Imperial régime in France which, it was expected, would involve him in a duel with Prince 'Plon-Plon' Napoleon. 'Plon-Plon', however, swallowed the affront and Aumale was the hero of the hour. The Comte de Paris, too, came to her for advice on the pamphlet he was writing on the Lebanon.

They made it difficult for Frances to find time for the endless rehearsals in the crowded life she led as a great political hostess, but there was also the building of the huge new rooms at Strawbery Hill to supervise, and the constant dread of her sister Josephine's next unscrupulous action. In addition to this Lady Waldegrave had to chaperone the two Money girls to parties and dances the whole season. Mr. Harcourt was not surprised that she complained of being 'fagged and harassed, like a hunted hare'.

Frances had, from the first, found the household at Little Strawberry Hill a constant source of anxiety. Brought up in the comparative isolation of Norfolk by a succession of indifferent governesses, the Money girls had suffered the further disadvantage of an invalid mother and an elderly father. Lady Laura had petted and spoilt her elder daughter and namesake at the expense of the younger, Ida, whom she entirely repressed and to whom she never showed the slightest affection. During the two and a half years that intervened between the deaths of their mother and father, Laura had used her position as mistress of her father's house to continue the repression of her sister.

Laura's attitude to her sister and her almost insolent assertiveness had always irritated Frances who naturally sided with Ida. Nevertheless, she had done her best for Laura, had chaperoned her through two seasons and had bored her other guests at Nuneham, Dudbrook and in town by the presence of a dull young dragoon because the girl appeared to be interested in him. It was for Laura that Henry Hervey had been asked to Dudbrook at the beginning of August.

A nephew of the Marquess of Bristol, Hervey had soon run through the money his father had left him and had distressed his family, and imperilled his position at the Foreign Office, by a rash early marriage.

After Chichester had taken to chastity, his obliging friend, Miss Polly Fleming, had found another admirer in Lord Ribblesdale, Lord John Russell's stepson. She had persuaded Ribblesdale to elope with her to Normandy, whence after a long pursuit by his brother-in-law, he was at last brought back to his wife. Meanwhile, Kitty Fleming had succeeded in marrying the Earl of Stamford, which suggested marriage as a possible future to her sister. Young Henry Hervey was her victim, but what little money he still had was quickly spent, and as Ribblesdale was pleasantly rich and was again weary of his wife, they repeated the elopement and Hervey obtained a divorce.

Since the divorce Hervey had settled down and become a very agreeable young man who soon won Frances's affection. She was a little amused by the presence at Dudbrook of both Hervey and Chichester Fortescue, as John Bidwell had rather meanly told her of the earlier liaison with Polly Fleming, though carefully omitting to tell her when and why it had terminated.

Unfortunately Hervey had almost no income except his Foreign Office pay, and though the Money girls had been left adequately provided for, Lady Waldegrave felt that Lord Bristol should in some way supplement his nephew's salary. On August 1 Hervey proposed and was accepted, whereupon his hostess summoned his uncle to Dudbrook to discuss settlements. On the same day the inevitable Aumales arrived and with them Alice Peel, her sister and Morier, who four days later proposed to Miss Peel.

Even for Frances, two engagements in one week was a record, and to add to her pleasure the ten-year-old Lord Waldegrave, whom Lady Chewton had brought with her, became great friends with little Constance. As soon as he arrived Lord Bristol fell a victim to the radiant Lady Waldegrave and was easily persuaded to make Hervey a small allowance. When, in the third week in August, Frances left with Mr. Harcourt for a tour of Switzerland, Bavaria, Austria and Italy, she felt that a number of her problems were solved.

Her sister, Mrs. Charles Wilson, was certainly still in England, but Pearson, Charles Braham and Fortescue had vowed that between them they would ship her back to America. Goldsmid, son of old Braham's friend, as trustee of the Wilson marriage settlements, refused to advance any money until Josephine's son came of age, and when she did finally leave in September, Lady Waldegrave had to pay her passage.

It was the last any of them saw of her. Four years later the miserable, squalid existence she had brought on herself came to an end in New York, possibly caused by the death of her child a few months earlier. Almost the only favourable aspect of her disastrous character was the affection she appeared to feel for her son.

Augustus was also thinking of crossing the Atlantic. His various operatic engagements had not proved lucrative enough to support his family, despite the allowance his sister made him. He felt that there might be some opening for him in Canada, and Frances was prepared to pay the family's passage. Mrs. Augustus, however, had no desire to emigrate and as usual Chichester Fortescue, Pearson, Charles and Ward had to listen to interminable discussions about it. Finally Chichester suggested that Lady Waldegrave should arrange a paymastership for him in England, and at the end of the following March Augustus became paymaster to the 7th Depot Battalion.

Mr. Harcourt was sincerely grateful to Fortescue for the trouble he took with the Braham family. At seventy-six he realized that he could no longer cope with all his wife's problems and had even resigned himself quite benignly to the August parties in 1861 being held at Dudbrook instead of at Nuneham. The prospect of having Frances to himself during their autumn tour gratified him, although they had arranged to meet Charles Braham, who had a winter engagement in Milan, early in October. Old Canon Harcourt and Chichester had also decided that October in Italy was essential to their well-being.

The tour was a success, though neither Frances nor her husband were especially delighted to find Lord Chelsea awaiting them at Geneva. To avoid him Mr. Harcourt welcomed the suggestion of a visit to Boisrond, a visit that amused his wife by the extraordinary contrast between her strange retired life with Lord Waldegrave and her present brilliant, crowded existence. Now wherever she went every embassy and legation fêted her and she found a crowd of old friends in each city they visited.

There was the additional excitement of buying furniture for the huge new drawing-room at Strawberry Hill which was nearly completed when she had spent a day or two there before they left England. It was in Vienna that she ordered the splendid parquet flooring which has magnificently withstood nearly a century of dancing feet.

During the first week of October they arrived in Milan from Venice to find old Canon Harcourt, Chichester, Charles and Ward to receive them. Fortescue had, after a few weeks with his old aunt at Ardee, returned to London to be best man at Morier's wedding to Alice Peel, and had then spent a day or two with Edward Lear before crossing to join the others.

Frances at once took her whole party to Como. Their visit there was rather spoilt by the presence of Lord Abingdon who was in a neighbouring hotel with his old love, Lady Jersey. Lord Villiers had died soon after succeeding to the earldom of Jersey, and everyone anticipated that the two lovers would at last marry. Even Mr. Harcourt was anxious to have the question settled as the scandal caused his grandchildren great unhappiness. Abingdon, however, appeared to feel no embarrassment about the situation, and eventually Lady Jersey ended the liaison by marrying a Captain Brandling.

The Harcourt family made their leisurely way through Parma and Bologna to Florence where Ward flatly refused to do any sightseeing and where Chichester was constantly 'blown up' for unpunctuality. The others spent their time visiting the various studios and exhibitions where Frances was anxious to buy pictures and statues for her new rooms. Among her purchases was Magni's 'Reading Girl', which attracted great attention in London, when it was shown at the International Exhibition of 1862, and a charming 'Tired Dancing Girl'.

For Chichester the climax of their visit to Florence was the evening he persuaded Lady Waldegrave again to visit Petraia as they had done in 1854. In those days he had thought it impossible for his devotion to her to increase, but she had become his entire life. She, on the other hand, still treated him with the affectionate friendliness of a sister, and refused to share his sentimental nostalgia about every place they had visited together seven years before.

Once again their journey home was through Genoa, Turin and Susa, where Ward and Fortescue parted from Mr. Harcourt and his wife and set off in the banquette of the courier over the Mont Cenis. The sight of the refuge reminded Chichester of the blissful night he had spent there, watching his beautiful lady as she slept in her chair while that fearful storm raged outside.

After a few days all together in Paris, Ward and Chichester left for London as their companions were to visit the British ambassador and Lady Cowley at Chantilly and the Persignys at the château they had so modernized that they could proudly boast of its containing every English comfort—'*des grands lits, des grands bassins, des* tubs *dans chaque chambre, de l'eau partout et vingt-cinq* waterclosets'.

On November 18 Mr. Harcourt and Lady Waldegrave landed at Folkestone. As she settled herself in the train Frances was profoundly glad to be back in England, much as she had enjoyed the past three months. It was a considerable responsibility for her to travel round Europe with an old man of seventy-six. Even as he got into the train at Folkestone his foot slipped and he fell heavily to the platform, but his devoted manservant soon helped him to his feet, brushed him down and all was well.

The splendid new suite of reception rooms at Strawberry Hill was nearly finished and delighted her when she went there two days after her arrival. Characteristically she immediately saw the one defect—that the new rooms were not high enough above the level of the lawns. She at once gave orders for the ground to be excavated to a suitable level.

There were all the arrangements for the Hervey-Money wedding to occupy her. Laura, as a Ward in Chancery and a minor, had to have the Vice-Chancellor's permission to marry which, in view of Hervey's first marriage and his earlier extravagance, would not be easy to obtain. Mr. Harcourt became 'very benign' when Fortescue agreed to undertake the negotiations, choosing of all extraordinary people Ward as his assistant.

On the 23rd, Chichester arrived at Twickenham to find Frances worried about her husband. His fall at Folkestone had apparently upset him more than he had realized at the time. The next day she summoned a doctor who agreed that the old man was 'quite off his balance from the fall'. Three days later the Duke of Newcastle, on his arrival at Strawberry Hill, told Chichester that he almost expected Mr. Harcourt to have a paralytic stroke before morning. It was that day that the news came that the Federal man-of-war *San Jacinto* had stopped the British steamer *Trent*, and seized the two envoys, Slidell and Mason, whom the Confederate States of America were sending to Europe.

The English, whose sympathies were largely with the Southern States in the American Civil War, were furious at this affront, and the possibility of war with the Federal States was freely discussed. On November 29 a despatch was sent demanding the immediate release of Mason and Slidell unless diplomatic relations were to be broken off. Troops were ordered to Canada and for the next few weeks the danger of war loomed large.

At Strawberry Hill the American crisis passed unnoticed. Frances was frantic with anxiety about her husband for whom all her affection revived whenever he was ill or unhappy. In his helplessness he was intensely grateful for her kindness, and she reproached herself bitterly for not having attached more importance to his fall at Folkestone.

Ward spent most of his time with his sister and was always glad when Chichester, Norreys or the Pearsons came, but he made no attempt to be polite to Willie Harcourt whom he detested as long as he lived. Although he caused her endless worry with his eccentricities and his debts, Ward would happily have died for Frances, and in spite of the many pretty ladies who fluttered through his life, he always considered her the loveliest and most fascinating woman he knew. After one of Mr. Harcourt's bad nights, Ward even grew poetical describing Lady Waldegrave to Chichester:

'She came into my room during the night with her great eyes fixed like a lovely oracle.'

By December 6, Mr. Harcourt was in a very weak state and asked to see Fortescue to whom he was most affectionate, telling him, 'I'm very ill, but I'm very happy.'

During the next three days his strength steadily ebbed, but he was consistently and touchingly grateful and affectionate to his wife. On the 11th there was a slight improvement and by the 14th Lady Waldegrave considered him to be out of all danger.

Till that day Frances had been too preoccupied with his illness to take any interest in the state of the Prince Consort's health, but on the 14th the whole country realized that the Prince was very dangerously ill. The following morning the news of his death aroused all Frances's sympathy for the Queen, but could not repress her happiness at Mr. Harcourt's recovery.

During the next day or two, however, her depression returned. It was obvious that Mr. Harcourt would be an invalid, if not bedridden, for the rest of his life. That she was prepared to face, but since his health had improved he had resumed his selfish ill temper. The charming, affectionate, grateful old man of the last few weeks had disappeared and she foresaw years tied to the bedside of a querulous, selfish invalid, with every moment of liberty absorbed by the Aumales.

Her neighbours at Orleans House had, with a sympathy she could well have foregone, been with her daily during his illness, oblivious of the fact that even at Strawberry Hill their presence caused a degree of formality that Frances in her anxiety found extremely irksome.

On the morning of Thursday, December 19, Chichester had a note from his hostess asking him not to return to London until she had seen him. At midday she appeared equipped for walking, and together they walked through the rosery and the grove to the far summer-house. In answer to Fortescue's enquiry she assured him:

'Mr. Harcourt is very much better this morning. I nearly agreed with Pethoud and Mrs. Bowne [her personal maid and the housekeeper] that he is well. As long as he lies there he looks almost well and very comfortable, and his voice is quite strong today, but the moment he moves or rather is moved, it is plain that he has no strength.'

They went on to discuss her probable life with him as an invalid, and whether she should take him to Ramsgate for a change of air, when a housemaid came running towards them and said: 'Madame Pethoud wants your ladyship to come in at once to Mr. Harcourt!'

She guessed instantly what it was and the blood rushed to her face. She could not run, but made Chichester run on to the house. Mr. Harcourt had fainted. By the time she reached her dressing-room, where he had been lying during his illness, he had recovered consciousness. She immediately called for brandy. He managed to gasp, 'I have had it already.' He struggled for breath, and in a few moments was dead.

LADY WALDEGRAVE'S certainty, during the previous few days, that her husband would recover, made his sudden death a terrible shock to her. She could think of nothing but her own selfishness at having let his ill humour annoy her, and her dread of his survival as an invalid.

Fortunately Seph, Ward and Chichester were with her and they sent at once for Pearson and Lord Norreys. Chichester felt that he should leave immediately, but neither the housekeeper nor Frances's maid would hear of it.

'*Le monde—le monde*,' they said, 'but you must think of my Lady —and everyone knows that you were Mr. Harcourt's friend. He was glad to see you to the last when he wouldn't see his own nephew [W. V. Harcourt].'

It was midnight before he returned to London, but within forty-eight hours he was again at Strawberry Hill.

Mr. Harcourt's will had been read the previous day, and his shortcomings were all forgotten in the appreciation felt of the wonderful tribute he had paid his wife. There were letters of the most affectionate sympathy from all her friends, but it was the letters from his brothers and sisters that were the most remarkable. Granville Vernon wrote of his brother's fortunate life 'how after having had his vanity so gratified by his first wife, he at an age when he had no right to expect it, had it still more gratified by his second'.

Chichester was every day at Strawberry Hill until he went to Ireland for Christmas. He travelled with the Lord-Lieutenant, Lord Carlisle, who told him that Mrs. Malcolm had written to the Duchess of Sutherland, that Mr. Harcourt's 'first wife had separated him from his family, and his second wife had restored him to them'. A few days later Georgie Malcolm wrote to Chichester that Mr. Harcourt's 'first wife was his bane—his second had been a blessing to him'.

On New Year's Eve, Lady Waldegrave, with Seph, Ward,

Constance, the Money girls and the Pearsons left for Dudbrook. Apart from her anxiety to get away from the scene of her husband's illness and death, she wanted a refuge from the everlasting visits of the Aumales. The little duchesse, who had already suffered the loss of seven of her nine children, had a morbid conviction that she herself would die young and had decided that the duc should then marry Frances. Possibly the fact that they were first cousins influenced the Aumales' married life, since the duc's devotion to her friend aroused no jealousy in his wife.

At Dudbrook, however, Frances's depression increased. At every moment she missed Mr. Harcourt's great good sense and counsel. As she herself described it, 'I feel like a horse trying to lean against the accustomed collar and finding none, missing both the restraint and the support.'

As he had promised to do in 1847, he had managed all the daily affairs of her busy life. There were a thousand details to settle about the new buildings at Twickenham, the Radstock mines and Laura Money's marriage settlements, and although Mr. Pearson had latterly devoted himself exclusively to her affairs, his health was failing rapidly and despite his presence at Dudbrook he was too ill to be of much assistance.

Once again the Aumales pursued Frances into Essex. Ward acidly described the visit.

'It is now 9-30 a.m. and I am the first down—and expect them *all* soon to breakfast. All consist of the following

> the Duke D'Aumale
> Aunt Seff
> Ida
> and Charles (arrived yesterday)

the following have breakfasts in their own rooms—

> My lady as usual
> the Duchess
> Mrs. Pearson
> Mr. Pearson

'Little old woman [Constance] breakfasts with the new maid. The whole affair of yesterday has completely upset me and I have taken a Seidlitz powder this morning.

'A telegraph came yesterday from the Duchess; to say that they would be at the Railway Station at 11-15 *"tomorrow"* of course the "tomorrow" my Lady thought must be today the 7th but what was her surprise to see them arrive in a cab. The telegraph was sent on the Monday night but was not delivered until the next morning (yesterday). I need not say my spirits sank immediately, my Lady sends all sorts of messages to me the last of all is that I am to be down to breakfast with the Duke.

'Old Charley Boy's arrival was a grand affair and made us all very happy.'

Even Edward Lear, wintering in Corfu, was irritated by the Aumales's persistence, and wrote to sympathize with Chichester about that and about scandal he had heard.

'I know exactly from whom the ill-natured gossip was derived, being the viddy of the late url. . . . I don't like a Bourbon Monopoly, & wish she [Lady Waldegrave] may go to some cheerful watering place for a little while—such as Torquay—or rather St Leonards. The low and damp situation of Essex is not good for her. It isn't. It isn't: it isn't, it isn't, t'isn't. . . . Concerning Bourbons, I had more to say: I do not like them being the first to see Lady W: of which more anon. Bourbons is Bourbons.'

A fortnight later he resumed the attack: 'What I said about Bourbons was not merely bosh: I heard abroad that she wished to marry C. de P. [the Comte de Paris] to the daughter of the Parma people—& that she was a great friend to all the B.s.: the A's will gladly enlist her interest & house as a help to them. That they should be friends is natural & right, but that she should in any way assist that effete & bad lot—as a sovereign family—to future power wd. be vexatious to all who know & like her. A year & a half ago I told her that the Duc D'A. had wrongly informed her as to the state of Naples (Kingdom): she however was sure that the B's were well looked on in the province.'

On January 14 Chichester's anxiety for his dear lady brought him back to England. His arrival at Dudbrook was not a success; 'Found the dear lady walking in the road by the beech walk with Charley', who had returned from Milan to comfort his sister. 'She looked very grave & serious at first, and was displeased at my coming, but after a time she began to talk, & talked a great deal before the day was over, which was good for her. Pearson was there & present during a great part of my talking to her.'

June 13. 1862.

3.30 PM. Waterloo Station. 4.15 At
Twickenham. Rain in torrents
Strawberry Hill. Many people. In a "harbour"
in the garden were L.T.W. - L. Chelsea, & others,
just as if it were 10 years ago, more or
less. She looks better & younger & prettier
than ever. Having looked at the new rooms
& alterations, went to my own, & after my
fashion, instantly 'penned out' some fiy
1857. small Albanian drawings.
Dinner at 8.

After the ladies went, Bidwell told a
story of Pelissier, who at some great party, where was
Lord S. de Redcliffe — he on the point of starting for
his last mission to Constantinople, shouted out — "I
"have a message to the Sultan, which I shall feel.
"glad if you will deliver from me." "Dites donc, —
M. le Marechal," said Lord S, & a dead silence
occurred, the whole company listening. "Dites au
Sultan que je lui conseille de dormer seul
pour au moins un mois, s'il ne veut pas mourir"
— Lord S's face was a sight. —

FROM A LETTER OF EDWARD LEAR'S
TO CHICHESTER FORTESCUE

Two days later he returned to find Pearson deep in negotiations with a parson, Mr. Bull, about the disposal of the advowson of Borley Rectory. This time he was allowed to stay for a week, and the party was increased by the arrival of the Malcolms, the Wardlaws and Lady Ida. Laura Money was to be married at the end of the month, which naturally created a more cheerful atmosphere.

The Aumales were again at Dudbrook for a few days at the beginning of February, but their announcement that they would return for another ten days decided Frances that she might as well face the world in Carlton Gardens since her attempt to escape from it in Essex was so unsuccessful.

The day after her arrival in London, the duc and duchesse came to dinner and persuaded her to accept an invitation to Wood Norton, their house in Worcestershire. She found that another of her friends was also missing no opportunities. Newcastle had taken 5 Carlton House Terrace, the house she herself had had twelve years before, within a stone's throw of her own front door.

At once a stream of visitors began. Lord St. Germans was constantly calling, though she would not receive him for some days. His behaviour reminded her strangely of Mr. Harcourt and the persistent calls he had paid at the Dover Street house at the beginning of '47. Newcastle was more tactful in his approaches, and his calls did not begin until she had returned from her week at Wood Norton.

Fortescue had little reason to grumble at the attentions his rivals paid Lady Waldegrave since he usually found some excuse to dine at Carlton Gardens almost every day of the week. None the less, it did not prevent his resenting her affection for the Duke of Newcastle who, he confides to his diary, 'had been telling her every conceivable thing, about himself, his family, his money matters, his will etc'.

In the Colonial Office itself, the Under-Secretary agreed well enough with his chief, but neither troubled to be particularly tactful. At a Colonial Office dinner which the duke gave at his new house, Chichester stayed behind after the guests had gone, to discuss colonial affairs, and then told his host how he had first met Lady Waldegrave in that very room. The younger man was doubtless right in suspecting, when he accompanied the duke through the Colonial Department of the 1862 Exhibition, 'that there was some change in his manner with me—something constrained'.

At one of Frances's Sunday levees the duke had his revenge. 'My Chief pulled out of his pocket a C.O. paper for me, & said "I thought I was likely to find you here, & brought you this for to-morrow's mail".' Their acquaintance thoroughly enjoyed the situation.

At the next Sunday levee Chichester arrived at Carlton Gardens to meet Lord Stanley of Alderley—an ardent admirer of Frances—coming away, 'who laughed and I soon saw why—because *my Chief* was going in. I retired to the Reform Club & returned in half an hour.' He found the Reform a most convenient club since from the library window he could watch the door of his idol's house.

Frances spent Easter with old Charles Harcourt at Rothbury, his house in Northumberland. With the exception of the old William Harcourts who had inherited Nuneham, all her husband's other brothers and sisters were even more affectionate to her than before his death. The new master of Nuneham, or rather his wife, infuriated Lady Waldegrave by raising every possible difficulty in the settlement of her affairs. She had been very liberal to them, but their pettifogging ways drove her to put everything in old Granville Vernon's hands to settle.

It was at Rothbury that she heard the news of Mr. Pearson's death. For twenty years he had been her devoted friend and ad-viser, and, since Mr. Harcourt had died, had been constantly with her. He had not been merely a lawyer in whom she had had com-plete confidence, but an intimate friend who had become part of her life. She felt utterly bereft.

Chichester's sudden return from Ireland, where he had been spending Easter, to attend the funeral greatly pleased her. He had been on very friendly terms with the Pearsons who had treated him in the same easy affectionate way that they did Ward and Charley. In the past few weeks Fortescue and Pearson had been much together about a parliamentary committee which was being held to decide whether the Great Western or the South Western Railway should build a line through Radstock, which would greatly affect the value of the mines there. It was not until three weeks later that the question was decided by the committee re-fusing both applications.

It was obvious that Mr. Harcourt's death had in no way affected

Lady Waldegrave's social pre-eminence or her political influence. Never had she been so courted and admired, yet she felt as desolate and as frighteningly unprotected as she was after John Waldegrave's death. Her brothers Charles and Ward were affectionate and amusing companions, but their advice on almost every subject was worthless, and the loss of her loyal counsellor Pearson within a few months of Mr. Harcourt's death left her with all the worries and responsibilities of her large estates.

The receipts from the Radstock mines had been very considerable with both her husband and Pearson to control them, but they had dropped most alarmingly and suspiciously the moment that control was removed. The palatial rebuilding at Strawberry Hill was always involving her in fresh expense as were the alterations she was having done to make Chewton Priory habitable.

Whenever she wrote a business letter she sadly felt the lack of anyone to congratulate or 'blow her up' about it. Although as she once said of Louis Napoleon, 'I know from my own feelings how much despots hate a check', yet it was exactly the check she had once hated that she so bitterly missed.

Except for the Nuneham people all her relations and in-laws were anxious to help her in any way, but none of them was in a position to devote the time her complicated financial, social and political affairs demanded. The most she could expect of them was already being done by Granville Vernon in his competent handling of the whole Nuneham question.

On July 19 Fortescue arrived at Strawberry Hill to find the Duke of Newcastle and Granville Vernon among the guests at a Saturday to Monday party. After luncheon old Vernon followed Chichester out on to the lawn ostensibly to admire the new fountain, and astonished the younger man by saying:

'Well—perhaps you will be surprised at my saying to you what I am going to say—but I hope that you will be the master of this place.'

As the only person with whom Chichester had ever discussed such a possibility was Edward Lear, he found it difficult to reply. Vernon assured him that 'all the Harcourt family were most anxious that Lady W. should make up her mind and to marry me —*and soon*. He spoke in the highest terms of my devotion to her— & conduct to her altogether. He said:

170

' "If it had not been for you I believe she and my brother would have been separated"—that he knew that society, he meant people of high standing, wd. think it quite right that she should marry me *soon*—that her case was most peculiar, . . . that her marriage with Mr. Harcourt had been nothing but "taking a temporary guardian"—that no one would expect her to act as a widow under ordinary circumstances wd. do—that his brother had *told him* that *he looked to me* to be her *protector when he was gone.*

'I told him how absolutely devoted I was to her—how desperately I loved her—how for her sake I had not known what a woman was for eleven years—that I had intended not to speak out to her until she took off her widow's cap—that I could not bear the thought of the world speaking disrespectfully of her. He said he honoured the feeling, but that there was no risk of the kind.

'Later G.V. after a talk with Lady W. spoke to me again. He said, "Well—the best thing will be that you should go on just as you are for the present, that you should go to Ireland, & *when you come back in September* you *shd. propose to her.* You will both remain free till then." Fancy *my* being *free!*—as if I weren't absolutely *hers* —now and forever, whether she marry me or not, whatever happens.

' "Then in January", he went on, "you can come quietly to Grove, [the Granville Vernons' Nottinghamshire home], be married there & face the season in London as man & wife." Really the seeming nearness & reality of this incredible happiness overpowers me as I write this, alone in the Tribune—and while I write, the darling lady is walking with the Duke of Newcastle.'

Apart from the Harcourt family, Chichester had powerful allies. Henry Grenfell, with whom he had for years shared rooms at 45 St. James's Place, and whose great devotion to Lady Waldegrave he had somewhat feared, entreated her to marry Chichester, saying it would kill him if she did not. Another adherent was the Duke of Sussex's daughter, Lady Truro, who had some time before assured Frances: 'You can never be loved as that man loves you.' She answered, 'I know he is quite devoted to me, and I like him very much, but I couldn't be in love with him.'

Lady Truro said, 'Never mind—*take him* when the time comes— you'll find *that will* come.'

Another counsellor was Frances's old governess, Miss Grant,

who had left the Grange at the end of 1838 because she had so violently disapproved of the marriage to John Waldegrave. Soon after Mr. Harcourt's death she had come, an impoverished widow, as governess to little Constance. When the question of an engagement to Chichester was first discussed, she besought Lady Waldegrave: 'Don't do it unless you love him. You have never really been married yet; you never yet really married for yourself. I want to see you *really married* at last.'

The Aumales, though they liked Fortescue, did all they could to dissuade Frances from remarrying, as they felt any husband would deprive them of her company. They tried to persuade her that her future lay in a far more exalted world than that of a political hostess. Princess Alice had asked the duchesse to invite her to Orleans House as she had 'taken a violent fancy to Lady Waldegrave and must stay at Orleans House to have an opportunity of going to Strawberry Hill, and that Mamma was anxious to know her, too, but didn't know how to manage it.'

Fortunately for Chichester the old Princess of Salerno was so desperately ill during the summer at Spa that both the duc and duchesse were obliged to join her there during the weeks that Chichester spent in Ireland.

It was partly Frances's anxiety to avoid a proposal from the Duke of Newcastle that brought her to an early decision about Fortescue. She was greatly attached to the duke and wanted to spare him the embarrassment of a refusal. At last she told him that if she married anyone it would be Chichester. He protested violently against it, and begged her not to allow the Harcourt family to talk her into it.

Despite the encouragement Granville Vernon had given him, Chichester was too worried by the presence of so many other suitors to leave for Ireland until Frances left Strawberry Hill for Dudbrook towards the end of August. It was an extremely painful period for him as not only had he to face considerable hostility from his lady's other suitors, but also the very delicate situation at the Colonial Office where his work brought him into almost hourly contact with Newcastle.

When Fortescue reached Ardee he found a family gathering. Lord and Lady Clermont, his widowed sister, Mrs. Hamilton, and their old aunt were frantic with anxiety at rumours they had heard of the possibility of Chichester's marrying. For years they had been persuading him to marry, but the prospect of the celebrated Lady Waldegrave as a sister-in-law terrified them. Although the Clermonts spent a few weeks at a London hotel every season, the hypochondriac Clermont avoided society as much as possible and the little they knew of Frances was really gathered from the gossip of their provincial neighbours.

They had no realization of her great political power—her remarriage even had become a political issue since her Tory friends were all trying to gain her to their cause by a Tory husband. Her wealth, her fascination, her brilliant social position could not compensate in the Clermonts' eyes for the gossip there had been at the time of her second marriage, for her Jewish father and for the host of devoted men whom scandal had for the last eleven years declared to be her lovers. Clermont was in his selfish way very fond of his brother, and had even resented his political career because it prevented his taking enough interest in the large Clermont estates to which he would eventually succeed.

Their opposition and total lack of understanding or sympathy for Chichester's complete enslavement drove him to propose sooner than he had intended. On September 11, in a letter of thirteen pages, he wrote to his 'dearest Lady' at Dudbrook a splendidly worded declaration of the passion that had dominated his life for eleven years. He ended by writing:

'If you allow me to come to Dudbrook next week, without answering this, I shall take it for a good sign.'

When, thirty-four years later, still obsessed by the love that had mastered him for forty-five years, Chichester, Lord Carlingford, found the letter among Frances's papers, he wrote on it 'God bless you, my love, my life.'

For two days Chichester was in an anguish of suspense. Then a note came from Dudbrook in Ward's tiny handwriting:

Sept. 11th.

'My dear Mr. Fortescue,

I have just received your kind letter—my Lady bids me say that she will not answer the one she received as she will see you here next week.'

The autumn, spent mostly at Dudbrook, was a time of almost

unbearable happiness for Fortescue. Charles Braham and Ward were there a great deal, both overjoyed that their sister had chosen their favourite. Frances's decision to keep the engagement secret until her year of mourning had ended caused almost the only difficulties that arose. At first Granville Vernon and Mrs. Malcolm, always the most attached of her Harcourt in-laws were, with Edward Lear, the only people told. They were all delighted, but Lear warned them of the difficulty of keeping it secret:

'I will take care to be silent about the subject. It is however *very much* talked of by those who know the parties—& I as a friend of one am probed and pumped. My reply has been all along—"My own impression is that she is more likely to marry C.F. than the D. of N."—but no more.'

A few days later he was again his nonsensical self. 'Write soon: now that the big event of your life is decided, I can fancy you say —what is there to write about? Write upon prawns, rheumatism, the Immaculate Conception, Armstrong guns, Birds of Paradise or raspberry jam, so you write.'

It was Chichester's radiant happiness that betrayed them, and by the end of October Lady Clarendon was writing to Frances:

29th Oct. 1862

'My dearest Lady Waldegrave,

We have heard from so many different people that your marriage is settled, that I cannot refrain any longer from writing to you, hoping that whether you have determined to declare it or not, your own mind is made up, and that you have decided upon a step that we think will certainly be for your happiness, as you well know what our opinion has long been of Mr. F.

'Pray write to me as we are intensely and affectionately interested in all that concerns you. . . .

'Clarendon sends his best love, and warmest congratulations upon the event which he feels quite sure must & ought to be oncoming.

> Ever dearest Lady Waldegrave
> Your's very affecly
> K. Clarendon'

It was typical of dozens of letters which Frances answered, admitting the engagement only to her closest friends but swearing them to secrecy, a secrecy that was indifferently respected even by Frances herself. As she told Chichester:

'After all my wishes are very moderate. What do you think I have been wishing lately? Only to be able to take your arm, and walk off alone with you anywhere, all down Regent Street, and no one able to say a word against it.'

At the beginning of November Fortescue had again to pay a short visit to his old aunt in Ireland. This time he refused to see the Clermonts about whose attitude he had been completely frank to Lady Waldegrave. His younger sister, Harriet Urquhart, was however staying at Ardee, and she alone of his family, despite her odd ways and, to her brother, obstinate and absurd political and sociological views, completely sympathized with him and was delighted about the engagement. She was even able to some extent to persuade the old lady to a more reasonable frame of mind.

Rumours of the engagement began to appear in the Irish press, and, on November 13, the *Dublin Evening Post* announced it in their 'Fashionable Intelligence'. Chichester at once wrote asking them to publish that 'We understand that the statement with respect to Mr. C. Fortescue which we copied from a Contemporary is made without authority.' To Chichester's misery Frances took exception to this and expressed her annoyance forcibly.

'The two Dublin papers have arrived. I see a certain amount of evil as likely to accrue from the sort of denial of the truth of the report. It is the near proximity of your imbecile relations which makes you so cautious & nervous.

'Don't be angry at my saying this, but really you are like most Irishmen more sensible in England than in your own Emerald Isle. If I have the patience to write half of what I heard from Lady A. you will see how silly it is to let the male part of the world be in any doubt as to the real state of things.'

Chichester's friends often teased him by humming the tune of *Strawberry Fair*, but like the young man in the ballad he sometimes doubted if he would find a tongue that was neither nimble nor tart, for all his tramping to Strawberry Fair.

There was some excuse for Lady Waldegrave's irritability. The previous month Newcastle had written from Clumber in a rather injured tone practically asking for an invitation to Strawberry Hill. His affairs were following their usual disastrous course. Lord

Lincoln's fantastic racing debts had infuriated his father-in-law, the millionaire Henry Hope, who was lying desperately ill at his house in Piccadilly. Until Hope's death three weeks later there was great discussion as to how he would dispose of his vast fortune. Frances was prophetic in her words to Chichester.

'I have a suspicion that Mr. Hope will leave nearly the whole of his property to his widow; she is clever, he is devoted to her & would like to improve her position in society, & at the same time he is wary as to giving too much into Lincoln's foolish hands. How annoyed the Duke would be! Another case for martyrdom.'

As it was impossible for Frances completely to avoid Newcastle, she decided to make the completion of the splendid new rooms the excuse for a large party. Lady Ailesbury, Willie Vernon Harcourt with his young wife, and a niece of old Mr. Harcourt's with her husband were among the guests. The day before the party began, the *Court Journal* announced that 'we understand that a marriage has been arranged to take place between the Countess of Waldegrave and Mr. Chichester Fortescue'. Guests and servants alike were agog with excitement.

Willie Harcourt behaved throughout as though neither Chichester nor the *Court Journal* existed, and once again treated his hostess to such a demonstration of the possessive affection that for years had caused so much trouble that his poor wife fainted at dinner. Lord Nevill, the husband of old Harcourt's niece, made the report an excuse for a passionate declaration to Lady Waldegrave. He swore that in 1847 he had found her 'the most lovely fascinating creature in the world', but that now 'she beat herself hollow' and was 'the most delightful woman God ever created'.

On the evening of the announcement in the *Court Journal* Lady Ailesbury had been surrounded at a party at the French Embassy by people asking if the report were true, especially by men anxious themselves to marry Frances. Lady Ailesbury with her good-humoured worldliness strongly advised her friend to settle the question of her marriage as soon as possible as 'you will find the men much less disappointed and bitter when they know the thing is settled—it is the uncertainty they detest'.

The general curiosity was such that Lord Russell—still 'Lord John' to his friends—cut a Cabinet meeting to drive over from Pembroke Lodge to cross-examine Frances. The melancholy presence of Newcastle added nothing to the gaiety of the party at Strawberry Hill and despite the fact that 'you forget my rule never to notice newspaper gossip', Frances decided 'that it does not do to have a party without my own darling Chichester to protect me'.

Chichester immediately returned to England escorting his sister Mrs. Urquhart as far as the Hammam in Jermyn Street, which her husband had recently built and which they were using as their London home. However mixed the feelings of the other guests may have been about Chichester's arrival, Frances and her household staff were overjoyed to see him. When a few days later she had occasion to send her personal maid to his room with a message before breakfast, the maid returned to assure her: '*Je suis bien aise de vous dire, milady que Mons. Fortescue est bein beau au lit.*'

The rest of the year was spent in a whirl of preparations for the wedding. Old Charles Harcourt insisted upon marrying them, though he announced that he wanted to leave out 'the indecent bits' from the marriage service. They decided that the wedding should be at Old Brompton Church where her disastrous marriage to John Waldegrave had taken place almost twenty years earlier.

There was little to disturb their happiness except the continued opposition of the Clermonts. Lear wrote to console Chichester:

'You vast owly mortle! why haven't you said on what day the marriage of yourself & Lady W. is to be. Confound it,—nor where it is to take place. . . . The C's & Mrs. H. [Clermonts and Mrs. Hamilton] will—I feel certain—be among the enthusiastic likers of Lady W. It appears the latter now knows their feelings— but she is too wise & kindly not to perceive that narrow early teaching & narrow modes of life produce effects not to be confounded with feelings which are initiated by people's own dispositions. Make every allowance for this—tho' I grant it is a gt. bother for you—& it will all come straight.'

Towards the end of December, Frances's eldest brother Hamilton died suddenly at Rochester where he was singing with the operatic company he had been touring round the kingdom for some years. Although his sister had been making him an allowance since 1847, she had seen little of him, and any affection that had existed between them was too slight for his death to affect her at all deeply.

During December even *The Times* and *Morning Post* published announcements of the marriage, but it was not until the New Year that it was officially acknowledged. Among the sheaves of congratulations that poured in, the letters Newcastle wrote to Frances and Chichester probably pleased them the most in view of the considerable affection they each felt for him. To Lady Waldegrave he wrote that:

'From my heart I wish you, and I can hardly wish more, a continuance of the prosperity which has been your portion in life and a full enjoyment of the pleasures both of domestic and social life— and that at the close of all a rare good fortune may succeed as little in spoiling you or rendering you careless of the lot of others as it has hitherto done.'

To Chichester:

4 Jany/63

'My dear Fortescue,
  I perfectly understood your silence, and though my friendship for you has often of late tempted me to break in upon it I would not do so—even at the risk of your supposing me to be indifferent to what so deeply concerns your happiness.

'My pen is now loosed, and I can assure you that nobody to whom you can have announced your marriage more heartily offers you every good wish which such an occasion calls for.

'Lady Waldegrave is kind enough to address me as one of her "truest and best friends". The first of those epithets at any rate I claim,—and if it were only for *her* sake my aspirations for your welfare would be most sincere,—but I must add that on your own account as a private friend and an Official Colleague you have my warmest sympathies.

I am ever
Yours very sincerely
Newcastle'

STRAWBERRY HILL: EXTERIOR

Showing the wing built by Lady Waldegrave, on the left of the picture

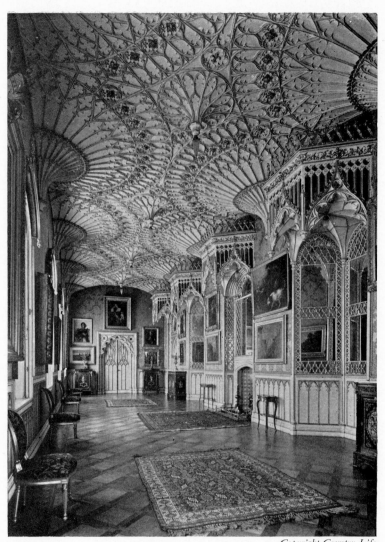

STRAWBERRY HILL: THE GALLERY

THE CONGREGATION that filled Old Brompton Church a little
before noon on Tuesday, 20 January 1863, must surely have been
the oddest assembly of in-laws that ever gathered at a wedding.
The bride's family was represented by Charles, Ward, Aunt Seph
and Frank Bolton. Her first and second husbands' two sisters,
Lady Horatia Wardlaw and Lady Ida, were there with their nieces,
Mrs. Hervey and Ida Money, and their cousins Beauchamp Seymour and Lady Laura Palmer. Lady Chewton brought her two
sons, the young earl and Noel.

The Harcourts were there in force; Mrs. Malcolm with her husband, Lady Johnstone with all her family, and Willie Harcourt
who brought his wife despite her imminent accouchement, but
only David and Harriet Urquhart were there to represent the
Fortescues.

Chichester had Henry Grenfell as his best man, while old
Charles Harcourt, quite incoherent with excitement, waited to
perform the ceremony.

At last the bride arrived, exquisite in a white lace crinoline, the
flounces trimmed with blue to match the feathers in her tiny white
bonnet. Looking even younger than on the day she married Mr.
Harcourt, she came up the aisle on the arm of her brother-in-law,
Colonel Francis Harcourt, followed by her attendants, little Constance, Ida Money and Lord Nevill's daughters.

The Wardlaws, with whom Frances had stayed the previous
night, gave a reception at their house in Prince's Gate, which the
bride and groom left early on their journey to the Granville Vernons' Nottinghamshire home.

They spent only a few days at Grove and within a week were
back at Strawberry Hill to find everyone discussing a letter signed
'Bluemantle' which had appeared in the *Daily Telegraph* three days
after the wedding, disputing Frances's right to call herself, Frances,
Countess Waldegrave. On the 26th there were two replies both
refuting the *soi-disant* 'Bluemantle'. The following day there was

an unpleasant letter in the *Telegraph* discussing her 'intermarriage with the brother of her deceased husband', but on the 31st a letter appeared from the real Bluemantle, indignant at the impertinence of someone assuming his official designation, and assuring the public that Frances was fully entitled to continue to be known as Frances, Countess Waldegrave. The attack on her, though it caused a great deal of talk, mostly aroused sympathy on her behalf.

George Augustus Sala, in his gossip column in the *Illustrated London News*, wrote:

'A very amiable, accomplished, and majestic grande dame de par le monde has just been married (en quatrième noces) to an Under-Secretary of State. The names of both bride and bridegroom are historic; the first particularly, the last aristocratically speaking; only in this particular case the gentleman happens to be a commoner, and the lady the widow of an earl . . . society, we believe, will see no harm in the beautiful and fashionable Frances, Countess Waldegrave, continuing a Countess to the end of the chapter.'

Chichester and his wife returned to Carlton Gardens in the middle of February, and there was little respite from Frances's usual tremendous hospitality. Willie Harcourt's wife had died suddenly at the end of January which naturally meant a period of mourning. In March everyone was engaged in the festivities in connection with the Prince of Wales's marriage.

Lady Waldegrave had scarcely begun her season with a dinner for the Duke of Newcastle when Chichester went down with an attack of measles. The Easter visit they had planned to old Mrs. Ruxton at the Red House, Ardee, had to be postponed for a week, but at last Frances met her husband's old aunt.

In spite of her previous distress the old lady was devoted to her new niece from the moment she saw her. As Mrs. Ruxton told Chichester, 'The moment I looked in her face I saw it was all right.' When Lord Clermont came to meet her, he was 'such a picture of nervousness, of terror, as his brother thought he had never seen, but Frances soon established friendly relations with both the Clermonts, who later admitted that she behaved about their previous attitude 'with great dignity, but with great magnaminity & generosity'.

The weekly dinners and receptions at Carlton Gardens were resumed at the beginning of May. The usual circle of intimates was there in force—the Orleans family not at all discouraged by the remarriage—and an increasing number of diplomats and politicians, since Frances was determined that her husband should at last be given an appointment where his very considerable talents could be employed.

Delane, of *The Times*, was gradually becoming one of her circle. He was still devoted to Lady Palmerston, but she, too, had come to realize Lady Waldegrave's great political and social influence, and on those few occasions when circumstances prevented her from holding her usual 'Saturday' at Cambridge House, she would at once advise her rival in case she should wish to give a Saturday party herself.

After the July gatherings at Strawberry Hill, Chichester and his wife paid a short visit to Chewton to inspect the new buildings, and then went to Dudbrook where the Aumales appeared for a long stay which they repeated in December. Chichester, a great bibliophile, had much in common with Aumale, but neither the duc nor the duchesse troubled to consider whether a newly married couple appreciated their almost daily visits.

There was some consolation for Fortescue in the different tone the press began to adopt about him. Shirley Brooks, a shrewd political commentator, drew a just picture of him, early in December. After speaking of his fellow members' attitude to 'the somewhat austere and cold hard oratory of Mr. Fortescue', he continued:

'Perhaps they do not understand how much of a model Under-Secretary he is. Representing his Department in the House of Commons, it is singularly safe in his hands. Always ready with the minutest details, at once simple and courteous in his manner, he is, yet, never turned aside from the current of his assertions, having the advantage in a ministerial explanation on matters just doubtful, of appearing to go into their discussion at considerable length; never really yielding a point against his department, and yet seeming to slip out bits of frank and candid admission—slow, measured, monotonous, in his utterance—so that it is difficult to catch a salient point with the ear if he should present one which he never does; he has the happy art—for an official—of making people think that he has given the fullest explanation that is possible, and yet, when he has concluded, nobody knows exactly what he has said, or what there is to rejoin to. The consequence is, he almost invariably has the last word, and there remains on the minds of his hearers a vague consciousness that whatever is right is all right, and whatever is wrong remains as it is, but that it is not so very wrong after all.'

January 1864, saw Strawberry Hill crowded to the attics with half the diplomatic corps and most of the Liberal Party, Lord Russell and Lord Clarendon discussing foreign policy in front of their hostess with all the freedom of a Cabinet meeting. Chichester was extremely busy the whole time on the question of the transportation of convicts about which the colonies were becoming increasingly hostile, but Frances would allow no politics to interfere with her gaieties. She gave a magnificent ball and, as always, the Aumales insisted on her bringing her party over to Orleans House to another dance.

By the middle of February her Wednesday dinners and assemblies had begun at Carlton Gardens, more brilliant and crowded than ever before, but the almost hopeless state of the Duke of Newcastle's health cast a certain gloom, partly because Frances and Chichester were both sincerely fond of him, and partly because it tied Chichester to the Colonial Office.

Just before Easter the duke was taken ill with fits and his resignation as Colonial Secretary could only be delayed a few days. Chichester was his obvious successor. He had successfully run the Colonial Office during his chief's absence in America, and had a passionate interest in all colonial affairs. His administrative abilities were first rate and, had his duties not involved him in public speaking, he would undoubtedly have been given the Secretaryship. Unfortunately his nervousness made him a dry, repetitive and at times wearisome speaker.

Palmerston, himself no remarkable orator, naturally dreaded the effect of Chichester's prosiness on the House, and could not help remembering that the member for Co. Louth had always given his allegiance to Lord Russell. Cardwell was the Premier's candidate, but Chichester had considerable support. Newcastle considered him his natural successor, and as Lord Clarendon wrote to Lord Granville:

'I think it is quite right that the Secretary of the Colonies should be in the House of Commons under present circumstances, but query whether Chich. plus Frank's most useful political hospitality is not a stronger man than Cardwell.'

At the beginning of April Newcastle resigned and Cardwell was appointed—even *Punch* said, 'We do not exactly know why.' Chichester immediately sent in his resignation, which Palmerston refused to accept, but two days later had Chichester made a Privy Councillor, so that Frances at least had the consolation of writing to Seph:

7 *Carlton Gardens S.W.*
April 6

'My dearest Seff,

Tell Mrs. Hickson, & Constance, & Muff that Lord Palmerston sent this morning for Chichester, & announced to him, that he was appointed a Privy Councillor & that the Queen had sent Lord P. a note this morning desiring Chichester to go down to Windsor tomorrow & kiss hands on his appointment. I am very much pleased.

In haste,
Yours dearest Seff most lovingly
F. W.

'You must direct to him in future *The Rt. Honble.*'

For the few months that remained to Newcastle, Lady Waldegrave and her husband were frequently with him, while both the Queen and the Prince of Wales demonstrated their appreciation of him by visits to his bedside. Two events occurred to comfort him a little. In June his daughter's degenerate husband, Lord Adolphus Vane-Tempest, died and in September Lady Lincoln gave birth to a son, but the duke had lost all desire to live from the moment of Frances's engagement.

His old friends the Dean of Westminster and Doctor Kingsley were with him at Clumber until on October 5 the Duke of Newcastle's tragic life came to an end. Chichester wrote of him, 'A truer friend we shall never have,' remembering the man who had loved Frances wholeheartedly for sixteen years, and yet who had done all in his power to help his successful rival in his political career.

Frances's other intimate friends in the meantime were taking up as much of her time as she would allow. At the end of May the Comte de Paris had married his cousin Isabelle, the daughter of the Duc de Montpensier, and the young couple had taken York House at Twickenham. Paris's brother, Chartres, with his young bride were living across the river at Morgan House, Frances being equally in demand at all three royal residences. To Chichester there was some solace in the visits to Ardee where at least the Orleans family could not pursue them, but Chewton Priory would not much longer be a refuge, since the rebuilding there was completed when they visited it in September.

Again in January 1865, there was a great party at Strawberry Hill and, in February, the usual Wednesdays began at Carlton Gardens. A young secretary at the American legation recorded his impressions of his first assembly there, and of his hostess:

'Although about forty years of age and so often married she is fine looking and attractive still. She is a blond and has a very bewitching manner . . . the reception altogether one of the most agreeable I have ever attended.' He was frequently there and a month later wrote:

'She had an attack of neuralgia in her side and received her company sitting, but was as fascinating as ever.'

There was consternation in society when Lady Waldegrave's assemblies had to be stopped, but six weeks later the press announced that 'Lady Waldegrave resumes her series of assemblies interrupted by her temporary indisposition'.

In June Chichester's fears about Chewton Priory were realized when Frances gave her first party there—Lear, the Malcolms, the Norreyses and the Clermonts who were becoming devoted to their sister-in-law. Later in the month the Disraelis came to Strawberry Hill for the first time. Chelsea had introduced him to Lady Waldegrave years before at Lansdowne House, but the curious affection that sprang up between them dated from this visit. Chichester had begun to reassemble many of the books from Horace Walpole's library that had been sold in 1842, and was delighted, a few weeks after the Disraelis's departure, to receive a small parcel with a letter enclosed.

'Dear Fortescue—

Here is the editio princeps of Gray's Odes, wh. when we were together, we observed was not in the Strawberry collection. It is more fitting that it should be there than at Hughenden.

'I have taken the liberty, therefore, of writing Lady Walde-grave's name in it, & I hope you may induce her to accept it, as a mark of my great regard for both of you.

                                        Yours sincerely,
                                        B. Disraeli'

Between the Disraelis' visit and the despatch of the book had come the upheaval of a general election. Frances had accompanied her husband to Ireland to the immense satisfaction of her adoring friend, old Aunt Ruxton. The excitement of Chichester's re-election, however, proved too much for the old lady who had a seizure the following day. She was devotedly nursed by her new niece who at once cancelled all the vast parties she had arranged for the summer, but after a month's illness Mrs. Ruxton died.

Their mourning for the old lady did not prevent a number of their more intimate friends from joining them in September at Chewton, including, to Fortescue's dismay, the Aumales with Frances's favourite, young Condé, and Newcastle's daughter Lady Susan, with whom Frances had resumed her friendship since Lord Adolphus's death. As soon as the Aumales left the usual family tribe arrived, a mixture of Brahams, Boltons, Waldegraves, Norreys, with old Mrs. Pearson and a nephew of Chichester's to add to the general confusion of cousins and in-laws.

It was while this party was in care-free progress that the news came of Lord Palmerston's death. Lord Russell became Premier, but no great changes were expected in the Government. Palmerston's appointment of his friend, Sir Robert Peel, to the Chief Secretaryship of Ireland had been both unfortunate and unpopular, and whatever esteem Lord Russell may once have had for Peel, it had long since vanished. Chichester's old friend Lord Carlisle had resigned the previous year and Lord Wodehouse had been appointed Lord-Lieutenant. Carlisle had been bitterly disappointed not to have Chichester as his Chief Secretary, but Wodehouse, though a personal friend, was not so fervent an adherent.

During the debate on the Roman Catholic Oath Bill in May, Fortescue had won great popularity in Ireland by his warm advocacy of the Bill, and by the well-reasoned forcefulness of his speech. His Irish friends besought him to press his claims. As soon as Frances heard that Lord Clarendon had succeeded Lord Russell at the Foreign Office, she wrote off to him.

The Priory
Chewton
Bath
Oct 22nd/65

'Très cher Cousin,

A thousand thanks for your kind & interesting letter. We are delighted to hear that you have accepted the F.O., tho' we understand the feeling you express so graphically upon taking that good Ship to Sea once more. I quite expect that the Govt will have more difficult times to deal with than have been known for years.

'The revival of party warfare, the necessity of a Reform Bill, the state of Ireland, the hatred of the Irish Catholics to Lord John & of the conservatives & whigs to Mr. Gladstone, & the difficulties which belong to your department will be enough to try very hardly the new firm without its old head.

'Now one word about ourselves. Chichester feels that there must be some limit to his present position, which is as odious to him as you know it is to me. There is nothing in it to compensate for the silence & inactivity in the House to which it reduces him, nor for his constant difficulties with his Irish friends, which will be greatly increased now that Lord Russell is head. I am sure you will agree with me that if nothing better can be found for him, he ought not to begin another Session as Mr. Cardwell's Under-Secretary.

'How is Lady Theresa? I fear, from what I hear, that she is in an unsatisfactory state of health. I am enjoying her Book immensely.

Ever your affcte Cousine
Frances Waldegrave'

For a month there were continually rumours that Russell was determined to rid himself of Peel and finally, on November 19, Clarendon wrote to Delane:

'I did not know that the Peel eviction was a fait accompli. Lady Waldegrave however will do better in Ireland, and if so minded, she may be of great use. The putting out of joint of Lady Wodehouse's nose may be a temptation.'

The Times leading article the following day showed that Delane shared Clarendon's view.

'Mr. Fortescue who has been for not less than seven years Under-Secretary for the Colonies, may well claim, after this weary apprenticeship, an opportunity of proving that he is capable of better things than supporting at second hand the policy of his Chief.

'. . . Mr. Chichester Fortescue will have ample opportunity of displaying the ability his friends attribute to him . . . his zeal and discretion are alike unimpeachable.'

Frances was delighted with the compliments both the English and the Irish press paid her husband, but was still more pleased to hear from her old friend Mary Bulteel, now married to Henry Ponsonby, an extra Equerry and future Private Secretary to the Queen:

6 *Cloisters*
Windsor
Saturday

'Dearest Lady Waldegrave

I was so glad to get your letter. I wished very much to know how you liked the thought of Ireland. It was so obviously the very best appointment the governt. could make, that I feared however much you disliked it, that you would not escape.

'However, you are not likely to allow a change of outward scene to depress your spirits very much & I daresay you will find a great deal to amuse you in the Irish world. My husband who was there (private Secretary) under 4 Lord Lts & had therefore a great deal of it always says that amidst heaps of twaddle & absurdity there is much to attract you to the place & people, but then he is an Irishman! Really Lord Russell seems to be looking about him & making some good attempts to bring in real men.

'I think the Whig Jeremiades I occasionally come across are among the most hopeful signs of the times! As you say, I suppose W. Harcourt will make his appearance now in public life. I have been surprised he has not done so sooner for somehow his name never appears as a *possible* statesman for the future & it is time it should.

'How sorry you will be to give up your pleasant parties, but you will leave Ireland to take care of itself in the summer I suppose & come & look after London a little bit. I am sorry for your sake Lady Wodehouse is not more amusing & agreeable. It would have made such a difference in the comfort of the whole thing. . . .

'Pray remember me much to Mr. Fortescue. I can scarcely fancy his having patience with all the stupidity in the bornéd R. Catholics & still more exasperating Protestants he will have to deal with! Do write to me from there.

Ever yours aff.
M. Ponsonby'

There was a large farewell party at Dudbrook and on December 9 the Chief Secretary and Lady Waldegrave left for Dublin.

It was rather Frances's wit than her radiant loveliness that won her the affection of the Irish. A few days after her arrival there was a 'bespeak' night at the theatre—the vice-regal equivalent to a command performance. It was a Dublin tradition that on 'bespeak' nights a considerable degree of freedom of speech was allowed to the gallery, who commented loudly on their likes and dislikes as the notabilities entered the theatre. Many years before when a Duke of Rutland was Lord-Lieutenant, a much quoted incident had occurred. The duke's liaison with the notorious Peg Plunkett had been much discussed by the Irish, and when he appeared in the vice-regal box, a voice from the heavens cried:

'Who slept with Peg Plunkett last night?'

Immediately another voice from the gallery shouted reprovingly:

'Manners, you dog!'

The same liberty was taken as Lady Waldegrave, superbly dressed, entered the Chief Secretary's box with her regal grace of movement. A voice from above shouted down the question half the kingdom wanted to ask:

'And would your ladyship be after informing us, which of your four husbands do ye like the best?'

With that exquisite and inimitable turn of her head, she looked up at her questioner and, without a moment's hesitation, her clear, lovely voice flashed back:

'The Irishman, of course.'

It brought down the house, and it was minutes before the deafening cheers died down. From that moment poor Lady Wodehouse had not a chance. By the beginning of January '66 Bernal Osborne was writing of Frances:

'She has castled King Wodehouse, and moves the Queen of Dublin Society.'

At the same time he wrote to tell Delane:

'Lady Waldegrave is incessant in her entertainments. 700 guests on Friday last. Last night public dinner of 30, tonight 18. The astonished inhabitants exclaim "There is but one Lady Waldegrave and Chichester Fortescue is her Secretary". '

Later he wrote:

'30 people to dinner 3 days in the week, and balls once a fortnight, ought to strike terror into the Conservative ranks. Lady Waldegrave has done more to upset the Vice-Regal form of Government than any Fenian conspirator and has quite snuffed our H.R.H. Lord Wodehouse and lady. Certainly Lady Waldegrave's talents for society are extraordinary; there is no rest for poor Chichester, he is worked off his head by day and danced off his legs by night. If he can play his part on the Treasury bench as well as his wife plays her character in the Phoenix Park, the Ministry will hold on for some time.'

It was small wonder that at the Dublin Lord Mayor's banquet it was the Chief Secretary's health that was drunk 'with the greatest enthusiasm'. The Aumales had, of course, come to the Chief Secretary's Lodge at the first possible moment as had the Duc de Chartres, and the Dubliners were utterly bedazzled by the prodigal hospitality, by the fascination of the fabulous Countess Waldegrave, and by her royal guests.

By the end of January Frances was writing to Lear that 'we are longing for the quiet of a London season', to which Chichester added that 'I agree with C. Lewis if it weren't for its pleasures life wd. be a very tolerable thing'.

The parties went on until the next parliamentary session recalled Chichester and his wife to London. In the middle of February the Irish correspondent of *The Times* wrote:

'Dublin has been enjoying a most brilliant season, with an al-most unprecedented number of balls, assemblies and parties of all sorts. This is to be ascribed in a great measure, if not altogether, to Lady Waldegrave. She has reminded the older citizens of Dublin of what the Viceregal Court once was. She has shown them what it should be. . . .

'On Tuesday night there was closed a series of the most brilliant entertainments at the Chief Secretary's Lodge that Dublin has enjoyed for many years.'

Frances at once wrote to Aunt Seph to draw her attention to the article, but added:

'The only thing I don't like in it is that it implies that Lady Wodehouse does not do enough for Dublin. The truth is that she could not receive until last month as her mother had only then been dead 4 months.

'She gives a great many dinners & is now giving balls. I like her very much & she shows no jealousy of me—which is much to her credit.'

A week later came the excitement of Ida Money's engagement to the Lord-Lieutenant's A.D.C., the Hon. Edmund Boyle. His brother, the Earl of Cork, had large estates in Somerset, and the young couple planned to live in the vicinity of Chewton. The marriage took place in April and eventually the Boyles settled at Chewton House within a stone's throw of the Priory.

Once back in London the weekly dinners and assemblies began again, but since Lady Palmerston was not holding her Saturdays at Cambridge House, Lady Waldegrave, who now became the principal Liberal hostess, chose that day for her receptions at Carlton Gardens. They were so eagerly attended that five hundred guests was no unusual number, all agog to pick up some scrap of political gossip.

Chichester had come back to England full of plans for the wel-fare of his own country. The disestablishment of the Church of Ireland was obviously essential, as was some Act to improve the condition of the Irish tenantry. The whole question of education there had to be reviewed and everything done to conciliate the moderate element who might otherwise be won over by the Fenian extremists. He had already explained his ideas by letter to Gladstone, who, like most of his Liberal colleagues, was too obsessed by the Reform Bill he hoped to introduce to realize how great a menace Fenianism had become.

On the very day that Wodehouse and his Chief Secretary were forced to suspend the Habeas Corpus Act in Ireland, Gladstone wrote his reply to Chichester:

Feb 13. 66

'My dear Fortescue

Your letter contains a Budget indeed of policy for Ireland and I fear you will have to abate much of it under the circs of the time. Unhappily we are pressed with the Cattle Plague and other subjects of great urgency in a Session which would not have been too much if undivided to give the question of Reform the fair chance it requires. We are therefore obliged to throw over whatever we can of disputable matter however excellent its aim. Please accordingly do consider first what can be done *out* of Parliament; viz. as to University & as to church schools. I suggest that you might by statistics exhibit what you describe as the distorted operation of those schools. Further if progress can be made in such a question as Landlord and Tenant I quite think it should be done by Bill.

'With respect to new money, if a gift is to be made to Ireland, I doubt whether the one you propose is the one which should be selected. I know of no way in which an effectual and permanent boon can be given to Ireland, as distinguished from particular interests in Ireland, except through the medium of the Railways. This is a subject which would require much manipulation, & a conjunction of favouring circs. but as [far] as I am concerned I am favourable to it in principle. Monsell is keen about it.

'It will I think require your presence here to be the propelling and organising agent of whatever is to be done: but would it not be useful if you set your Law Officers to work to think over the subject of Landlord and Tenant and see if they can get any useful amendment into shape.

'These of course are all matters for Ld. Russell & the Cabinet but I have indicated what seem to [be] our preliminaries. Meantime I circulate your letter with copy of my reply.

'I am very doubtful about any Commission on the Established Church. I fear it would be misinterpreted both ways: one never really gets to know the facts.   Yours sincerely,

W. E. Gladstone

I hope Lady Waldegrave is pleased with her Irish experience.

'I take it for granted we shall in any case propose new Scholarships for the University.'

Once in London Fortescue was able to convince both Lord Russell and Gladstone of the gravity of the situation in Ireland. The questions of disestablishment, tenant rights, and education were urgent and could best be furthered had he, as Chief Secretary, a seat in the Cabinet. The Lord-Lieutenant was expected to spend the greater part of the year in Dublin, and could therefore not attend many Cabinets, whereas the Chief Secretary's duties were mostly in the House of Commons and in the Irish Office in London.

The Premier sympathized with this view, but Wodehouse, who in May was created Earl of Kimberley, was able to avenge the resentment he felt at Lady Waldegrave's immense success, as his correspondence with Chichester proved. The latter had written to him:

'My dear Wodehouse

I wish to tell you that before you returned to Ireland I spoke to Ld. R. again of my desire for a seat in the Cabinet. I thought your objections to continue in the Lord Lieutenancy if I, as Chief Secry were to be admitted into the Cabinet wd. be probably removed by the fact of your being created an Earl as a mark of the great value of your services in Ireland. The result of the two conversations with Ld. R. shewed me that I was mistaken, that you still gave him to understand that you wd. resign if my application were complied with, and also, that your opposition was the only obstacle to such compliance. I admit the anomaly of the relation between Lord Lt & Chief Secry when the latter is in the Cabinet, from which the former from the nature of his office is absent.

'But on the other hand I know by experience, what anyone might know without it, that the inconvenience and disadvantage of the Irish Govt. not being represented in the Cabinet is intolerable. And in practice the relations between the two officials under the circs must depend upon themselves. I can conceive this to be very objectionable to a Lord Lt. In our case—I think I may say it now that we have worked together for some months—they ought not to be so.

'In short—considering that I sh. represent in the Cabinet an Irish policy on wh. you & I are heartily agreed—& considering the dignity wh. you are about to receive, and the notorious fact that you are certain of high office whenever opportunity offers, I feel that I might fairly expect you to take the handsome & friendly course of waiving in my case your objections to acting with a Ch. Sec. in the Cabinet.'

The Lord-Lieutenant was adamant in his reply:

Viceregal Lodge
June 1/66

'My dear Fortescue

I am exceedingly vexed that I should be an obstacle to your obtaining a seat in the Cabinet, but I cannot depart from my determination. If an Earldom or any other mark of distinction had been offered me on condition that I should remain here with the Chief Secretary in the Cabinet I should have declined it at once. Nothing would induce me to consent to such an arrangement.

'Lord Russell spoke to me on the subject before I left London and I told him I would not consent. At the same time I said I was most willing to resign if he wished it in order that you might be put in the Cabinet, and I begged him in considering the point to rest assured that I should not complain in the least if he asked me to resign for this purpose.

'Indeed I should be delighted to withdraw from this office if I can do so honourably not only because I dislike the office itself, but because it is to the last degree irksome to me to feel that I stand in the way of your wishes. You must remember however that I was already here, when you accepted the Chief Secretary's office, and that you might easily have ascertained from me that I would not remain with the Chief Secretary in the Cabinet. If there had been a Chief Secretary here who was in the Cabinet when Lord Palmerston offered me the office of Lord Lt. I should have refused it.

'The true solution of the difficulty is the abolition of the Lord Lieutenancy.   Yrs sincerely
Kimberley'

As soon as Lord Russell became Premier he determined to bring in a Reform Bill. He had always considered Palmerston lukewarm on the question of electoral reform and Lady Palmerston's opposition to it was public knowledge. In March Gladstone introduced a Reform Bill to the House of Commons which met with considerable opposition not only from the Conservatives but also from a few Liberals, particularly Edward Horsman and Robert Lowe.

As a young man Lowe had spent some years in New South Wales where he had been a member of the Legislative Council. Australian politics had given him a remarkable distrust of democracy, and, since he was a brilliant speaker, his attack on the Reform Bill had very great influence.

On the second reading on March 13 John Bright scornfully referred to Horsman retiring to his Cave of Adullam. *Punch* took up the name, and the 'Cave' eventually proved to contain thirty-three rebels from the Liberal ranks.

To a great many moderate Liberals, both Russell and Gladstone, after Palmerston's almost conservative leadership, appeared to be, to all intents and purposes, Radicals, and neither of them had at that time the immense personal popularity Palmerston had enjoyed. Lord Elcho, Lord Grosvenor and Lord Dunkellin were among those who had no faith in their new leaders; in fact, the amendment to the Bill that Lord Grosvenor introduced was tantamount to a vote of no-confidence in the Government. His amendment was thrown out, but the amendment Lord Dunkellin introduced in June caused the defeat of the Russell Ministry.

It could scarcely have happened at a worse time. That same week Austria had declared war on Prussia in reply to Prussia's attack on Hanover, Saxony and the Electorate of Hesse. Italy and Bavaria were soon drawn in and no one was certain what attitude France would adopt. The Queen herself was in despair. Two of her daughters were involved in the war, as Prussia was attacking Hesse. Moreover she was devoted to her cousin, the blind King of Hanover whose little army stood no chance against the strength of Prussia. She felt that it was no moment for a change of Government, and did all she could to persuade Russell to remain in office.

Although Lowe, Grosvenor, Elcho and Dunkellin were frequently his wife's guests, Chichester was unswervingly loyal to his chief. Lord Russell probably realized that this was not always easy for him, since Frances had made no secret of her preference

STRAWBERRY HILL: THE DRAWING ROOM, 1865   From a painting by Desanges

(*Back row, standing—except* Lady Hislop) H.R.H. Le Duc d'Aumale, the Earl of Clarendon, A. Hayward, Esq., Lord Stanley of Alderly, the Rt. Hon. Chichester Fortescue, Mr. Bernal Osborne, the Marquis of Clanricarde, H. E. Monsieur Van de Weyer, the Duke of Newcastle. (*Front row, sitting*) Frances, Countess Waldegrave, Lord John Russell, the Marchioness of Clanricarde, Madame Van de Weyer, H.R.H. La Duchesse d'Aumale, Maria Marchioness of Ailesbury, Lady John Russell, H.R.H. Le Comte de Paris, the Countess of Clarendon.
(The portrait of the Duke of Newcastle is posthumous, as he died the previous year.)

FRANCES, COUNTESS WALDEGRAVE, 1871

From a painting by French

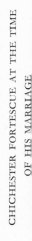

CHICHESTER FORTESCUE AT THE TIME
OF HIS MARRIAGE

for Palmerston. At the beginning of May, Russell showed his appreciation without causing Chichester embarrassment. Lord Clermont was very conscious that his was only an Irish peerage and that he could therefore not take his seat in the House of Lords. After twenty-six years of childless marriage there was little chance that his brother would not inherit the title, and so on May 2 Clermont became Baron Clermont in the peerage of the United Kingdom.

There was a very large Saturday to Monday gathering at Strawberry Hill on June 23. The Gladstones, Stanley of Alderley with most of his family, the Goschens, Charles Villiers, Bernal Osborne, Delane and Hayward were the more politically minded guests, and the constant coming and going between Pembroke Lodge and Strawberry betrayed the political crisis.

As Abraham Hayward wrote to a friend on the Monday:

'I was at Strawberry Hill from which I have just returned with the Gladstones. There were four members of the Cabinet there who kept such a watch on one another that even Lady Waldegrave could get at nothing definite, except that we are to have no revelations till they have seen the Queen, who is to be at Windsor at nine tomorrow.'

The following day the Queen accepted Lord Russell's resignation.

FRANCES was overjoyed that her husband was no longer in office. After seven years as Colonial Under-Secretary and the last seven exhausting months of Irish affairs, he was seriously in need of a complete rest. She would not even allow him to go over to Dublin to arrange for the disposal of their many possessions in the Chief Secretary's Lodge. Fortescue's nephew, 'Chi.' Hamilton, the only surviving son of his widowed elder sister, had for some years been managing the Red House estate at Ardee, and since Mr. Pearson's death had gradually undertaken the management of Lady Waldegrave's estates in Essex and Somerset. He offered to see about their things in Phoenix Park, enabling his uncle to enjoy an untroubled July at Strawberry Hill.

At the beginning of August they went on a little tour in Cornwall, reaching the Priory in the middle of the month. There they spent an enchanting autumn almost alone, except for those Frances considered her family circle. For once they were spared the company of the Aumales, though the reason for the separation caused Lady Waldegrave great unhappiness. Their son, the young Prince de Condé, whom Frances had liked best of all the Orleans princes, had died of fever in Australia in May. Since then the Aumales had been living in retirement at Wood Norton, where Chichester and his wife visited them before they returned to Carlton Gardens in December.

If they could no longer meet in Downing Street, most of the ex-Government were quite happy to arrange rendezvous with each other for the January parties at Strawberry Hill. In view of the Conservative minority in the House, the Liberal attitude to them was of an almost parental indulgence. As Delane expressed it to Frances, he wished 'the Tories to stay in till we are ready to come in'.

Although Lord Derby was Premier, as the Queen herself said, Disraeli was the directing mind of the ministry, and was determined to introduce a Reform Bill to which even the Opposition would be forced to agree. He was more nervous of the reactionary members of his own party than of the Liberals, and since Robert

Lowe had been largely responsible for the downfall of the Liberal Government, Disraeli, who apparently completely misjudged his motives, hoped to gain him to the Conservative cause.

Lowe, however, was genuinely horrified at the prospect of extending the franchise to the illiterate, and realized from the first that he would find Disraeli's plan for Reform as distasteful as Gladstone's had been to him. It is doubtful if Disraeli would have made any approaches to him had he known of the lines Lowe had written on reading the other's famous 'side of the angels' speech:

> *Nor ape am I, nor angel*
> *But quite another shape,*
> *For who has ever circumcised*
> *An angel or an ape?*

Lowe's opposition to the Tory Reform Bill was quite as effective as was Gladstone's, but the Bill had a reasonably favourable reception when Disraeli introduced it in March '67. On April 8 a considerable number of Liberals informed Gladstone that they could not follow him in his opposition to the Bill, and the Queen hastily advised Disraeli in view of this victory to be as conciliatory as possible. Gladstone and Lowe continued to oppose it, but Lord Derby and Disraeli accepted amendment after amendment until the Reform Bill received the Royal Assent in August.

The fact that she was no longer the Government hostess made no difference to the success of Lady Waldegrave's parties during the '67 season. As she liked to go down to Strawberry Hill when possible on Saturdays, she had reverted to Wednesday for her dinners and assemblies at which there were invariably some of the Orleans family.

Other royal neighbours were, however, becoming increasingly interested in her. The gardens of her town house backed on to the gardens of Marlborough House, where during February and March the little Princess of Wales lay desperately ill. The prince's behaviour aroused all Frances's ire, and she wrote to Seph who, was living at Little Strawberry Hill with Constance and her governess, that 'the Prince is the most selfish of Brutes—He does nothing but amuse himself & pay no attention to her'. At the same time she had always great faith in the good nature that underlay all the young prince's excesses and follies.

The season culminated for her in a crowded house party she held at Strawberry Hill at the end of July with a dinner and ball for the Prince of Wales on the second night. The princess was still not strong enough to attend, but Frances was consoled for her absence by an engagement that began on the night of the ball. The Russells had brought their family over from Pembroke Lodge as had the Peels from Marble Hill. Archibald Peel, whose friendship with Chichester dated back to their Oxford days, proposed to the Russells' daughter, Georgiana, though their tête-à-tête was interrupted at a critical moment by the tactless intrusion of the Duke of Argyll. 'Just like his beastly perversity,' as Peel sourly remarked.

The rest of the year was spent at Chewton Mendip, except for September which they passed in Ireland as Chichester had some political campaigning to do. In October the big Priory parties began. The Comtesse de Paris had been unable to go to the Strawberry Hill ball, so a ball was held in her honour at Chewton, where the delighted villagers became fervent Orleanists overnight, and insisted that the Comtesse was the rightful Queen of France. Since the enlargement of the Priory, the quiet little village had become utterly blasé about ambassadors and minor royalties, but on this occasion all the cottagers stayed up most of the night to cheer the guests on their arrival and departure.

The happy months in Somerset came to an end in the second week in February '68 when, as Frances expressed it, 'We are grousing at being obliged to leave this dear place . . . for hateful London. We have been immensely happy here in spite of all sorts of little worries, broken chilblains, Mendip Mists, East winds, weak eyes, a grand row in the Steward's room etc. etc.'

By the end of the month there had been two great changes in the political world. Lord Derby's health had been failing for some time, and on the 24th he resigned. Disraeli became Prime Minister to face an Opposition led by Gladstone to whom Lord Russell had handed over the leadership of the Liberal Party. To express his personal views on the Disestablishment of the Irish Church, which as leader of the Liberals he would have been unable to do, Lord Russell published a letter nominally addressed to Chichester Fortescue as ex-Chief Secretary.

A few weeks later Gladstone gave notice of a resolution for the

Disestablishment of the Church of Ireland, which was carried by a large majority at the end of April. Disraeli was, despite this, persuaded to carry on the government and to deal with essential and non-controversial measures until the end of July, after which there was to be a general election.

For once, therefore, the election did not interfere with the London season, which was also somewhat simplified for Frances and Chichester by the absence of the Aumales who had gone to their estate in Sicily. Apart from her usual social and political activities Lady Waldegrave was much occupied with a scheme in which Pearson's nephew and successor had involved her. He had decided that Teddington had a great future as a riverside suburb, and had persuaded her to transform that side of the Strawberry Hill park into a great housing estate to be known as Waldegrave Park.

Whether it was sharp practice or simply inefficiency on the young lawyer's part it is difficult to decide, but his advice was eventually to lose Frances a very considerable part of her fortune. Both Mr. Pearson's nephews were engaged in a lawsuit with his widow, which was embarrassing for Lady Waldegrave as she was very fond of Mrs. Pearson, but the young lawyer died in the early summer of '68, and the case was dropped. Possibly Waldegrave Park might not have proved financially so disastrous had he lived, or had Chichester had a fraction of Mr. Harcourt's business acumen.

Frances fully intended to leave the Essex and Somerset estates eventually to young Lord Waldegrave, and though she destined Strawberry Hill for Chichester, as she had no children that, too, would one day presumably pass to the Waldegraves. She felt that all the building she was having done at Dudbrook, the Priory and Twickenham was increasing the value of the estate, and though she had frequently to raise money to pay for more construction, such loans could probably be repaid from the coal profits.

Chichester was less sanguine. He was acutely conscious that on the Essex estates alone there were still mortgages of over £50,000, but he could not bear to dash his wife's childlike happiness in her plans and projects. It had been considerably easier for old Mr. Harcourt as he had been on much the same footing financially as his wife. Fortescue's income, on the other hand, was negligible when compared with Lady Waldegrave's, and until such time as he came into the Clermont estates he had little wish to criticize her financial arrangements.

The tremendous outlay on entertainment Frances felt was amply justified by the exigencies of her husband's political career, though at times her only desire was for a quiet life with him at one or other of their country homes. For the first time she knew what was a completely happy marriage, and real daily companionship. A number of their friends had wondered how Chichester's almost pedantic scholarliness would adapt itself to the social whirl that was apparently her life, but they did not realize to what an extent Mr. Harcourt had made her conscious of the gaps in her education and so driven her to mask her more intellectual interests.

Somehow she found time for a great deal of reading and though her criticisms were generally vehemently for or against they had an instinctive shrewdness that appealed to Chichester. Her enthusiastic appreciation of Ellis Bell's poems astonished people who found even *Wuthering Heights* hard to comprehend. She slightly shocked her contemporaries by preferring the full-blooded Chaucer to Mr. Tennyson, yet she loathed *Les Misérables* as much as she was to enjoy *Middlemarch*.

In '62 while reading *Orley Farm*, she noted that 'All Trollope's works are healthy & sound. They will be read for years hence as good pictures of what I suppose Lady Ailesbury would call the middle classes of the English in the 19th Century. . . . I never read Trollope without longing to make him write better English. He is always making mistakes à la Henry Grenfell & as I am sure he is an imitator & admirer of the Tom Jones style of writing I wish he would be equally vigorous in his grammar.'

However alluring the Fata Morgana of a quiet country life may have appeared when she was pestered by continual callers at Carlton Gardens or Strawberry Hill, Lady Waldegrave had become too involved in social and political life; yet she had really only embarked upon it 'to show the Bulteels' during her estrangement from them in 1854, and in order to escape from 'Harcourtism'. The whole Orleans family had come to depend on her advice and influence, and Chichester was by no means the only politician whose career she hoped and intended to further.

Among the guests at the 1868 Whitsun party at Strawberry Hill were Sir Edward and Lady Strachey. He was the eldest of six brilliant brothers and had, as his second wife, married Maribelle Symonds, whose own family was equally brilliant. She was the daughter of the Doctor Symonds of Clifton who had attended Lord Waldegrave at Harptree Court in 1846, and her brother was John Addington Symonds who, like Chichester Fortescue, had won the English Essay prize at Oxford, and whose writings were beginning to attract considerable attention.

The Stracheys had, since their marriage, led a retired life at Sutton Court, their beautiful home in Somerset. Sir Edward, a frequent contributor to the *Spectator*, was so engrossed in editing Malory's '*Morte d'Arthur*', that his wife, though devoted to him and to their three small sons, was glad of the distraction afforded by the winter months they spent abroad on account of her health.

Sutton Court was only a short drive from Chewton Priory and it was at the Priory that they first met Lady Waldegrave. Lady Strachey herself described the meeting:

'The first time I saw my beautiful Lady—(Frances, Countess Waldegrave)—was at the Priory Chewton Mendip in Septr 1865. I thought that I had never seen anyone so beautiful, so attractive, or so charming—or who was such a gracious, delightful Hostess; she seemed to be so happy herself & to enjoy everything so much, that it made everyone else happy & pleased with themselves, & she had the most wonderful power of sympathy & of bringing out the best qualities of those who were with her.

'Lady Waldegrave was dressed in black & it was most becoming to her exquisite skin, & the wonderful beauty & radiance of her face. I thought her the most perfectly beautiful woman I have ever seen, & I was immensely impressed by her loveliness.'

Sir Edward, who was himself delighted to find a neighbour of Fortescue's intellectual calibre, was pleased that his young wife should make so charming a friend as Frances. With the exhausting obsessive friendship of the Duchesse d'Aumale occupying so much of her time, Lady Waldegrave had remained only on neighbourly terms with her new friend until the duchesse's departure to Sicily left her with a little more freedom for other interests.

The brilliant circle at Strawberry Hill was another world to Lady Strachey and she went back to Somerset, impatient for the

Priory to reopen its hospitable doors. It was not, however, till the end of September that the parties began there, as in August Frances and Chichester paid their first visit to Nuneham since 1861, and in September there was political campaigning to be done in Essex.

Frances probably found the canvassing in Essex more exciting than Chichester's election proved to be in Louth. She crossed to Ireland with him at the end of October and spent November partly at Ravensdale with the Clermonts and partly at Ardee. She had gone over full of determination to fascinate even the most recalcitrant electors into voting for the Liberal candidates, but Fortescue's popularity was such that, though the Liberal candidate for the second seat had little following, both their elections were uncontested.

Frances and Chichester reached Chewton Priory on December 2. After the turmoil and bustle of the election the prospect of a few days of peace and solitude in Somersetshire delighted them. It could only be a few days as they would have to return to London when Parliament assembled.

The next morning their peace was shattered—Disraeli had resigned the previous day. With the news of his resignation came a hasty note from Abraham Hayward:

'It seems all but certain that the Government intend to resign without meeting Parliament. Why don't you come up?'

On the 6th Lady Waldegrave wrote from Carlton Gardens to Aunt Seph:

'We arrived here last night. Chichester saw Mr. Gladstone in the evening & accepted the Irish Chief Secretaryship with a seat in the Cabinet—We were very nearly getting the Colonies, which is what we wanted—Lord Granville is to have that post.'

It was a great disappointment, but Gladstone could scarcely be blamed. For the moment there were no urgent colonial problems and the whole election had been fought with the Disestablishment of the Irish Church as the principal issue. In the book, *The Gladstone Government*, which appeared a few months later, the author explained Gladstone's position.

'And to that now more than ever prominent office [the Chief Secretaryship of Ireland] he at the same moment determined to reappoint the administrator who had already, under far less propitious circumstances, won a large amount of popularity for himself, even while in the very act of suppressing—how shall we express it?—the tendencies at least towards an insurrectionary movement.' He went on to point out that the Liberals had come in with an 'overwhelming majority . . . pledged to the abolition of the Irish Church, pledged to its disestablishment, pledged to its disendowment'.

Frances herself counted for a great deal in her husband's appointment. Years before she met him she was already vehement about the injustice of a rich established Protestant Church in so Catholic a country as Ireland, and had been from the first a keen advocate of disestablishment. Again the great popularity that her charm and hospitality had won her in Dublin was of considerable assistance to Chichester. The Irish considered it a compliment that the Liberal Government should send over their principal hostess and, much as London might bewail her departure, Dublin looked eagerly forward to a renewal of the festivities of 1866.

It was with very mixed feelings that Lady Waldegrave accepted the situation. She knew that her husband, however disgusted he might be at the Fenians' methods, was as determined as they were to obtain justice for the Irish tenantry, for the Irish Catholics, and to raise the standard of education for all denominations, but she also knew that he was not physically strong enough for the exhausting work the various Bills would entail. His seat in the Cabinet, though great political advancement, meant that he would have frequently to cross from Ireland to attend Cabinet meetings, a journey he dreaded as much as she did.

The Chief Secretary's Lodge, though a charming house had, during her previous residence there, proved quite inadequate for her prodigal hospitality, and she lost no time in arranging with the Office of Works to put a number of improvements in hand. In the meantime she gave her usual New Year parties at Strawberry Hill and tried to forget 'how I hate the thought of two crossings in three weeks', since they had to be in Dublin in the middle of January to prepare for the new Lord-Lieutenant's entry, before Parliament reassembled early the following month.

The new Lord-Lieutenant, Lord Spencer, was in a strange position. His honours were purely nominal, since a seat in the Cabinet was allotted only to the Chief Secretary. Fortunately Chichester and Spencer were on excellent terms, while Frances and Lady Spencer had for years been great friends.

The session of '69 was largely taken up with the disestablishment and disendowment of the Anglican Church in Ireland. From the time of his appointment Chichester had almost daily letters from Gladstone urging him on with the Disestablishment Bill. On Christmas Eve, '68, the Premier wrote suggesting that Fortescue should go to Dublin as soon as possible as 'how unless you are there can he [the Irish Attorney-General] have your help & superintendency or how are you to have the share in preparing the measure that clearly should belong to you'.

The Chief Secretary and his law officers duly drew up the Bill, which the Premier himself introduced at the beginning of March. As it was one of the most important measures the Government was to introduce it was only natural that the Premier should introduce it, and that his superb oratory should be employed rather than Chichester's uninspiring delivery.

It was, however, a little unfortunate that Gladstone should have forgotten to give any public acknowledgement to Fortescue for the brilliant work he had done in the preparation of the Bill. If Chichester noticed the discourtesy, it apparently did not affect him at the time, for he wrote to Lear in May:

'I am sure you have watched the progress of the great Bill. It is something to have taken a share in its formation & enactment, tho' of course the lion's share has been Gladstone's.'

There were endless amendments and counter-amendments, but towards the end of July it received the Royal Assent.

Not all the press was prepared to believe that the Bill had sprung fully framed from the Prime Minister's outsize head. In August *Vanity Fair* published a caricature of the Chief Secretary with the usual commentary by 'Jehu Junior':

'It is appropriate that at this time the Secretary for Ireland should be an Irishman who has so full a sympathy for his countrymen, and so honest a desire to act justly towards them, as Mr. Chichester Fortescue; it is fortunate that the new order of ideas should have been introduced under the guidance of one who knows so well as he the necessities of the country, and who has so deservedly won its confidence. There has been much parade of late among politicians of a new-born desire to do justice to the long-oppressed sister isle; but Mr. Chichester Fortescue is no modern convert to that desire, and he will entertain it longer and carry it farther than many of those to whom party exigencies have introduced it for the first time. This it is that has made him that most acceptable and successful guide of Irish affairs that this generation has seen; this it is that gives him at this time a greater power to work good for the Empire than has yet been wielded in his native island.

'It is not the least of Mr. Chichester Fortescue's advantages that he is the husband of the lady who holds undisputed sway as the social leader of his party, nor would her grace and tact be the least of the qualifications he would take with him should he ever go as Viceroy to a country where grace and tact win hearts and secure devotion; and it will be no small thing to say of him, as History will say, that he married Lady Waldegrave and governed Ireland.'

All her vast circle of friends were delighted with the compliment to Lady Waldegrave, which Delane promptly twisted into 'the lady who married Chichester Fortescue and governed Ireland'. The only malcontent was the somewhat sententious old Aunt Seph who complained of Pellegrini's sketch of the handsome Chief Secretary. Frances's reply was prompt:

'My dearest Seff,

You were so occupied with the ugliness of Chichester's caricature that you did not say what you thought of the very flattering article upon us both in the letter press—We were delighted with it.

'Ugly as Chichester is made, he is not so frightful as all the other caricatures in *Vanity Fair*. You say that there is only a step from the sublime to the ridiculous. That is true, but in this case, that step is *Fame*.'

It had been the usual exhausting season for Lady Waldegrave; Wednesday dinners and assemblies, Sunday levees, an Easter party at Dudbrook, and a Whitsun party at Chewton Priory with Saturday-to-Mondays at Strawberry Hill. The season practically came to an end with the enormous fête she gave there at the end of June in honour of the Viceroy of Egypt, with a ball at night to which the Prince and Princess of Wales came.

The parties at the Chief Secretary's Lodge in Phoenix Park began early in October. Aumale of course was there, but his little duchesse was not well enough to face the journey. His devoted friend, the Comte de Jarnac, who had Irish estates, came with him, and most of the Strawberry Hill circle found their way over during the autumn. The Stracheys came from Sutton Court, the Vicar of Chewton Mendip—wide-eyed at the *beau-monde* in which he suddenly found himself—the ubiquitous Abraham Hayward, the Wardlaws with Lady Ida Waldegrave, the Norreyses, the Boyles and the Herveys. Ward Braham had been pressed into service to run the amateur theatricals, and even little Constance made herself useful at the tea table at the weekly afternoon receptions.

There were endless dinners, receptions, theatricals and balls, interrupted by a 'family' party at Red House, where the ghost of old Mrs. Ruxton must have been slightly startled to see the whole gathering playing roulette all day long. The Spencers enjoyed Frances's hospitality as thoroughly as she enjoyed her visits to the Vice-Regal Lodge, but there was one great drawback. At the end of October and again in December the Chief Secretary had to attend Cabinet meetings in London.

Old Lady Truro had prophesied correctly when she had told Lady Waldegrave that the day would come when she would be desperately in love with Chichester. When he left her at the end of October to lay his Land Bill before the Cabinet, Frances wrote to him:

'It is a terrible thing to love so completely & engrossingly one object in life. I often wish I had some of the Ravensdale coldness, or what the Inhabitants of that establishment would consider—and would serve my purpose equally well—a reasonable & calmly regulated affection for you. This highly respectable luke-warmness is certainly not in my line. . . . Don't let the Cabinet worry you & remember that it is better to resign than hurt your health & so make me the most miserable of wives instead of the happiest. I can assure you that this separation is a *tremendous* price to pay for this most odious & most thankless office.'

If her husband had accepted Gladstone's taking all the credit for the Disestablishment Bill, Frances most certainly had not, and bitterly resented the Premier's attitude. Two days after the foregoing letter she warned Chichester:

'Pray take care that when the proposal for the Land Bill is laid before the Cabinet that *you* are the *person to do it*. I am delighted to see that the papers now treat you as *the* person in this matter.'

The Irish Attorney-General had all her sympathy when he accused Gladstone of being a hard taskmaster who would wear out his best men in his service. When Chichester was again in London in December, she wrote that:

'As the Bill made progress & you got your own way as to the principle of "compensation for disturbance" I think it was worth being more or less tired from the fight. . . . I long for a quiet life with you, at the Priory, Dudbrook, or anywhere out of the official & representative world.'

A few days after that she informed him that Lord Spencer was not well pleased to hear from her ally the Irish Attorney-General that the Premier had told him 'that the Irish Government had a very easy play of it. Mr. Gladstone does continue to make himself odious to his most friendly admirers. . . . I am so glad that Spencer has begun to see what sort of a Prime Minister we have as to *not* appreciating the *hard work* of his colleagues. . . . I told Spencer to-day that I should do all I could not to come back here with you as C.-S. He was horrified & said "Oh pray, pray, don't say anything so dreadful." The fact really is that the work, wear & tear & anxiety are too much for both you & me, & you see what thanks we get for it, from the observation of Mr. G. to Sullivan. I say *again* I am *delighted* that Spencer was so put out by it.'

The Premier's ingratitude, Chichester's frequent absences, and the endless Fenian outrages were only partly the cause of Lady Waldegrave's unhappy mood. Although it was a relief to her to escape from the Aumale intimacy, she was extremely fond of the duchesse, who like herself was the driving force behind a brilliant, scholarly but retiring husband. Frances always hoped that, should the Imperial régime in France fall, Aumale would become a great figure in the politics of his country, but she feared that without his wife to urge him on, he would prefer the quiet of his vast library and metaphysical discussions with his more intellectual friends.

The Duc d'Aumale's stay in Dublin was cut short by the news that the duchesse was suffering from heart disease. The deaths of all her children except the Duc de Guise had left her with no will to struggle against her illness, and at the beginning of December came the news of her death. Frances was naturally miserable at the loss of her closest friend, and went into mourning, but the entertainments at the lodge were of an official nature and could not be postponed without making her grief seem ostentatious.

She found little pleasure in the success of her parties, in Ward's brilliant stage management or even in the affectionate sympathy of her vast adopted 'family', when her one wish was to be at Twickenham to console poor Aumale.

A frequent guest at the Chief Secretary's Lodge was Bernal Osborne, whose wife and daughters had for years been devoted to Lady Waldegrave. Osborne was a sort of licensed wag in the House of Commons where his wit, and sometimes the unconscious humour of his political speeches, amused the members. Some years before his wife had written to Frances of him:

'Are you aware that Mr. Osborne is under the delusion that one of his conspicuous qualities is justice? for I am under the impression that he is the most superlatively unjust character I ever met. He is dead to all influence save one & that is his *vanity* being flattered. This avenue is open to you but closed to me, so if you will accept the trouble, my goodwill hands him over to you as regards this power, in toto, and it could not be in better hands or more gratifying to me.'

It was Osborne who, at the beginning of 1870, wrote an epilogue to one of Ward's dramatic productions which half Dublin was invited to see at the Chief Secretary's Lodge. His verses ended:

> *But one there is for whom I gladly claim*
> *Your special notice; need I tell her name?*
> *Whether by Twickenham's classic site she dwells*
> *Or near the Phoenix weaves her social spells,*
> *Where'er she goes she adds new zest to life*
> *A generous hostess and true hearted wife!*
> *Long may she live, these revels to renew*
> *And grace the genial home of Fortescue.*

A few days later Chichester's duties took them back to London where they were welcomed by a gratifying notice in the *Daily News*, quoting Osborne's poem and complimenting Frances on her superb entertainments:

'Elegance and unaffected geniality make the perfection of refined society; they have been the perfection of the Countess's evenings 'at home', and we have no doubt that she will always be made at home in Ireland, as it has been her unfailing success to make Irishmen and Irishwomen at home with herself.'

The pleasure such comments must have given her in no way compensated Frances for her dislike of the Irish office or for her increasing indignation at the Prime Minister's lack of appreciation. On February 15 it was Gladstone who introduced Chichester's Irish Land Bill which was at last to bring some degree of justice to the Irish tenantry. The Chief Secretary and his law officers had produced a measure which John Stuart Mill considered the most important passed by the British Parliament since the Catholic Emancipation Act. The previous November, before any plan whatever had been adopted, Fortescue had sent Gladstone a memorandum which contained the whole substance of the Bill, yet Gladstone omitted to give him any credit for his work.

Once again, as he wrote to Lord Clermont, Chichester was prepared to remain behind the scenes. 'That is my fate in this matter, partly from circumstances, as it was necessary that the Prime Minister sh. carry the Bill through the Cabinet, and partly from the nature of Gladstone himself, who is not a man ready or anxious to give credit to others.'

Frances was less forbearing in her letter to a friend:

'The Bill is an immense success. The Irish extreme Liberals were silent and angry, as they did not understand Mr. Gladstone's explanation, which was not astonishing as he was not quite *well up* in *Chichester's* Bill. . . . It is certainly hard lines for Chichester that Gladstone should carry off all the *public* honours of Chichester's work. All the Landlord Tenant part of the Bill, which is *the* Bill, is his. The rest is Bright, etc. & I believe will most likely go to the wall.'

The Land Bill was bound to gain the Premier great popularity with the majority in Ireland. At the same time the Fenian outrages called for some very strong measure which would scarcely endear its promoter to the Irish. Gladstone therefore left it to Chichester to introduce the Peace Preservation (Ireland) Bill four weeks later.

Lady Waldegrave was determined that her husband should have his work duly recognized, and left none of her innumerable acquaintances in any doubt as to the authorship of the Land Bill.

The public, however, she was unable directly to reach, and so intensified her efforts to win over the Press. Delane and Hayward were old friends, E. H. Pigott of the *Daily News* was a staunch ally, and Sir Edward Strachey could always influence the *Spectator*. Now she also cultivated Greenwood of the *Pall Mall Gazette*, and Thornton Hunt, and was annoyed with Chichester for doing nothing about the Levys of the *Daily Telegraph*.

Another important newspaper soon came under her influence. A niece of Lord Clarendon's, a sister-in-law of Willie Harcourt's, had become engaged to Algernon Borthwick of the *Morning Post*. They were married early in April and by offering them Strawberry Hill for the honeymoon, Frances all unwittingly won yet another editor's allegiance.

Her fantastic hospitality in Dublin caused not the slightest decrease in the scale of Frances's entertainment during the London season. Dudbrook was the scene of her Easter party, and for Whitsun her guests assembled at Strawberry Hill.

There was again a great fête in honour of the Prince and Princess of Wales at Strawberry Hill on June 22. Ward produced a play for the royal guests, after which there was a ball. The American Minister, Motley, whose two daughters were present, wrote to Frances that he heard her party had rivalled the most magnificent scenes in *Lothair*. The Clarendons as usual were staying in the house, Lady Waldegrave's *très cher cousin* as amusing and affectionate a companion as ever. His sudden death three days after he had left Twickenham was an overwhelming shock. Her grief made it difficult for Frances immediately to grasp the political implications. Lord Granville was the obvious man to succeed him at the Foreign Office, which meant that the Colonial Office would need a new chief.

When, in December 1868, Gladstone had offered the Irish office with a seat in the Cabinet to Chichester, the latter had said that he hoped to become Secretary of State for the Colonies. Gladstone had replied that he was sure the other would not press the subject as Granville had been offered his choice of offices and had chosen the Colonies. Gladstone added:

'Lord Clarendon's health is very far from strong, and if he should be unable to go on at the Foreign Office, we have an admirable Foreign Secretary in Granville.'

Chichester naturally took that to mean that in the event of such a transfer the Colonial Office would be his, and he told Frances so when he returned home.

The day after Clarendon's death, Fortescue called on Lord Granville at the Colonial Office, and asked him to tell the Premier of his, Fortescue's, claim, which Granville promised to do. This call was confirmed by a letter from Chichester which Granville sent to Gladstone. The next day the Premier replied:

'My dear Granville   *June 29. 70*
    I return Fortescue's letter.

'I am not aware, & could not admit, that anything passed between him & me, on our taking the Government, which ought to influence the disposal of the Colonial Office in the event of your becoming Foreign Secretary on the vacancy which this lamentable loss has brought about.

'I do not recollect any reference to a vacancy in the C.O. If there was such a reference, I probably said that there would be nothing to prevent him from urging his claim, but I did not say & would not have said, anything which could approach to a promise or to giving anyone an expectation.

'Fortescue has held his office with great credit, & has done excellent & distinguished service. I am happy however to say that service of very high order has not been uncommon during the short existence of the present Government, among its leading members, extending the phrase a little beyond the Cabinet.

'His office is a very high one. From various circumstances, it has, while in his hands, escaped entirely from the control of the Home Secretary. It has stood in *fact*, not very greatly below a Secretaryship of State. It has afforded greater opportunities of distinction than some of the Secretaryships of State. It *may*, I do not say it will, rise even somewhat higher. I dwell more upon this; the work for which Fortescue took it is not yet complete, though I hope it may deserve that epithet next year. One of its branches, if the smallest not the least difficult, remains untouched.

'Were the C.O. to go for service only, Fortescue has, it might be contended, one very formidable competitor in the House of Commons.

'But the occasion is one on which we must consider the relative

P   211

strength of the Government in the two Houses. It is plain to me that the C. Secretaryship should go to a Peer. If so, those who are Peers already may be thought to have the first claim.

'Of course it is not to be expected that Fortescue should take my opinion of what his fame requires, rather than his own. But nothing can prevent me from having an opinion: and it is that his character and reputation have much more to gain by his remaining for the present where he is, than by any transfer to any office whatever.

Sincerely yours
W. E. Gladstone'

Granville saw Chichester and told him the contents of the Prime Minister's letter, doing all he could to prevent the younger man from resigning. The next day Chichester called on Gladstone who stuck firmly to what he had said in his letter. Chichester asked him to clarify two points in it. One was that the Irish office might 'rise even higher'.

The Premier explained that there was a plan in embryo to get the Prince of Wales to Ireland either by providing him merely with a residence there—Granville's suggestion—or by making him Viceroy as Gladstone wished to do. In either case the Chief Secretaryship would increase considerably in importance.

The other point was 'those who are Peers already'. Gladstone explained that if the only obstacle in the way of giving Chichester the Colonial Office had lain in his not being in the House of Lords, there would have been no difficulty whatever in making him a peer, if he desired it.

Chichester continued to protest, pointing out the great services not only he rendered but his wife also. It was she who had first broached the question of a royal Viceroy to the Prince of Wales, when she had suggested Prince Arthur, but Wales had said, 'Let me have first turn.' Chichester also pointed out that he 'could not go on dragging Lady Waldegrave over to Dublin winter after winter.'

The interview ended by Gladstone assuring him that he by no means wished to assume that Chichester was to be a fixture at the Irish Office, and that in the case of any future changes he had a full right to consideration.

The annoyance that both Frances and her husband felt was considerably aggravated by the appointment the Premier made to the Colonial Office—a man who had already stood in Chichester's way in another important connection—Lord Kimberley, the erstwhile Lord Wodehouse. Nevertheless their loyalest friends could understand Gladstone's difficulties, and The *Times* comment was very fair:

'The considerations which made it impossible to move Mr. Forster rendered it also impossible to recognize Mr. Chichester Fortescue's claims, based on seven years' apprenticeship at the Colonial Office, to be appointed Colonial Minister. He will have more than enough on his hands initiating the operation of the Irish Land Bill, with the original idea and passing of which he has been so intimately connected.'

The *Daily News* expressed very similar views and both provided Chichester with the slight consolation of admitting his great part in the Land Bill. All the same there was throughout the Government an embarrassing feeling that Chichester had been somehow victimized. The Queen herself, in an endeavour to show her appreciation of his work, hastily summoned the Chief Secretary and his wife on a visit to Windsor, thoughtfully choosing as her only other guests their old and close friends the Van de Weyers.

IF, as Chichester suspected, 'Puss' Granville had not been over-sincere in his sympathy, he soon had trouble enough of his own. The day after the announcement of his transfer to the Foreign Office, the Cortes offered the throne of Spain to Prince Leopold of Hohenzollern, an offer which led to the outbreak of the Franco-Prussian War in the middle of July. The whole Orleans family descended on Frances for advice. Fortunately she left for Chewton Priory the day before Louis Napoleon surrendered to the King of Prussia.

Aumale, who with his brothers and his nephew Chartres had gone in vain to Paris to offer their services to the French army as soon as the Second Empire had fallen, wrote to her a week later:

'Je suis arrivé de Paris hier soir et j'ai bien regretté de ne pas vous trouver ici; car vous êtes la personne du monde avec qui j'aime le mieux causer en tous temps et vous êtes, de tous vos compatriotes, la seule avec qui je pourrais causer en ce moment.'

He wrote every two or three days to ask her advice, and the Orleans Pretender himself, the Comte de Paris, wrote twelve-page letters to Frances discussing every aspect of the Orleans hopes and plans. It was, however, difficult for her to do much, as her knuckles had been smartly rapped by a Conservative Irish newspaper some weeks before:

'Lady Diplomatists
     (from our Paris correspondent)
'The most bitter feelings have been excited here by the sudden conversion of some of the London journals from being staunch Imperialists to being the most scurrilous abusers of the Emperor. A distinguished and brilliant lady, whose receptions are fre-quented by royal as well as by diplomatic personages, and who, as the wife of a Cabinet Minister, possesses power which adds weight and influence to her opinions and suasions to her assem-blies, gets credit for much of this. To her, diplomatic men here

attribute the pro-Orleanist tendencies of more than one of the leading journals of England. A devoted friend of the Orleans family, and strong in her position and her fascinations, she has, it is said, been in the habit of making use of her great power and status to secure adherents to the exiled princes. She is said to have been particularly gracious to certain members of the press. At the outset of the Hohenzollern affair, the chief editor of a London organ of much celebrity, wavered as to the part he must take in the pre-shadowed difficulties, but a watchful interest was taken in his decision, and luckily for the tactics of the fair politician she was seconded by a speculation in which the journalist was minus some thousands. Other journalists have also succumbed to the soft influence of the persuasive diplomatist; but somehow those things do transpire, and it is said that the occupant of the former residence of the dethroned railway king has sent to the Foreign Office a very full account of the little intrigues which have led to the pro-Orleans policy of the London press. This affair may be trifling in appearance, but I am by no means certain that there will not yet be a more full development of the disagreeable results which would-be kingmakers may bring about.'

Apart from her sincere desire to see the Orleans family again in control in France, Lady Waldegrave had begun to find Aumale's open devotion to her a little too reminiscent of the ten years that Chichester had spent in that weird companionship with Mr. Harcourt. Her first marriage had so accustomed her to a *ménage à trois* that she had scarcely realized the situation in the Nuneham days, but now the less friendly of her acquaintances were obviously amused that Aumale was unconsciously avenging Mr. Harcourt, and on Chichester's behalf she found their amusement extremely tiresome.

For once it was almost a relief to leave for Ireland. Before they crossed they spent a few days with old Charles Harcourt at Carlisle. They found their old friend touchingly happy to see them, and immensely gratified to witness the success of a marriage he had done so much to bring about.

The Norreyses and the Stracheys joined them soon after their arrival at the Chief Secretary's Lodge, on a six weeks' visit. The Spencers, the Clermonts and the Boyles all gave them a great welcome back, but what Frances considered Gladstone's injustice to Chichester after Clarendon's death had killed all her enthusiasm for the Irish Office.

Early in December she wrote to Constance who was to spend Christmas with Seph at Strawberry Hill.

'You were mistaken in thinking I was going to give a *great many* parties here. I am doing what I said I would do, only asking those people to dinner Mr. Fortescue wishes to see & asking a few people instead of *many*, as I used to do in the evening. We danced after dinner on Friday from $9\frac{1}{2}$ to $12\frac{1}{2}$, so there was no supper, only refreshments & we were not tired after it.'

On December 18 Chichester had a letter from Gladstone:

'My dear Fortescue   *Dec. 17. 70*

'Bright's resignation is now as good as accomplished; and you expressed to me very recently your sense of the domestic & social sacrifices entailed by your present office in terms so decided, that I should not like to make any effort at an arrangement for filling the Presidency of the Board of Trade in any other quarter without saying first to you that if you think fit to take the office I shall on public grounds be very happy to propose you to the Queen as I am sure the arrangement will be in every way efficient and satisfactory. I have no idea what your view of it may be, perhaps I myself regard with partiality a post which I have filled. Should your aye or no be at once clear to you I shall be glad of an immediate reply here; but should you be disposed to take time to consider the matter pray do not scruple to do so.

Believe me

sincerely yours

W. E. Gladstone'

Frances was delighted although she felt that her husband's health could not stand the long nights in the Commons. If he went to the House of Lords, an Under-Secretary could relieve him of a good deal of the drudgery of his new office. Gladstone would be prepared to recommend him to the Queen for a peerage so Chichester wrote off to his brother, enclosing Gladstone's letter, and explaining his own views:

'And indeed to speak openly to you, I greatly doubt whether I would take a peerage with the small income of my own wh. I now possess. I sh. be very sorry to have any painful discussion with you on this subject,—but I am bound to say that if I could reckon on a reasonable addition from you to that income, I should feel free to go to the Lords at any time, when health or other circs. might make it advisable.'

Clermont's reply was extremely cautious.

Dec. 19th. 70

'My dear C.

I quite understand your case pro and con as between Ireland and the Bd. of Trade, and can see that there are weights in each of the scales. As to promotion—there is no doubt that the latter is considered by the world, and perhaps by all but some officials who know the details, as the higher place. Perhaps you could hardly have expected Gladstone to put the offer in different terms from these which he has used, because you asked in the summer for a change on the grounds to which he refers, and he does say something civil about the Govt being benefitted by your acceptance, still there is no hint at a further step hereafter. I think that if next year should prove troublesome in Ireland from Fenians or Repealers, you would be sorry to have to face it, and in any case Frances would not like to come again.

'Then as to income (I do not now refer to the more remote and larger question as connected with the Peerage) would not the difference of necessary expenditure in entertaining, journeys etc, be so largely in favor of the Bd of Trade as to make up for the loss of £2000 a year?

'I imagine that with your power of taking up various subjects, you would soon find an interest in the work which must be, I should suppose, in some sense cosmopolitan—but as to the amount —whether it would be heavy, and as bad or worse than the Irish Office I am quite ignorant, but you certainly ought to consider that point cautiously. I can understand that you would not like to leave the H. of Commons at present on changing office, but surely if you ever take a Peerage during my life it must be because as the husband of a very rich wife you are and are considered by the world to be able to accept it.

'I was in hopes that any expectation that you once thought reasonable to indulge about an allowance from me had ceased when you got Red House estate, so that without knowing what

217

your feelings and ideas upon that matter now are I cannot say anything. If you care to write them down I will promise to think all well over. We shall be most anxious to know how you decide to answer Gladstone.

Love to Frances
Yours very afftly
Clermont'

Fortescue's first letter to Gladstone was mostly an attack on him for having announced the release of some Fenian prisoners although he had previously agreed to the announcement being made by the Chief Secretary. The letter continued:

'I am not able to write to you today about the Board of Trade. Only let me ask you a question which I should have asked if I were talking instead of writing to you on the subject, namely, whether this is an isolated change in the Cabinet, or whether there are others going on, or in contemplation.

'I hope you have got back to Hawarden.
Yours sincerely
C. P. Fortescue'

The attack so flustered the Prime Minister that his next two letters were devoted to excusing the premature announcement of the Fenians' release, and Chichester had already accepted before Gladstone, in his third letter, returned to the question of the Board of Trade.

Dec. 23. 70

'My dear Fortescue
You must have been surprised at my not replying to the query contained in your letter of the 19th which unfortunately miscarried. The answer is quite unequivocal. There is no movement in the Cabinet except to fill Mr. Bright's place, and my letter to you was the first and only step taken. I am very glad you find the change acceptable, though the loss in the Irish Office will be severe. Your name has not yet been to the Queen; and I should much wish to fill the Irish Office before anything is divulged. I have telegraphed to you to request secrecy. I see that in naming the Irish Office I have employed a phrase which is too narrow. I meant office with a small o—and had in view all the duties of

what is & must continue to be a very important & critical place. I am writing to Hartington to offer the appointment to, and indeed press it upon him.

'There can be no difficulty I think about your postponing the actual change for the period which you name. . . .

'A happy Xmas to you & Lady W
Ever yours
W. E. Gladstone'

Chichester certainly 'must have been surprised' since he had already received two replies to the first part of the letter the Premier claimed had miscarried. On December 30 Gladstone was able to inform Fortescue that:

'I telegraphed today to Spencer, who has so large an interest in the matter, the satisfactory conclusion of the conferences with Hartington who has behaved extremely well in a palpable sacrifice of inclination to honour and duty.

'I think we may make known your & his appointments on *Monday* morning.'

The typically Gladstonian remark about Hartington's 'palpable sacrifice of inclination to honour and duty' did little to endear the Prime Minister to the new President of the Board of Trade.

It took Lord Clermont over a month to make any further comment on the peerage question, but it was very much to the point when he did make it:

'I confess to have been rather startled by the suggestion that I was to help to support another title, knowing that my fortune is unequal to such a burden, and because judging in the only way that I can, that is to say from apparent expenditure, you are in the full enjoyment, if not in the full possession of very much larger means than I have. You and Frances live in a style quite good enough for a dukedom, and such that if Louisa and I were to attempt it I should be speedily ruined.'

The press, including even the Tory papers, was gratifyingly sorry that Chichester should be leaving the Irish Office, after his great work on the Disestablishment and Land Bills. The *Times* Irish correspondent wrote:

'The retirement of Mr. Fortescue is sincerely regretted by the friends of the Government here. He has administered the duties of an anxious and ardous office during a very trying period with a mingled firmness and forbearance which did much to inspire respect and disarm hostility. . . . The hospitable kindness of Lady Waldegrave will also be long gratefully remembered.'

The question of Irish education had still to be dealt with, and in some quarters it was felt that without him in charge such a measure might bring down the Government.

Frances and Chichester arrived at Holyhead with the last of their guests on 12 January 1871 to find that three six-wheel railway carriages had been provided for them, 'one for the Chief Secretary & 2 for the President of the Board of Trade. . . . I think for the future all our friends will wish to travel in our company if they like civility & tender *empressement*. We laughed a good deal at the double arrangements for the double capacity'.

The Gladstones were anxious to dispel any ill feeling Lady Waldegrave might still have towards them, and before the end of the month Lady Strachey was told that:

'I was amused today to see Mrs. Gladstone flying in here from a friend's carriage, whilst we were at luncheon. I went out to her in the Library & she kissed me & looked so happy because she felt I was "all right again". She came & sat with us whilst we finished our luncheon & tucked into some Maccaroni tho' she had just finished her own repast.'

A few days later Mrs. Gladstone brought her son and daughter to dinner at Carlton Gardens—'the People's William' was in bed with a cold, and early in February Chichester told Frances that she 'must go tonight to Mrs. Gladstone's. This bores me awfully . . . if I don't go there it will look as if I took no interest in the Govt'.

That night 'at Mrs. Gladstone's small and early the Duke of Cambridge had a long confidential chat with me . . . he told me that Mr. G. & Mr. Cardwell wanted to make a whipping boy of him . . . & he said that in all the years he had held office he had never come across two men so utterly devoid of gentlemanlike feeling as this Prime Minister & the War ditto'.

The Premier managed to raise himself a little in Frances's estimation when, early in March, in reply to a criticism of the Board of Trade, he said:

'I ask my honourable friend whether he marked the course of my right honourable friend the late Secretary for Ireland during the last session of Parliament throughout the discussion of the Irish Land Bill, and, if he did, if he approved the discretion, the ability, the consideration, the firmness with which my right honourable friend conducted himself throughout those difficult discussions—I only ask him whether it is really rational to suppose that the capacity of my right honourable friend is unequal to dealing with the Trades Marks Bill.'

Two days after that, Mr. and Mrs. Gladstone were 'in the best possible form' at one of the Thursday dinners, that Frances had instituted for Members to come up from the House in morning dress, to meet various notabilities who were however expected to change.

Mrs. Gladstone's 'small and earlys' were no attempt to rival the political entertainments at 7 Carlton Gardens, though Frances was, for the moment, more interested in foreign affairs than in the troubles of the Liberal Party. In February the Belgian Minister had assured her that in Brussels they expected Aumale to be elected President of France, so she at once began to work on the German ambassador and Countess Bernstorff to prevail on Bismarck to offer France more reasonable terms of peace. The Bernstorffs had, however, no influence with the German Chancellor, who preferred Louis Napoleon to any of the Orleans princes.

At the French elections the same month both the Prince de Joinville and Aumale had done well, the latter's electoral address having, of course, been first submitted to Lady Waldegrave. As Orleanist Pretender the Comte de Paris was unable to take any very active part, but his brother Chartres had aroused a good deal of enthusiasm by fighting in the French army under an assumed name. The new French ambassador, the Duc de Broglie, was an old friend of Aumales' and immediately became an intimate of Frances's.

For the next three months the French political situation was of absorbing interest to Lady Waldegrave. From March 18, when the Commune gained control in Paris, until Thiers succeeded in restoring order at the end of May, her Orleans friends were frantic with anxiety. In June, however, Thiers's government rescinded the decree of exile against them, and one by one they came to take leave of her. Napoleon III had confiscated the Orleans estates, but Aumale's fortune had been left him by the old Prince de Condé and was therefore untouched. He it was who had now to provide for his brothers and nephews, and on June 22 he set off for one of his French estates, having for weeks spent every moment she would grant him in Frances's company.

Other royalties were on hand to take their place. Princess Mary of Cambridge, firmly determined to remain in England, had discouraged a number of foreign suitors, and had been on the point of accepting Lord Hood when the Queen had vetoed the match. The Cambridges' sympathies had always been rather pro-Austrian than pro-Prussian, and so the princess had been prepared to listen favourably to one of the most attractive princes at the Austrian Court, when she heard that he had no objection to settling in England.

Franzi Hohenstein, with the striking good looks he inherited from his Hungarian mother, could, had he wished, have been a great favourite of the impressionable Empress Elizabeth. Early in the sixties his uncle, the King of Wurtemburg, had created him Prince Teck, and in 1866 he had married Princess Mary and settled down happily in England.

The Tecks had been asked to the usual July ball for the Waleses at Strawberry Hill, but had not been included in the dinner list as both the Duke of Edinburgh and Prince Arthur were dining, as of course were the Waleses, that night. However, the Duke of Coburg fell ill, and Edinburgh as his heir had to go to him. To Frances's amusement and pleasure Teck called at Carlton Gardens to ask if he and Princess Mary might take Edinburgh's place.

Lady Waldegrave described the ball in one of her almost daily letters to Lady Strachey:

'I was too tired yesterday to write to you even a line. I am going off to a Breakfast at Chiswick the Prince & Princess of Wales give to the Queen. I can't tell you how immensely successful the Ball was. The Waleses said they never enjoyed anything so much. I never saw the Princess so happy, she quite took my fancy which she never did before as I thought her too stiff for my taste, but she was radiant & full of "beans" this time. She looked very pretty & was beautifully dressed in white covered with rosebuds. My dress was much admired, white net & Brussels lace with no end of white roses & loads of green leaves. Princess Mary was quite *flirtatious* with me & got into tremendous spirits when I asked her to be one of my two ladies at the M.P. dinner on the 20th. Lady Ailesbury is to be the other. . . . The Waleses stopped to the end 4 ½ a.m. tho' they had to be at Harrow that morning at eleven. He told me he was very nearly sending an express to ask me to let them sleep here or at all events the Princess, but he found they would be no nearer Harrow than if they were in London. I suspect this was a hint to ask them to stay here next time. They both said they liked my parties better than anything else in the season.'

The royal compliments were no consolation to Frances when a few days later Chichester had to go to Osborne as Minister in Attendance and she wrote that she hated the House of Commons and the Board of Trade more than ever, but when, despite the Queen's pressing him to stay another day, Chichester made his excuses, Frances wrote, 'What a darling he is, after eight years of marriage.' It had been a busy session for him, though he found his new work dull after the Irish Office, and he yearned for the peace of Chewton Priory, now a large establishment, as three wings had been built on.

His sister's passion for building had infected Ward, who decided to enlarge the cottage he had acquired at View Island near Reading. Being Ward, he had made the alteration to the building out of champagne cases, and at the end of July it was completed. Frances promptly took her guests down from Strawberry Hill to inspect it. Ward rose superbly to the occasion, and even had his Militia band on a barge moored beside the cottage to play during dinner. His guests were enchanted and declared that it was like a scene from *La Somnambula*. From then on Chichester and Frances invariably broke their journey to Chewton at View Island.

There was the usual succession of guests at the Priory during the autumn, interrupted by a short visit to Bournemouth where the Stracheys had taken a house for the winter. The two elder Strachey boys, Edward and St. Loe (Doodle Doo), were being coached by the Vicar of Chewton Mendip and were Constance's inseparable companions, though they were respectively three and five years her junior. Although Constance was only sixteen her matchmaking aunt was already writing, 'If Eddie had been two years older than Constance I should have liked that immensely.'

In December the Cabinet was summoned to London by the Prince of Wales's dangerous illness. With the fateful fourteenth of

December only a few days off, and the illness the same that had killed his father, everyone was despondent, but it was on the 14th that he rallied and a week later Chichester and Frances were able to return to Chewton for Christmas. Their festivities were a little dampened by the news that their old and good friend Evelyn Denison had resigned from the Speaker's chair, as he told Chichester from 'disgust at the Task-master'. Gladstone's candidate for his successor was a man both Chichester and Frances disliked and distrusted, the former Liberal whip, H. B. W. Brand. Frances's comments were acid:

'I don't like the idea of an ex-Whip for that post. It seems to me the very worst school for an impartial judge & the habit of obedience to the Master of the Hounds must have become 2nd nature. The Premier's love of Slaves is on a par with his other "nigger"dly proclivities.'

Three days later she returned to the attack. The Queen had issued a letter thanking the nation for their sympathy over the Prince of Wales's illness, which Lady Waldegrave discussed:

'Are you not delighted with the Queen's letter? We are immensely pleased with it. Lord Torrington writes to Chichester cutting up its style. What we like so much about it, is that it has *no style*. She is a clever woman & knows her subjects hearts & minds much better than "the people's William" does & I suspect he has begun to find this out.'

The January parties in 1872 were at the Priory followed by a reluctant return to Carlton Gardens when Parliament reassembled. Chichester was again in attendance at Osborne in February which encouraged Frances to hope that his duties in that respect might be over for the year. There were few of Gladstone's ministers for whom the Queen felt much affection, and she found the society of some of his Cabinet utterly distasteful. In March Her Majesty decided to visit her half-sister at Baden, and was determined that the minister in attendance should be a creditable representative of her country. The President of the Board of Trade was very good-looking, charming and polished, so to Lady Waldegrave's dismay the choice fell upon him.

The year 1872 was not a pleasant year for Frances as it was the only period in her life that her health failed her. Her nerves were affected with the result that her outlook upon everything was a little gloomy. She could bear less than ever to be separated from her husband and was greatly relieved when he persuaded Lord Halifax to accompany the Queen. A few days later, however, she was again in despair; and confided in Lady Strachey:

'That dreadful Queen is after Chichester again. Last night a note from Lord Granville saying that Lord Halifax had settled to go with her, but now was laid up with lumbago—upon which the Queen remarked "Speak to Mr. Fortescue again. I wish him to go with me." Chichester went off to Lord G. to tell him to write at once to ask Hartington. Hartington complains that he has had no holidays, the Queen did not ask for him, but like a brick, he says that if I am really not well, he will go, but he hopes that I shall be all right by the middle of the week. C. has now gone to the House, & hopes to get Goschen to go. If *he does*, the Queen will be furious!!! One of her great friends told me yesterday, that she could not bear to show one of the men abroad, out of the Cabinet, who was not a gentleman in every respect, manners, looks etc.

'. . . Fancy my astonishment yesterday at receiving a note from Chichester written at the House of Commons to say that Mr. Gladstone had just said to him—"It is so very long since I have seen Lady Waldegrave that I must ask you to let me know if I may call upon her at 6'o'clock & ask her for a cup of tea." C. came in with him & he remained talking extremely agreeably for an hour & a half. We both saw that he wanted to say something to me alone, but I would not give him the chance.

'I *suspect* it was to ask me if I would consent to going to Ireland with C. if he were made Secty of *State* for it. I have made up my mind now that I would *not*. If it had been *last year* I should have consented. . . . I forgot to say just now that Mr. Gladstone sent me a present of a book last night with his best regards. Wonders will never cease—The Queen running after Chichester & the Prime Minister after me. —Mind this long scrawl is *private*.'

Chichester did at last find a substitute and was able to spend Easter at Dudbrook with his wife. He found the work at the Board of Trade increasingly uninteresting and had yet another disappointment about the Colonial Office. Lord Mayo, the Viceroy of India, had been assassinated and his post had been offered to Lord Kimberley who, however, refused it. Even before that, Frances had written that 'Chichester is so sick of the Board of

Trade that he would give anything for the Govt. to skedaddle'.

Two months later she complained to Seph:

'It is a horrid bore being kept in London when the nightingales are singing at Strawberry Hill. I was in hopes that the Govt. might have been turned out on Mr. Fawcett's motion upon Irish education but I fear there is no such luck.'

For Gladstone the whole period of this administration was a trying time. The Liberal Party was still by no means united, the Whigs, the Peelites and the Radicals disagreeing on every conceivable point, and the Premier himself making things more difficult by trying to force too many important measures through. He was well aware how discontented a number of his ministers were, and at times he, too, longed to be out of office. Not the least of his troubles was the consciousness that the Liberal hostess was out of sympathy with him. He felt that he showed her every consideration—only recently he had made her nominee Governor of Ceylon—and could not understand that the only serious obstacle in the way of any friendship lay in his own total lack of graciousness and charm.

Towards the end of June Lady Waldegrave and Chichester were summoned to dine and sleep at Windsor. It was a little awkward as they had already accepted for the concert at Buckingham Palace on the same night. They felt they could scarcely excuse themselves from dining with the Queen on the grounds that they were going to her concert. At Windsor they were given the 'same beautiful rooms' they had had the previous year. The Queen forgetting entirely about the concert, had asked their friends, the Duchess of Sutherland and Lord Bessborough, to dine with them, but they were both in waiting on the Waleses at the palace. The dinner party was therefore only the Queen, Prince Leopold, 'two highly respectable slow Biddulphs', a lord-in-waiting and the lady-in-waiting, Lady Clifden.

Frances was to sit next Prince Leopold, and before dinner Lady Clifden told her: 'I am so sorry for you that you will have to sit next the Prince as he never utters.'

The first ten minutes were awful—not a sound above a whisper. The Queen looked black and, after saying a few words to Chichester, turned to Frances who was sitting next but one to her and talked about the Orleans family. After that Frances realized it was up to her, and from sheer desperation, began telling Prince Leopold a funny story almost in a whisper. The Queen, half hearing, said, 'Oh, Lady Waldegrave, what is that, tell it to me.' To everyone's delight the Queen laughed till she cried at the anecdote and from that moment the dinner went splendidly. After dinner the Queen talked to Frances for twenty-five minutes, and for a quarter of an hour to Chichester, devoting exactly five minutes to the others.

After a dinner party the Queen normally retired soon after ten, but on this occasion to the annoyance of her weary staff, she stayed till nearly one o'clock, enjoying herself as thoroughly as did Prince Leopold.

The following day Gladstone offered Chichester the G.C.B. The offer was for once made graciously and the Premier accepted Chichester's refusal of it equally pleasantly, with the odd remark: 'This offer was by no means intended as a balancing of accounts between us.'

Both Frances and Clermont agreed with his refusing the knight-hood, though the former wrote a little regretfully:

'I think he would have looked very handsome in his ribbon. It is a curious thing that I should have said to him at Windsor when he was in his Court toggery that he looked so well in it, he should have a ribbon & star to make it perfect. The *very next* night the offer came.'

The Queen had discussed the Orleanses with Lady Waldegrave knowing the immense influence her guest had on that family. Since the Orleans princes had taken their seats in the French Assembly, Frances was swamped with letters from them all consulting her about everything. The Comte de Paris wrote begging her to persuade the Duc d'Aumale to take a more dominant part in French politics, and a fortnight after the Windsor visit Aumale arrived in London to spend a few days with her to discuss his plans. A week after his return to Paris his last misfortune befell him. His only surviving child, the Duc de Guise, died of typhoid.

Apart from the shattering blow it was to Aumale, it directly affected the chances of an Orleanist restoration at the one time the possibility existed. Aumale was by far the ablest and most influential of the Orleans family, but was no longer able to play any effective part in their fortunes.

The news from Paris deprived Frances of most of the pleasure she would have felt when some days later a deputation of Irish admirers led by the Duke of Leinster came to Carlton Gardens to present her with a portrait of Chichester by Tissot. The young French pointer had also done a portrait of Frances herself, at the window of her boudoir at Strawberry Hill, but it was a poor representation of her. Although she spent a fortune on pictures she was never herself painted by a first-rate artist.

The excitement of the autumn at Chewton was Constance's 'coming-out'. Her own family had caused Frances endless anxiety and expense, but from the moment the five-year-old Constance had kissed away her tears on that drive through Bushey Park, her aunt had adored her. Now in the comparative seclusion of the Priory the girl was to appear in her first low cut gown with her hair up, and Frances was quite as excited as if it were her own début. From the very first dinner party Constance was a success, and her beauty, charm and thoughtfulness doubled the popularity of her aunt's parties to the end.

It was Constance's house party in September; Edward Lear, who had illustrated an alphabet for her before she could read, was there to caricature the other guests for her as parrots; the Stracheys, whose sons were devoted to her; the Netherlands minister and his wife; the Clermonts; old Abraham Hayward; the Tom Hugheses; the Belgian minister; the Archie Peels; and among others the American minister, General Schenck.

The American minister's stay in England ended disastrously for him, but at the Priory he achieved great popularity by teaching the whole party the new game of Poker, and before he left Chewton, Poker had established itself as the game of the century. The Wardlaws, the Boyles, the Swedish minister and his wife, eccentric old Lady Molesworth—all arrived in their turn and all were at once introduced to Poker. Chichester, who detested all card games, was the only one who objected and for the rest of his married life he continued, quite uselessly, to object.

The Priory party in October was amused at their hostess when Chichester was summoned to Balmoral. Her loyalty to her sovereign was sorely tried.

'Fancy *any woman* wishing a man to travel for two days, including one night at this time of year'—it was early in a rather mild October—'after a fatiguing Council of many hours duration

—entre nous I think it quite abominable. Don't tell Elise Stonor that *"them's* my sentiments", as she would be sure to tell the Waleses, as it would be nuts to them, & I should get into a scrape. . . . She is certainly a first-rate Queen & a good clever woman, but I wish she would let Chichester stay at home with his own first-rate Queen.'

Chichester, however, quite enjoyed his visit, and he found the former Mary Bulteel and her husband Henry Ponsonby, of course, there. Another close friend of Frances's was in attendance, Jane, Marchioness of Ely, and the Waleses and their children were all very pleasant when he went over to Abergeldie.

The highlight of his stay for Chichester was at the Council, when Sir Roundell Palmer, who had married Lord Chewton's sister, was to be sworn in as Lord Chancellor. Chichester had to act as Lord President of the Council. When the Queen handed Palmer a red velvet bag containing the Great Seal, Palmer, to his palpable dismay and to the Queen's uncontrollable amusement, proceeded to drop the Great Seal with a resounding crash to the floor.

The day after Chichester returned to Chewton, Frances was enchanted to hear from Lady Ely:

'The Queen told me yesterday she was so much pleased with Mr. Fortescue's visit. She had found him so pleasant & agreeable & his voice so gentle, that she had been interested & not tired & spoke with much pleasure of his appreciation of Balmoral & Scotland. You know I was always to tell you what I liked, dearest Lady Waldegrave, so you must let me add the Queen spoke so much of you & said she knew you had always been so friendly & of the weight you carried in society & of your talent & influence which was always directed for good. This is for yourself but I cannot help telling you for I know how true it is. You will I am sure believe the pleasure it was to me to have you both so much appreciated.'

TO WHAT EXTENT the troubles in Gladstone's first administration were caused by Lord Granville it is impossible to say. As leader of the Liberal Party in the House of Lords and as Foreign Secretary, he had in any case great power, but in addition he had by his suavity completely won the Queen's confidence. Almost all his colleagues suspected him of intriguing against them, and his letters to Her Majesty were scarcely remarkable for fervent loyalty to the Premier.

As Mr. Harcourt's cousin, he had for years been thrown into close contact with Frances, but she trusted him as little as Newcastle had done. She coupled 'his pussy cat softness' with 'the treachery of that animal'.

Granville's brother had, in the sixties, become a regular visitor at Lady Waldegrave's various homes. He was completely won over by her irresistible *bonhomie* and greatly appreciated Chichester's fine intellect, but the account of her he wrote years later was incompatible with the admiration he had expressed during her lifetime. The most surprising of his statements was that she 'did not much care for politics in the abstract'. Since he had frankly admitted to her early in their acquaintance that he wanted all the political gossip she could tell him to repeat to his brother, she was hardly likely to give him the benefit of her political opinions.

Lord Granville was well aware of the great power Lady Waldegrave wielded in the Liberal world, and as Foreign Secretary he knew how much the various embassies and legations in London were influenced by her. He was too shrewd to offend her in any way, which would be a charitable reason to assign to his never attempting to encourage in her a more sympathetic attitude to the Premier.

In February 1873, Gladstone introduced, as his own, an Irish University Bill. Fortescue, with considerable assistance from William Monsell, the Liberal member for Limerick, had in 1869 drawn up an Irish University Bill which they had presented to the

Premier. During the intervening years Gladstone had made a number of alterations, with a High Churchman's confidence that he alone understood the Roman Catholic clergy. Chichester, in whom the heads of the Catholic Church in Ireland had great confidence, realized how disastrous the Premier's alterations would prove, but, though for days before the Bill was presented Gladstone had consulted Chichester on every conceivable point, he obstinately stuck to every change he had made.

Protestants and Catholics alike were prepared to support a measure that would reform education in Ireland, but the Bill as Gladstone introduced it succeeded in offending both Churches, and was seized upon by the new Home Rule party as a weapon against the Government.

Knowing the Irish as he did, Fortescue saw from the first that Home Rule must lead to secession, which he sincerely believed would not be to the advantage of his own country. Gladstone, however, had as yet come to no decision on that point, and in his endeavour not to offend the Home Rulers succeeded in offending everybody else. Chichester had recently had to bring before the House an extremely difficult Railway Bill which he had managed so competently that it had successfully got through the second reading. It was a small personal triumph, but the Premier pretended to be totally unaware of it. Frances was furious and wrote:

'He certainly is a miserable man to serve under. He thinks of no one but himself, & is jealous of any success for the Members of the Govt.'

When Gladstone, at a Cabinet meeting, asked Chichester to speak for the Bill before Hartington, Chichester for once lost his temper. He shared his wife's annoyance about the Railway Bill. As Hartington was Chief Secretary, he would resent another man speaking before he did. The Premier had made no acknowledgment of Chichester's work in framing the original Bill and yet expected the Irishman to endanger his position as Member for Co. Louth by speaking in favour of a measure which as it stood must offend most of his constituents. Fortescue angrily told him that he had no right to ask such a thing and that he certainly would not speak before Hartington. Gladstone said nothing, but looked majestically down his nose.

Chichester did eventually speak for the Bill with some success, but on the second reading the Premier decided that Cardwell should speak for the Government. His speech was so injudicious with regard to the Irish that he turned the undecided Catholic votes decidedly against the Government which was defeated in the early hours of March 12 by 287 to 284. Later that day the Government resigned. Gladstone had a few days before prepared the Queen for such an eventuality, assuring her that the end of that administration would be the end of his own political career. That prospect must have made the Queen view the fate of the Bill with very mixed feelings.

The Conservatives however refused to take over as a minority a second time, and on the 18th Gladstone was again in office. Frances reported that 'Mr. G. is *not* in good spirits, & seems much vexed & worried at being obliged to be Premier once more with *his* Irish Bill non-existent,' but she considered that he 'behaved very well'. Gladstone had succeeded in weeping at the Cabinet meeting when the resignation had been decided upon, and his powers of oratory were such that, when he had spoken of his profound gratitude to them, his ministers had actually believed him. Even Frances's customary common sense temporarily forsook her and she, too, sympathized with the Premier.

The members of the Carlton Club and of the Reform claimed that they could always assess the exact political situation by watching from their respective windows, the personalities who called on Lady Waldegrave. None the less her hospitality was not primarily political. She was quite as happy giving dances for any of her young friends as she was when her dinner table looked like a Cabinet meeting. Her clothes were still discussed, envied and copied by most of her acquaintance, and in 1873 she had the pleasure of planning Constance's wardrobe for her first season.

In her letters to Lady Strachey, Frances would break off the most lucid dissertation on some international crisis, to describe a new bonnet that had just arrived from Paris. In the middle of the Irish University Bill dilemma she wrote that:

'Chichester & I have fallen in love with a beautiful diadem Garrard has brought to tempt me, & I think we are rapidly giving way to the temptation. I shall make Constance sketch it for you if we buy it. I have to go to so many Court festivities & do not always like to appear at them in the same diadem, so there is very good reason if we do indulge this fancy.'

Apparently she found the 'very good reason' quite incontestable since a fortnight later she was at a ball at Marlborough House wearing 'my new diamond diadem & diamond necklace'.

At the end of the month there was another long description of a Marlborough House dinner which had given Lady Waldegrave great pleasure:

'I sat next the Prince of Wales & we had no end of jolly confidential chat. He told me that he had heard so much of the M.P. dinners & would very much like to come to one, so we are to fix one for him as soon as we can after Easter & he is to learn Poker in the evening. He & the Princess are to come to a dinner & ball at Strawberry Hill in June. My new billiard room is to be built by that time & will be used for their supper.

'*Quite Private.* I told him that I had thought when I saw two good portraits of him & the Princess for sale that I would buy them for Strawberry Hill, but I would not do so without first mentioning it to him. He said, "Why, my dear Lady Waldegrave we should be *quite proud* to sit for you to be put into the Gallery at Strawberry Hill. . . ." He had heard of Constance's beauty & asked when she was to be presented at Court . . . it was arranged that I was to present her to them tonight at Mrs. E. Baring's.'

At Easter there was a party for a fortnight at Dudbrook. Two days before Frances returned to Carlton Gardens, London was horrified to read in the new Conservative paper, *The Hour*:

'Death of the Countess Waldegrave

We regret to announce the death of Sarah, Countess of Waldegrave, wife of the Right Honourable Chichester Fortescue, M.P. for County Louth, and President of the Board of Trade. The late countess was the daughter of the celebrated singer Braham. As the widow of the late Earl Waldegrave she married Mr. Harcourt, and some time after his death Mr. Chichester Fortescue. Her ladyship's receptions and entertainments have been, of late years perhaps the most frequent and most frequented in fashionable life, and have probably not a little contributed to the cohesions of the Liberal party. Her death took place at Hastings yesterday evening, after a brief illness.'

It was, of course, the evangelical widow of the eighth earl, but, as the editor of the Liberal *Echo* wrote to Frances, it was interesting to read 'the curiously expressed opinion of even an unfriendly critic upon your services to the Liberal party'.

The season was the usual sequence of brilliant entertainments for Frances—Sunday levees, dinners for British or visiting royalties, assemblies with 700 guests, M.P. dinners, dances for Constance, all ending in a magnificent ball at Strawberry Hill, which was postponed till early July so that the Waleses could bring their brother-in-law, the Tsarevitch, and his wife with them.

At the beginning of August Gladstone was forced considerably to reorganize his Government. He frankly admitted that he had originally made Robert Lowe Chancellor of the Exchequer because he could do less harm in the Cabinet than out of it, but even so, he now felt that Lowe would be less of a problem at the Home Office. There had also been trouble at the Admiralty and the Post Office, and the First Commissioner of Works had not been a success. Knowing how discontented Fortescue was at the Board of Trade, the Premier was nervous of attempting any reshuffle before pacifying him.

Chichester had done a great deal for the Liberals in Essex—until his marriage a Conservative stronghold—and as the Lord-Lieutenancy was vacant, Gladstone offered it to him on August 2. Frances was delighted and persuaded her husband to accept it, but Chichester had no illusions as to why it had been offered. The transfers in the Government were duly made, though the *Morning Post* considered that Fortescue would have made a better Home Secretary than Lowe. The end of the session brought Frances the additional gratification of hearing two difficult Bills—Merchant Shipping and Railways—which Chichester had successfully carried, mentioned in the Queen's Speech.

Lady Waldegrave had reached the point in her career that was described at some length in the *Graphic* twenty-five years later.

'Frances, Lady Waldegrave was one of the last ladies who ruled over the West End world. Witty, well read, taking a keen and intelligent interest in interesting things, worldlywise without being worldly, Lady Waldegrave reigned as no living lady can, considering the altered circumstances of social life in London. In her day, Strawberry Hill was the Mecca towards which the eyes of the ambitious turned with longing looks, for it was there that Lady Waldegrave held her court, and very carefully did she choose her courtiers. The mere possession of money, if it influenced her at all, did so to the disadvantage of the candidate, and almost the same may be said as regards the possession of the title. Around her sofa throne crowded the men and women who were making the history of the time, the men who had influence because of their intelligence, the women who, on account of their wit, or beauty, or wisdom, wielded power.

'It was at Strawberry Hill, in those days, that political programmes were discussed and decided upon; that differences were patched up which otherwise might have switched history on to other lines; that promising converts were received; that promising postulants were examined, and were accepted or rejected according to the judgment passed upon them by Lady Waldegrave and her experienced friends. This one craved for place, Lady Waldegrave procured it for him; that one was eager to obtain a title, Lady Waldegrave obtained it for him; another yearned for social recognition, in an instant every door in Mayfair flew open to receive him and his. It was an especial honour for a young man to be invited to visit Strawberry Hill on a Sunday, for it meant that his elders perceived that he possessed qualities which, if properly cultivated, might be useful to the State or to the party.'

One of the very few who had the honesty, after her death, to admit his great debt to Frances was W. V. Harcourt. Although none of her circle much cared for him, Frances's affection for and interest in him never diminished. Since 1868 he had been Liberal member for Oxford, and though he had little sympathy with Chichester's plans for the improvement of conditions in Ireland, Frances was always anxious to help him.

The historian Motley had been succeeded as American minister by General Schenck, but had remained in Europe. His widowed daughter, Mrs. Ives, and Willie had fallen in love, but her parents strongly disapproved, with the result that the lovers' meetings were mostly at Carlton Gardens or at Strawberry Hill, though Chichester was a little annoyed when they occupied his study for three hours on end. Parental opposition proved too strong and, after months of alternate despair and hope, the whole affair dwindled into silence.

Harcourt's greatest friend, the brilliant barrister, Henry James, had become Solicitor-General in September 1873, and at the beginning of November there were rumours that he was being considered for the Attorney-Generalship. Frances at once thought of William Harcourt and wrote off to Gladstone putting Willie forward as Solicitor-General, quoting Roundell Palmer—now Lord Selborne—and Henry James as supporters of her suggestion. Gladstone's reply, though non-committal, was affable and ended: 'I need not keep you long in suspense.' Three days later Frances was able to write:

'We have succeeded about William Harcourt. It was a very difficult matter as he has so often wantonly & outrageously offended Mr. Gladstone publicly & you know how disagreeably he has offended him privately—Don't mention this appointment till you see it in the papers as it is just possible Mr. G. may offer it in so ungracious a way that Willie may refuse it in a pet.'

Her fears were groundless. Willie accepted with alacrity and a month later had a knighthood to increase his self-esteem.

Among the guests at the Priory during the autumn was young Lord Waldegrave, whom years before Frances and his mother had destined to be Constance's husband. He had, however, fallen in love with his cousin, Mary Palmer, Lord Selborne's daughter, and their marriage the following year put an end to Frances's dream. It affected her very little as she was determined in no way to influence Constance on the question of marriage. In any case Constance was only eighteen and was already immensely popular and admired.

Another romance was intriguing London when Chichester and Frances arrived there in November. For some months Trollope's *Phineas Redux* had been appearing in the *Graphic* and everyone was trying to recognize the characters. Plantagenet Palliser had already been decided on as the late Duke of Newcastle. Disraeli and Gladstone were easy enough to spot, and though some people had previously thought Lady Glencora was based on Frances, they now felt that possibly Madame Max Goesler was taken from her, especially as there were points of resemblance between Phineas Finn and Chichester.

Lady Waldegrave refused to see any reference to herself or her husband, but was extremely enthusiastic about the novel as a picture of political life, and she enjoyed the portrayal of Mr. Daubeny. Her curious friendship with Disraeli continued—in December that year he wrote of her as 'our dear friend—and, alas, my fair foe'—and the Tories from the Carlton Club windows were frequently aghast to see their leader disappear into the Liberal citadel, 7 Carlton Gardens, for an hour's talk with its chatelaine.

The lack of harmony within the Liberal ranks could not be kept secret, and gradually the country's growing uneasiness about the Government manifested itself at various by-elections at which even notoriously Liberal constituencies returned the Conservative candidate. Gladstone was exhausted by more than five years of power, and with a sudden feminine capitulation to circumstances decided that the country should be forced to settle his difficulties. On 23 January 1874, he announced the immediate dissolution of Parliament to his startled Cabinet.

Three days later Chichester left Dudbrook for Ireland on his electoral campaign. The two seats for Co. Louth were to be contested by Home Rulers, and he realized that he would have a hard fight. John Bright, who had no confidence in the Louth electors, tried to persuade him to stand for Frome where the election would almost certainly be uncontested. Frances confessed that such a prospect made her mouth water, but her husband was determined 'to stick to Ireland as long as Ireland would stick to him'.

At Dudbrook Lady Waldegrave was ill with anxiety when she read of Liberal candidates being kicked and stoned in various Irish constituencies, as she knew that Chichester was incapable of realizing that he was in any physical danger from those he believed to be old friends and neighbours. He was, however, from the first very dubious about his prospects and wrote of his doubts to the Premier. The Home Rulers were making great play of the Peace Preservation Act that Fortescue had been forced to bring in in March 1870 to contend with the Fenian outrages. One of the contestants, Callan, had been bitterly disappointed that Chichester, as Chief Secretary, would not help him to some lucrative official position and had no scruples about employing the vilest methods in his campaign.

Polling day at Louth was not till February 12, by which time the electorate there had been greatly influenced by the news of the

Liberal collapse throughout the kingdom. The declaration of the poll on February 13 announced Chichester's defeat. The sheer, black ingratitude of it dismayed him far less than it did the general public, but what sickened him with his compatriots was that he and his nephew 'Chi' Hamilton were pelted and hissed through the streets of Ardee.

The result of the poll was considerably lightened for him by a letter he had received from Gladstone the previous day:

> 10 *Downing Street*
> *Whitehall*
> *Feb.* 11. 1874

'My dear Fortescue

I receive with great concern your dark prognostication of the result of the Louth Election. It would be so painful in a public view, with reference to the gratitude of Irishmen that I will still hope for a better result. But, with reference to the latter part of your letter, I at once write to say that in the double event of your rejection and your wish I consider your claim to a Peerage indisputable.

'It would be hard to name the man who has done for Ireland all that you have done, or any man that knew the greatest Irish questions as you knew them.

'After all, in some points of view, it is better to be rejected outright, than to be hitched in, like me at Greenwich, between Boord and Liardet—one of the heroes of the Tichborne trial as I am told.

> Believe me
> Sincerely yours
> W. E. Gladstone'

Gladstone himself was the principal victim of his inability to give encouragement and praise in everyday life. At any time of crisis he could rouse all his colleagues' devotion by showing how profoundly he appreciated their work and loyalty, but in the ordinary course of events he seemed to begrudge them the least sign of encouragement, praise or gratitude.

The comparative merits of a peerage or a safe English constituency could only be discussed after Chichester had returned to Carlton Gardens, where his wife, Constance, Charles and Ward gave him such a tremendous welcome that he felt he must some-

how have won the election after all. Frances was strongly in favour
of the peerage since all the posts he liked best were usually in the
Lords, and there was so much less wear and tear there than in the
Commons. Clermont, surprisingly enough, sided with Frances.

Chichester was very undecided. It seemed certain that Gladstone would retire from the leadership of the Liberal Party, which
would presumably go to Lord Granville. A Liberal leader in the
Commons would be needed, and the man most likely to suit the
various factions could be Chichester himself. A great number of
his friends in the Commons pressed him not to desert them.
Chichester's solution was to leave the decision to his doctor, Du
Pasquier.

To Frances's great pleasure, Du Pasquier told him he had not
the strength to take office again in the House of Commons, but
that he might live to a good age if he went to the House of Lords
and took office there.

The following day, February 18, the Government resigned, but
Frances's political cares were not over. That evening the Comte
de Paris and the Duc de Chartres dined at Carlton Gardens. They
had come over to ascertain how much the British change of
government would affect the immediate future of France.

On March 3, as Lady Waldegrave was dressing for dinner, a
little note was brought her:

'This will be the last letter I shall sign as C. P. Fortescue. Under
whatever name for the outside world,

always your own
most loving
C. P. Fortescue'

The following morning another message came from her husband's study:

'My dearest love
I was going to answer F. Peel's letter—but I pulled myself up,
—in order that I might sign myself for the first time

Your loving and devoted
Carlingford'

Carlingford was a little town with a ruined castle on Lord Clermont's estate on the shores of Carlingford Lough. Lord Dufferin

had fancied the title for himself when he was created an earl in 1871, but had naturally changed his mind when he had discovered that the place was Clermont's property. The Queen told her private secretary that she thought it 'a very pretty title', while Edward Lear expressed his feelings in verse:

1. *O! Chichester, my Carlingford!*
   O! Parkinson, my Sam!
   O! S.P.Q., my Fortescue!
   How awfully glad I am!

2. *For now you'll do no more hard work*
   Because by sudden pleasing jerk
   You're all at once a peer,—
   Whereby I cry, God bless the Queen!
   As was, and is, and still has been,
   Yours ever, Edward Lear.

Apart from his letter to the Queen at the time of the Irish University Bill crisis, Gladstone had so frequently spoken of his anxiety to withdraw from any prominent political position, that his party naturally believed him. Lord Granville led the Liberals in the House of Lords, but as General Peel told Frances, he could not believe that they 'would be satisfied to act under such a weak old cat as Granville'. The most urgent problem was to find an Opposition leader for the House of Commons, a question that Gladstone was expected to decide. One after another the principal Liberals called on him, but his disappointment at the result of the election had thoroughly disgruntled him.

In December '72, Frances had told Lady Strachey:

'Gladstone sent me this morning Dr. Dollinger on the reunion of the Churches. It is *awfully stiff*. For a man in his senses & Governor of this Kingdom what do you think of this opinion he gave me the other night on the efficacy of continual prayer—"that it was impossible to know the effect of the constant beating of the air *physically* on the Higher Power". Please *don't* either of you repeat *this* to *anyone*. There must be, I think, a *considerable* screw loose somewhere.

'*Private*. I can't help thinking that he is aware of his failing powers & that fear is influencing him in his anxiety for rest. It is quite unmistakable that he longs to throw up the cards & does not much care who takes them.'

By 3 March 1874 Lady Waldegrave had begun to doubt if his longing to throw up the cards was so unmistakable after all. Lady Strachey was told how 'all the M.P.s in town rush off to us to unbosom themselves from Mr. Gladstone's state of high sulks'. Arthur Kinnaird was selected to call on him '& advise that he should either consent to continue to lead the party, or to express his wish that they should choose some other leader. He was in an amiable mood as to *tone*, but the contrary as to matter. He said he would not communicate with his party out of the House of Commons, would not lead them, but would sit in his old seat & speak only when he felt inclined to interfere in the debate, & that he entirely declined to speak to Hartington or any other person on this Head, in any sense as indicating his desire that anyone but himself should lead the party, tho' he felt certain he would not consent, at the end of a few years to be again Prime Minister. Kinnaird said Mrs. G. made three raids into the room to try to stop the conversation but on each occasion she was requested to take herself off.'

For the next week there were frequent meetings at Lord Granville's to discuss the position, and on March 9, Frances reported:

'There is another meeting at Lord Granville's going on now of the old Cabinet to consult what is to be the next step in the treatment of the unwilling Liberal Leader. My opinion is that he will continue to say No, & mean only *yes*, if the Public should, after 2 or 3 years of disgust at Tory rule, make a great outcry for the "people's William" to reappear at the head of affairs. In the meantime I do not expect he will do the generous thing to his party & ask Hartington to lead at once . . . Lord Hartington told me that when Dizzy heard Mr. Gladstone had dismissed the Whips & broken up the machinery of the party, private printing press etc. etc., he said "Well there has been nothing like this since Overend & Gurney" (the disastrous bank failure in May 1866).

'We had an immense levée yesterday—most of the M.P.s getting very cross at the long delay of Mr. G's answer. They say they would rather have a less clever Leader, who would give his whole heart & mind to the work, than be governed by a sulky genius. The English hate to see a beaten man show that he had been punished & sneak away from the fight like a cur with his tail between his legs. . . . Carlingford has just come home. . . .

'*Quite Private.* The result is so far satisfactory that he has almost consented to lead the party till the end of the session next year upon the understanding that he is not to be expected to lead either in opposition or in office after this time.'

The Marquess of Hartington's devotion to Lady Waldegrave amused and puzzled their friends. She had first been interested in him when, at the age of twenty-six, his motion for a vote of no-confidence had brought down the Derby Government in 1859. He appeared to be a dull, pompous young man, and as such had startled London by taking the notorious and beautiful cocotte, Skittles, under his protection, installing her in a Mayfair mansion and settling a large income upon her. It had led Frances, in February 1860, to rush off one evening to the St. James's Theatre when she heard his mistress was to be there.

Hartington had soon tired of the liaison and had made the American Civil War his excuse for a visit to that country. Skittles pursued him there and foolishly made a public scene in New York, for which he never forgave her. On his return to England he fell in love with the Duke of Manchester's German wife, one of the most beautiful women in Europe. Neither he nor the duchess made the slightest attempt to conceal their great affection for each other. Few hostesses were tactless enough to invite one without the other, and the duchess's great charm generally surmounted any disapproval that may have been felt. After the Duke of Manchester's death they did eventually marry in 1892.

The duchess took little interest in politics and was as pleased as was Hartington himself that his political career should be Lady Waldegrave's responsibility. He was Carlingford's loyal supporter, and had a great admiration for the latter's fine intellect and administrative abilities, while he himself had none of the sensitiveness and diffidence that often made public life distasteful to Chichester. Hartington was not an inspiring speaker, but that did not worry him unduly. Disraeli said that the only man he had seen in all his political life who yawned at his own speeches was Hartington, and that he respected him accordingly.

Gladstone's dog-in-the-manger attitude continued throughout 1874. Whigs, Peelites and Radicals alike were disgusted with him.

Lord Clarendon's brother, Charles Villiers, who as one of the instigators of the Repeal of the Corn Laws could scarcely be called a reactionary Whig, wrote to Frances during the autumn that:

'Our party are no doubt *now* hoping that Lord Palmerston's last words have become true & that Mr. Gladstone is in a state to be put under restraint.'

Although Lady Waldegrave claimed that 'there is no human being, I believe, hates visiting as much as I do', she and Lord Carlingford were obliged to accept an invitation to Chatsworth in December. Hartington was anxious to discuss his position with her. He assured her that he had made up his mind to sit on a back bench in the House, if Gladstone did not decide before the meeting of Parliament either to lead the Opposition himself or to announce that he retired entirely as Leader of the party.

Like a great many of his colleagues, Hartington was afraid that Gladstone would say that he would retire, and then, when any important questions came on, he would rush down to the House and upset all the arrangements of the Opposition front bench. Frances's comment on the ex-Premier was that 'it is too bad the way he goes on at present as it entirely destroys all order & discipline in the Liberal party'.

At the 1875 New Year party at Strawberry Hill a number of representative Liberals decided that, though they were willing and anxious to serve under Gladstone again, they would not go on their knees to implore him to return, nor would they consent to allow him to treat the party as he had done the previous year. Cardwell was deputed to tell him of the party's feelings.

On January 14 there was again a meeting of the ex-Cabinet at Lord Granville's. There a letter from Gladstone to Granville announcing his resignation was duly drawn up, to appear in the press the following day. As Ward Braham with his unexpected shrewdness remarked: 'I read it—You have bad cards now, when you have a good hand I will play it.'

Granville remained leader of the Opposition in the Lords, but he wrote to tell Chichester that he would accept no further responsibility. The two candidates for the leadership in the Commons were W. E. Forster and Lord Hartington, of whom the latter appeared to be the more reluctant. Frances, vehemently pro-

Hartington, used all her influence both to persuade him and ensure his election.

Matthew Arnold, Forster's brother-in-law and an old friend of Chichester's, told him that neither he nor his sister at all wanted Forster to be leader, and on February 1 Granville was surprised to hear from Forster that he would decline even if he were chosen by a majority. Frances at once wrote to Lady Strachey:

'Do you remember *The Times* saying the *Salons* had *no* influence now? That *put my back up* & I am *very* glad we came to Town in time to be of use.'

A fortnight later:

'Mr. Gladstone made me a two hours visit. He was perfectly delightful & did not in the least make me nervous by his over-whelming power of intellect tho' he was in great force. . . . How-ever I took precautions, the moment I saw him, to get aid & sent off a servant in a cab to beg Carlingford to come home immedi-ately as luckily I knew he was on books intent at Bush's. In the meantime I gave him a slopbasin full of tea & told him all that he was longing to know of the ins & outs of his late Govt. As he had never seen any paper but the *Echo* since Parlt met, you may imagine how avid he was for news.

'. . . In spite of his ultra devotion to religious subjects I can't help seeing that a great political issue would bring him to the front again as Leader of his party. At our Sunday levee all the old hands said they were sure he would take his seat behind the front opposition Bench.—I was the *only* one who said he would sit with his old colleagues & I was right. He sat next to Bright. . . .

'Dear old Hartington is taking to his work bravely, & all last week gave up his dinner & his Duchess like a hero. . . . At present he sits on his chalk egg with exemplary patience & good temper.'

As Chichester was no longer in the Lower House to act as her informant, Frances resumed her attendance at debates there, greatly to the agitation of the Liberal speakers, who were im-mediately summoned to Carlton Gardens to be 'blown up' if their speeches were not up to standard in policy and delivery. The un-official leader of the Liberal Party expected her flock to be 'states-manlike' to a high degree.

ON MARCH 10 Aunt Seph drove up to Carlton Gardens to spend the afternoon with her beloved niece and great-niece. Though it was only a few weeks to her seventy-second birthday, she had lost none of her youthful enthusiasm, and none of her delighted amazement at finding herself living in such a world of splendour. It was sometimes a little lonely at Strawberry Hill when the family was not there, and she enjoyed a visit to London to see Frances's or Constance's new clothes, for which she had such a passion that her niece hoped that in the next world the angels indulged in an occasional change of plumage. Seph had been feeling a little out of sorts, but drove back to Twickenham as happy as a child. The next morning she was found lying peacefully in her bed, dead of heart failure.

Frances could hardly bear to think of Strawberry Hill without her old aunt's ecstatic welcome. She at once cancelled the ball she had planned to give there for Constance during the summer and would have gone to Dudbrook for some weeks, but her Essex home was being considerably enlarged, and would only be ready in time for the Whitsun party she had invited there.

At Carlton Gardens Lady Waldegrave was pestered all day long by visitors, and while she was there it was not easy to refuse the endless invitations that flowed in. It was no longer essential for Chichester to spend so much time in Parliament, and both Dudbrook and Strawberry Hill were accessible enough for him to go to the House of Lords from either. By the middle of the season Frances was always anxious to escape from London to the gardens of her riverside or her Essex homes. Tenants were easy enough to find for Carlton Gardens, and the enormous rent they were prepared to pay helped towards the mounting costs of her endless entertainments.

A tenant was found for two months from the end of May so, to console Constance for her cancelled ball, Frances hastily arranged a 'little dance'—possibly a slight understatement since the Prince

245

of Wales and the Duke of Cambridge were among the guests.

By the beginning of June Frances and Chichester were established at Strawberry Hill. For once the fête there for the Waleses was not favoured with good weather. Over a thousand guests were soaked to the skin before they could reach shelter, at the garden party which preceded the evening's entertainment. A few days later the brilliant, unhappy Queen of Holland came to dine, more anxious to study her remarkable hostess than to inspect the curiosities of neo-Gothic architecture. The event of the season which gave Frances the most pleasure, however, concerned Lord Carlingford rather than herself. In May he presided at the Royal Literary Fund dinner, and sixty of the most notable men in London volunteered as stewards. The Austrian Ambassador, responding to the toast to the Ambassadors and Foreign Ministers, paid Carlingford and his 'noble lady' a very charming compliment, and Chichester's speech was enthusiastically received.

Out of office, Chichester could devote more time to his non-political interests—the re-establishment of Horace Walpole's library, the activities of the Philobiblon Club, his duties as Lord Lieutenant of Essex, and his researches into the problem of the Junius letters. However gay and frivolous the majority of Frances's guests might be, there were invariably a few men such as Hayward, Henry Reeve of the *Edinburgh*, Dr. Smith of the *Quarterly*, Knowles of the *Contemporary*, Sir Edward Strachey, Matthew Arnold or Lord Houghton whom he could tempt away from the tennis court, the poker tables or the dance floor. After twelve years of marriage he was still obsessed by the same passion for his wife, yet he was one of the few Liberals whose political views were not a faithful echo of hers.

Carlingford was well aware that the Duc d'Aumale hoped one day to become Frances's fifth husband, yet he was fond of him and greatly regretted that he had so little personal ambition. The duc's admirers were anxious for him to enter the Senate, but the position of the Orleans family had considerably changed in the last two years, and the chances of a restoration of the monarchy had been diminished by the intransigence of the old Comte de Chambord. The Comte de Paris's prospects had suffered in consequence, and a large party had formed who wanted Aumale as President of the Republic. As usual the duc could decide nothing without Frances's advice, and he appealed to her to come over to Paris to discuss the whole situation.

Enthusiastic accounts of the new channel steamer, *Castalia*, tempted Frances to go in the autumn. They arrived at the Hotel Mirabeau on October 23 without having notified any of their friends in Paris of their intention. From the moment their arrival became known, their little excursion assumed the proportions of a state visit.

Frances reported:

'We arrived here safe & sound on Saturday evening & I fired off a line by the late post to Chantilly to let the Duke d'Aumale know we were at Paris. On Sunday morning arrived a delighted telegram saying that he should come to Paris in the afternoon & begging us to let him call for us at ½7 to come & dine with him at 7 & that we should only find the Duke de Chartres. Of course we accepted. I then sent a line to the Count de Paris who found it on his arrival at Paris at 5 o'clock & off he came & made us a long visit, to insist upon our going to them at Chateau d'Eu for as many days as we could spare & at our own time. So we have arranged to go there on our way home. . . . We met at dinner the Duke de Chartres, the Duke de Montpensier & the Count de Paris. . . . We go with the Duke to dine at the Café Anglais tonight & then go with him to the Française to his Box, tomorrow we lunch at Chantilly & return with the Duke to dine at his house in Paris & go with him to the Palais Royale. Wednesday we dine with the Duke de Montpensier. . . . Carlingford says he seems *never* to be *alone* with me *anywhere*.'

Four days later 'I begin to despair of getting any time to my-self. . . . We had a wonderful dinner at the Duke de Montpensier's. His 3rd daughter, I believe the future Queen of Spain, aged 15 did the honours charmingly. She is pretty with such soft taking large brown eyes. We went with the Duke to the Opera, & the Duke d'Aumale & one of the Princes of Cobourg who had dined with us joined us there. The Opera House is the most splendid thing you can possibly imagine, but too much gilding for perfect taste. . . . The Duke d'Aumale calls for us on Sunday at ¼ 10 a.m. to take us to a private view of the Louvre & dines with us in the evening at this Hotel tête-à-tête à trois. . . . I have ordered a dress at Worth's, a black morning one for Thursday as one must dine in a quiet dress to go afterwards to a small theatre, & I must get a bonnet to go tomorrow to the Institut.'

There had been a great dinner in their honour at the British Embassy the previous night, which they had both enjoyed, but at the Institut 'We were awfully bored ... when we tried to get away at 3½ we found there was no possible outlet short of fainting as one lady did & was carried out over heads & under legs in the most fearful manner'.

The Duc Decazes gave a banquet for them at the Quai d'Orsay, and there was another dinner at the Montpensier's which 'was as usual perfect. The Duchess had come home from the Château d'Eu & she & the 2 Princesses & Prince Louis of Cobourg went to the play with us *Le Voyage dans la Lune*. The Duke had taken the Imperial enormous box with a fine large room behind it. . . . Princess Christine & Princess Mercédès were sent home with the Lady in waiting at the end of the 1st Act with an ice each to console them. The rest of the Play was *quite impossible* for young ladies but *we* all enjoyed it *immensely*. The fun is intense & the Music most charming from the beginning to the end. I am sorry that Constance must not see it until she is married as it would not do for any girl to be seen at such a play. . . . Madame Thiers made me a visit the other day. She was grown quite old, ugly & cross.'

The Worth dress arrived and 'the fit of it is such perfection that I have ordered the dress-maker to make patterns for . . . demi toilette & grande toilette'. There was a visit to the Assembly at Versailles where they 'found the Debate wonderfully dull', and every spare evening dinners with the Duc d'Aumale and more theatres where a royal box was always at their disposal. By November 12 Carlingford, and even Frances, were glad to leave for a few days of comparative quiet with the Parises at their vast Château d'Eu, before they returned to Dudbrook for the rest of the year.

Meanwhile in England the Conservative Government was in trouble. Austria and Russia were quite willing to acquire the Christian provinces still within the Ottoman Empire, and actively encouraged them to revolt against the rule of a more than usually degenerate sultan. Bismarck, who preferred that Russia and Austria should involve themselves in as much trouble as possible on their furthest frontiers from Germany, was pleased to give them his moral support.

In July 1875 Bosnia and Herzegovina had revolted, and by the end of the year the situation had become sufficiently serious for Austria, Russia and Germany to send a note to the Sultan urging a number of reforms. It was Britain's traditional policy to support the Ottoman Empire, but the incompetence and bankruptcy of the Turkish Government forced Disraeli early in 1876 to agree to the Note.

The financial collapse of Turkey had affected Egypt, still nominally a part of the Ottoman Empire, and in November '75, Disraeli had made his brilliant *coup* of buying the impoverished Khedive's Suez Canal shares for £4,000,000. As Lady Waldegrave wrote it took 'people's breath away. . . . Gladstone would never have had the courage.' Gladstone, Granville and Lowe were loud in their opposition, but Carlingford thoroughly approved. Unfortunately the purchase of the shares, and the influence it had on communications with India encouraged the Queen to think of assuming the title of Empress of India.

The bitterest parliamentary struggle during the spring of '76 was over the Queen's new title. The Liberals were violently opposed to it, and thereby immensely increased Her Majesty's affection for Disraeli. Frances joined in the fray and was a little disappointed in Hartington who had no very vehement feelings on the subject. 'Carlingford told me that Hartington failed to get his way last night with Dizzy, but Gladstone came gloriously to the rescue & completely routed the Govt. He certainly is the *only giant* in the House.'

For once Gladstone appeared to be winning Frances's reluctant friendship. Only three days before she had written that 'I had a visit from Mr. Gladstone on Thursday of an hour, three quarters of which we were tête à tête. . . . He was *immensely* agreeable & strange to say he did not make me nervous, his manner is so much subdued & he is so much less full of fight than he used to be.'

An offer of 1,200 guineas from April 20 for three months for 7 Carlton Gardens persuaded Frances to leave for Dudbrook a little earlier than she had intended. A succession of parties had already been arranged there until early June, and she was always thankful to escape from the exhaustion of London. Apparently Disraeli had not known of the letting of Carlton Gardens at the end of May the previous year, since he wrote to Lady Bradford a week later assuring her that:

'If it were not for the mysterious letting of the house of my friend Lady Waldegrave, I think we must fall to pieces.'

At the end of June the *Daily News* published a sensational account of Turkish atrocities in Bulgaria; ten thousand Bulgarians massacred, to say nothing of countless castrations and rapes. At first the account horrified the civilized world, but Disraeli, who well knew that the Christian communities in the Balkans had nothing to learn from the Turks on the question of maltreating enemies, refused to be stampeded into action. The *Daily News* account proved to be fairly accurate, but, soon after, other reports came of horrors inflicted on the Turks by the Bulgarians and, it was rumoured, by the Russians, though the latter did not officially enter the war until the following April.

Although David Urquhart had never succeeded in winning Chichester over to his adoration of the Turks, neither Chichester nor Frances was prepared to believe that the Slavs were any more humane than their foe. To Gladstone, however, it was a magnificent opportunity to reinstate himself as 'the people's William' by appealing to their sentimental prejudice and ignorance. In September he published a violent denunciation of the Turks which convinced the more gullible of its readers that the Conservative Premier was little better than Anti-Christ for showing an interest in the future of the Ottoman Empire.

Disraeli, who the previous month had gone to the Upper House as Earl of Beaconsfield, was less damaged by Gladstone's onslaught than was Lord Hartington. The rank and file of the Liberal electorate had always resented Hartington's dry, reserved, aristocratic manner, and had missed the demagogue who invariably paid the gallery the compliment of playing to it. Hartington, who had accepted the Liberal leadership in the Commons with great reluctance, felt that Gladstone was trying to oust him, and Frances and the Duchess of Manchester had an anxious time preventing his resignation.

Socially for Lord Carlingford and his wife, 1876 was the usual round of vast gatherings at Dudbrook, Strawberry Hill and Chewton. In October Frances was pleased with a long article in the *Quarterly Review* that Abraham Hayward had written on Strawberry Hill, containing a charming tribute to her, though a number of her friends felt that he tended to give Horace Walpole credit for a great deal that was entirely her doing. Another article appeared in the *Whitehall Review* in December with a very indifferent portrait of her. The text was a very charming account of her by Henry Grenfell.

The only other event of the year that much concerned Frances was the marriage of Willie Harcourt to Mrs. Ives. They had met again in November, and at last decided to ignore the protests of old Motley. Her father scarcely had time to realize that they had met, as they were married seventeen days later. Frances, who was as fond of Mrs. Ives as she was of Willie, lent them Strawberry Hill for the honeymoon—a kindness of which Harcourt showed his appreciation by doing all in his power to steal her cook.

For Christmas 1876 the usual family party gathered at Dudbrook. A close friendship had grown up between Ward Braham and Carlingford's nephew, 'Chi.' Hamilton, but the latter's health was causing great concern, and it seemed that he had inherited his father's ghastly disease. He was no longer capable of managing his uncle's Irish estate, and though, as he was at Dudbrook, he was able to assist with the Essex tenants, Frances and her husband could no longer rely on his help.

'Chi.' Hamilton and Ward stayed on at Dudbrook after the family party broke up, and Ward as usual helped to entertain the guests who arrived for the shooting week in the middle of January. Frances always dreaded the return to Carlton Gardens for the parliamentary session, and in '77 she had the additional sorrow of knowing that Ward's militia duties would keep him from her till June. He spent the first week of February in London and then decided to go down to View Island for a night to see what damage the winter's floods had done to his cottage.

The cottage had not suffered much, but the swollen river enabled Ward to fish from his windows, and it amused him to go boating over what were normally fields and roads. He forgot his promise to return to London the following day, though on hearing that 'Chi.' Hamilton's condition was serious, he wrote to Frances on February 16 offering to look after him. Hamilton, however, was trying a new treatment in London, so Ward stayed on in his cottage thoroughly enjoying his solitude in spite of a cold that his endless boating and fishing had given him. On the 21st Frances wrote:

'I hope you are not *really* ill. Take care of yourself & don't do anything at all imprudent.'

Two days later Charles went down to the cottage to nurse his brother, but when the following day Carlingford arrived, Ward was suffering from congestion of the lungs and could scarcely speak. On February 26, as Carlingford was preparing to leave Carlton Gardens on a second visit to View Island, Charles arrived with the news of Ward's death.

It was a shock from which Frances never entirely recovered. Since the days of her first marriage Ward had always been the most welcome visitor she could have. In spite of his endless financial scrapes, she had never succeeded in staying angry with him for long, and since her marriage to Chichester, who was devoted to him, Ward had become an almost essential part of their life in the country. Carlingford wrote to Lear:

'She & he had been devoted to one another from childhood, but I don't think I sh' have known beforehand that it wd. be the greatest loss caused by death that I had ever suffered. But so it is. He was quite a man to be missed, full of original fun & humour, & at the same time most tender & sympathetic. He seemed a necessary part of our home life especially in its quietest and happiest parts in the country.'

From the time of Mr. Harcourt's death, Frances had persuaded Charles to make Carlton Gardens his home but even his daughter Constance saw comparatively little of him. The disastrous picture dealing and his moderately successful compositions took him a great deal about the country and across the Channel, while his vagueness and the mixture of demonstrative affection and pugnacity made him far more unpredictable than the eccentric Ward.

Of all Lady Waldegrave's houses, Carlton Gardens held the fewest memories of her youngest brother. At Dudbrook, Chewton and Strawberry Hill he had been Lord of Misrule at all her parties, and more poignant for her still, he had been so much with them when there had only been herself, Chichester and Constance. For the next two months, therefore, she stayed in London seeing almost nobody.

Carlton Gardens was again let for the second half of the season, so it was at Dudbrook at Whitsun that she began again to receive friends, at first only the Stracheys and the Duchess of Manchester, but by the beginning of June most of the ex-Cabinet had collected there.

Half-way through the month Frances moved to Strawberry Hill. She had meant to spend the next two months quietly there, but the Comte and Comtesse de Paris wrote to propose themselves from June 30 to July 2 and again from July 7 to 9, which necessitated asking parties to meet them. An M.P. dinner for the Prince of Wales had been cancelled on account of Ward's death, and the Prince now suggested a visit to Strawberry Hill before the end of the season. The Tecks proposed themselves for July 1 and Princess Louise and Lord Lorne for the 21st. In despair Frances wrote to Lady Strachey:

'The Royalties seem to have Strawberry Hill upon the brain. . . . I am driven nearly wild with the invitations for all these double events.'

By the time she had dealt with the dinner to the Prince of Wales —the last party of the season—Lady Waldegrave was so breathless for a less rarefied atmosphere, that she insisted on Chichester taking her to Margate for a few days to restore her to normal, before the Chewton parties began.

The year 1877 was Constance's fifth season, and yet no one had apparently made any impression on her heart. She was greatly admired, both for her looks and for the charm and quiet efficiency with which she handled all the complications of her aunt's fabulous hospitality. She was asked to every ball in London and was never allowed to sit out one dance. She had refused to become Marchioness of Tweeddale, Lady St. Leonards, and Lady James, and had quietly discouraged any number of other offers.

She was happiest when there was a family party at the Priory, with her vague affectionate father always convinced that his latest discovery was an old master, and that the last song he had written would be an international success; Lady Horatia Wardlaw and Lady Ida Waldegrave whom she always considered as her aunts; Lord Norreys and his youngest sister; the Vicar of Chewton Mendip and his family; and, best of all, the Stracheys. Eddie, the eldest boy, seemed to prefer the idea of running his father's estates to an army life. He loved Sutton Court and was always a little resentful to be dragged away from it to spend his winter vacation at Cannes. St. Loe, the second son, had inherited his father's literary talents, while the youngest boy, Harry, was obviously destined to be a painter.

For nearly ten years Eddie and Constance had confided all their troubles and pleasures to each other. They were equally devoted to Sutton Court, once the home of the great Bess of Hardwick and considerably enlarged by her when she was Lady St. Loe. Constance actually appreciated the lovely old house more than Lady Strachey did, and always enjoyed her frequent visits there. Sir Edward and his wife were extremely fond of her, Lady Strachey considering her 'much the most charming young lady that I know'.

Frances decided to give a ball at Dudbrook in November, and as the house was already full of visitors, the two hundred and fifty ball guests booked every available room in the village inns for miles around. Two thousand peacock feathers to decorate a corner for sitting out was only one item of the vast preparations. The Stracheys had left Somerset in October for Cannes with the youngest boy, and Frances determined that the two elder sons should get away from Oxford for the dance. St. Loe succeeded in arranging permission for himself, but in spite of Lord Carlingford's application, the Dean of Christ Church was adamant about poor Eddie.

Of the three Strachey boys St. Loe was unquestionably Chichester's favourite—Frances said she had never known him so enthusiastic about anyone except Ward. He predicted a brilliant future for him and already found him a witty, clever companion. St. Loe had an adolescent passion for Lady Waldegrave, and describing the Dudbrook ball to his mother, told her that 'Lady Waldegrave and Constance were very lovely', whereas Mr. Cornwallis-West's astonishingly beautiful young Irish wife, he only considered 'very nice'.

Frances was enchanted with her young Irish guest whose beauty and gaiety reminded her of herself in the early Nuneham days before politics and royalties had taken their toll. Everyone fell in love at once with 'Erin' Cornwallis-West. Even pompous Willie Harcourt carved out a turnip as a cap and dared her to wear it to dinner. 'She came down to dinner looking most beautiful in it. The bows were fastened down in front of the turnip by a large diamond brooch & she had a spray of the leaves in the body of her frock.' The Austrian and German Ambassadors were 'quite silly about her'. Old Abraham Hayward was another guest, and he wrote a verse which he slipped into the bouquet she carried on the night of the ball. The verses appeared in the *Morning Post* three days later headed 'Lines dropped in the ballroom at Dudbrook with a bouquet. Author and owner unknown'.

The long accounts of the ball that appeared in the daily papers made pleasanter reading than the other news they contained. The Turkish fortress of Kars had surrendered to the Russians.

The British had been frantically anxious to remain neutral during the early months of the Russo-Turkish war, and were convinced that Lord Beaconsfield only drew attention to the dangers of a Russian-controlled Bosphorus because he was an inveterate war-monger. The very serious trade recession in the second half of the seventies made Gladstone's emphasis on internal affairs so extremely popular that his total lack of any foreign policy to support his criticism of the Government passed unnoticed.

On December 10 the Russians captured Plevna. Suddenly Great Britain realized that the Russian army was at the walls of Constantinople. By the end of the year Gladstone found that many of his former supporters were fervently singing the new music-hall song, 'We don't want to fight, but, by Jingo, if we do'.

Everyone besought Lord Beaconsfield to persuade the Tsar to agree to an armistice. The Premier, however, felt that Russia would pay little attention to this country unless we were in a position to meet any threat of force by even greater force. By chance the third volume of the *Life of the Prince Consort* had just been published. In it the Crimean War was dealt with at some length. Nine days after the fall of Plevna, Frances wrote:

'I have no doubt that the 3rd volume of Prince Albert's life will have an *immense* effect on the country upon the Eastern question. H.M. shows up the Russians, *Gladstone* etc in the most calm & efficient way. Mr. G. will be furious. The volume is *the* most fascinating book I ever read.'

Beaconsfield summoned Parliament to meet on 17 January 1878, exceptionally early, officially to discuss the eastern situation, but in reality for the Chancellor of the Exchequer to move a supplementary estimate for naval and military supplies. By an injudicious speech at the end of January at Oxford, Gladstone so seriously embarrassed the Liberal Party that once again Harting-ton was on the verge of resignation.

Schouvaloff, the popular and level-headed Russian Ambassador, was on very friendly terms with Frances, so she invited Glad-stone to dine with him at Carlton Gardens on February 8. The Russian discussed the whole eastern question very frankly with his hostess, but of the other guest she wrote:

'Mr. Gladstone is more odd & more impossible to manage than ever. He seems to be bent upon bringing utter ruin on the Liberal Party. He looks quite painfully *mad* & I was told that his conduct at the House of Commons, before he came on here to dine, was most extraordinary. He made faces & loud noises at Sir Stafford Northcote & was called to order by the whole house. . . . Mr. Childers whispered to me that evening he feared the end had come to that fine brain.'

Three days later Lady Waldegrave was able to write:

'I am glad to say Hartington does *not* resign but Gladstone's conduct is most unfair to him & most provoking. Even Glad-stone's admirers here are ashamed of him.'

Frances's fierce loyalty to the Orleans family had stopped her from having any contact with the Empress Eugénie or the Prince Imperial. Since her arrival in England in 1870 the Empress had led a very secluded life, but the twenty-two-year-old Prince Imperial had become a very popular member of society, and it was no longer possible for Frances to refuse invitations to houses where she might meet him. Algernon Borthwick and his wife were as devoted to the young Bonparte prince as they were to Frances, and it was at their house that the introduction finally came about in February 1878.

Lady Strachey was told all about it:

'As soon as I came in Mrs. Borthwick rushed up to me & said she must mention that the Prince Imperial had made a mistake & accepted for *dinner* instead of after dinner music & she hoped that I would not mind it. We had refused over & over again to meet him on account of the Orleans family. In the evening he insisted upon being introduced to me & sat & talked for an hour. He is *very* nice, gentlemanlike & sympathetic. I have written to the Duc d'Aumale & told him all about it, at the same time saying, that as the introduction has come off by accident, I must *occasionally* show him some civility chez nous, but that it was easy to avoid any intimacy. I wish he was not so taking nevertheless.'

A few days later the Prince Imperial was at the first ball Frances gave that season. There were 450 guests present, and their hostess was very proud that they included the eighty most beautiful women in London. To Constance's sorrow Eddie Strachey's doctor would not allow him to go, but Eddie made his non-attendance the excuse for so many morning calls on Constance that Frances wrote to his mother that 'I must say these young people seem to be very fond of each other'. St. Loe was again luckier than his brother and reported to Cannes that Lady Waldegrave was more beautiful and charming than ever and that her dress was a triumph of good taste and splendour, a thing, he sagaciously commented, very difficult to attain.

That night Frances played poker with her non-dancing guests, but towards the end of the month at a ball at Marlborough House, she danced with the Prince Imperial to the great amusement of the Prince of Wales, who threatened to telegraph the fact to the Duc d'Aumale. The Prince was equally amused when he found Lord Beaconsfield deep in conversation with her at a table for two in a secluded corner of the supper room—the head of the Government conferring with the leader of the Opposition. The Marlborough House ball was, however, rather spoilt by Mrs. Cornwallis-West having hysterics and then fainting when two young men had a violent quarrel as to which should dance with her.

Truth, whose editor lived at Pope's Villa, practically adjoining Strawberry Hill, announced that it was tired of reading the lists of guests at Frances's parties, though as she said 'not half as tired as I am of giving them'. The editor's wife had tried in vain for an invitation to any of the parties in question. The Prince of Wales certainly had attended a party at Pope's Villa, but Frances, in spite of her growing intimacy with Marlborough House, was not by any means prepared to receive all the Prince's extremely assorted acquaintance.

In March The Prince was at another M.P. dinner at Carlton Gardens, and so much enjoyed it that he informed his hostess that he would dine again with her three weeks later, when there was to be a dinner for Princess Louise, 'and he says he must come to Dudbrook either in the Spring or the Autumn & he & the Princess think of sleeping at Strawberry Hill for the masked ball & dinner in June. He played Poker, Whist & Nap till ¼ before one o'clock'. By Easter Frances and Chichester were almost too weary to enjoy the quiet of Dudbrook.

Their stay at Dudbrook was interrupted by a summons from the Queen to dine at Windsor. They 'were *astonished* as H.M. never shows any *intime* civility to the "outs" '. The banquet was held in the Waterloo Chamber and the Queen was charming to all her seventy guests. After she had withdrawn the Princess Royal introduced herself and her husband, the Crown Prince of Germany, to Frances and was very affable. The Prince and Princess Christian announced that they would like to spend an afternoon in July at Strawberry Hill and dine there in morning dress. There were times when Frances heartily envied her cottagers' wives.

During the summer there were no great political issues to worry either Frances or Chichester. The country had considered the Congress of Berlin a triumph for Lord Beaconsfield, and even the majority of the Liberals were forced to admit that he had handled a very difficult situation well. In the autumn, however, with the outbreak of the Afghan war, the political turmoil began again. Half a dozen editors, including Chenery, the new editor of *The Times*, were promptly asked to the Priory. Prominent Liberals were busily attacking the Government all over the country for its handling of the Afghan problem, but the only Opposition speech that provided any constructive criticism was the one made by Carlingford at Bristol in November. It was very favourably commented on in the press, the first notice being the *Times* leader the following day. The Chewton guests had been thoroughly put through their political paces.

A splendid party gathered at Dudbrook in December to meet the Prince of Wales who was coming for a few days' shooting. The local farmers, in their enthusiasm, offered Frances's gamekeepers £1 a head for the privilege of acting as beaters to the prince. The day he was expected, came the news that Princess Alice, his favourite sister, was desperately ill with diphtheria. The prince, with the ill-fated 14th only a few days off, had to wait in London for news. All the other guests did their best to console Frances for the disappointment, but the general anxiety for Princess Alice dispersed the party the day before her death.

THERE were no parties at Dudbrook in January '79. Apart from the court mourning for Princess Alice, Frances and Chichester wanted a month's quiet before the season began, although Frances's conception of a quiet life did not preclude her from scribbling a dozen letters a day to her social, political and literary acquaintance in England and France, with the inevitable daily letter to Lady Strachey.

Harriet Grote, the bluest stocking of her time, had died at the end of '78 and in the middle of January, Frances was amused to hear from one of her most regular correspondents, old Abraham Hayward, that:

'Now that Mrs. Grote is gone, I have hardly any friendly and discriminating critic but you to hit off my best passages.'

A fortnight later she again heard from Hayward, and reported to Lady Strachey that 'Lord Hartington made a capital address & even Hayward writes in great praise of him & says that he now understands why I pin my hopes upon him. . . . Hayward is so devoted to Gladstone that he never likes to imagine that the Liberals can have any other leader during his life time. I am firing off these few lines with the Postman waiting with his mouth open. It would be rather fun to put it down his throat, only then you would not get it.'

Hayward was far less pleased in another connection. In spite of his visit to Chewton Priory, Chenery, the new editor of *The Times*, had not allowed the policy of his newspaper to be swayed by the fascination of his hostess. Oddly enough the daily newspaper on which Frances at that time had the most influence was the Conservative *Morning Post*, and she had no difficulty in persuading Algernon Borthwick to publish the early journalistic efforts of her sixteen-year-old admirer, St. Loe Strachey. The Tories were again aware of her influence when she persuaded Beaconsfield to appoint her great friend, the Liberal Lord Dufferin, to the embassy at St. Petersburg.

S   259

When Lady Waldegrave arrived at Carlton Gardens in February the whole political situation seemed a little more satisfactory. If Granville would, as Frances quoted, 'rest and be thankful', there was a chance that Gladstone would eventually agree to serve as Chancellor of the Exchequer under Hartington. She was still full of enthusiasm for the latter, but was upset by a plot she had discovered. The night after her return to London, she met her friend the Duchess of Manchester at dinner and learned that the duchess was leaving in a few days for the South of France to shake off a persistent cough. Her absence was to be utilized. Frances wrote indignantly of her discovery:

'*Private*. H.M. has got *Mrs.* Teck to try & get up a marriage between Lord Hartington & the King of Hanover's sister. This is *the cause* of her visit to England. It is to be tried on whilst the Dss. is abroad. *Don't* mention this to anyone. Did you ever hear of such a silly plot? I wonder whether the Dss. knows of this.'

The Queen's effort to cure Hartington of his duchess did not succeed, and as soon as she returned to England and could safeguard her love life, Frances relaxed sufficiently to have the Tecks with Princess Frederica of Hanover at a dinner where Hartington was among the guests.

The season at Carlton Gardens began with a typical Sunday levee that lasted from half-past two to a quarter to seven. The German ambassador, the Spanish, Netherlands, Danish and Swedish ministers; Lords Kimberley, Sydney, Orford, E. Fitzmaurice, Airlie, O'Hagan, Halifax and Houghton; Sirs Thomas E. May, Erskine Perry, William Gregory, Charles Dilke, Henry James, and Charles Russell; Messrs. F. Leveson-Gower, Henry Reeve of the *Edinburgh Review*, Dr. William Smith of the *Quarterly*, J. T. Knowles of the *Nineteenth Century*, Henry Grenfell and Abraham Hayward made up the list, all of them regular Sunday visitors throughout each season.

Frances complained that it had been very tiring but 'you may imagine how much good talk we had'. It was on that Sunday that Sir Henry James, on behalf of Hartington and those Liberals who considered Lady Waldegrave their leader, besought her to begin sitting to Millais for the portrait with which they were anxious to present her. Unfortunately she was always rather impatient of sittings and, when three days later she saw Millais, she only arranged 'that he is to make a sketch of me at Strawberry Hill for the picture some time this year'.

Early in March Frances and Chichester dined at 10 Downing Street. Much as they both disapproved of Lord Beaconsfield politically, socially they found him charming, whereas their sincere efforts to like Gladstone were never to succeed. Lady Waldegrave wrote enthusiastically of her host 'who talked to me for an hour after dinner. He is delighted to sit for a miniature for Strawberry Hill. I am told he has refused everyone but the Queen, & would not sit to Watts for the national collection of great men he is painting. He & and I have always been great friends with one *interlude*—the time he jumped upon Gladstone when he was down some years ago & then I told him *why* I did not care to see him. We talked over all sorts of subjects in a most open & confidential way.'

A series of bad harvests and the critical international situation had had a disastrous effect on the prosperity that had lasted since the early fifties. Telling his brother of their unsuccessful attempts to let Carlton Gardens for the second half of the season, Carlingford wrote that 'we want it badly'—the £1,200 rent—'as we, like other traders, have had a bad year' (with the Radstock coal). As Frances expressed it, 'The Govt. are in a nice mess, but unfortunately the country is in a worse one, so it is impossible even to wish for a mere party fight or success.'

The older Liberals complained bitterly to Lady Waldegrave of Gladstone's behaviour. Lord Kinnaird 'was full of the misfortune to the party in having such a mad man as W. E. G. always doing or saying insane things at critical moments which saved the Govt. from the full odium they so fully deserved'. Old Lord Grey voiced an opinion held by many Liberals who dreaded a Liberal return to power since it might mean putting Gladstone in a responsible position. None the less Frances decided to give a dinner to meet the Gladstones towards the end of March, though she could not resist a few days before it telling Lady Strachey that Hartington 'made the most wonderful progress in speaking & influencing the House. Fancy Mary Gladstone writing the other day . . . "My Father & Mother have been in bed together for four days with influenza." Everyone who hears it, pictures the Awful Sight.'

March was an extremely exhausting month for both Lord Carlingford and his wife. On the 14th 'our levee got into a state of flutter when the Graceful [the Groom of the Chambers] opened the door & announced "His Majesty the King of the Belgians". I forced the men to stay & told the Graceful not to let coming visitors know that H.M. was with us. A few came in, but others smelt a (royal) rat as they saw the Queen's carriage at the door & skedaddled in the most cowardly way. He said all sorts of civil things and said at the end "I must see if we can throw anyone over to dine with you". I hope he won't as we shall see plenty of them.'

Her hopes were not realized, as a few days later Lady Strachey learned that 'all the Royalties are in such a state of activity that I have not had a moment to devote to you. The King & Queen of the Belgians sent M. Devaux to tell me that they would not leave England without either dining or lunching here & as all their evenings were taken they proposed to lunch here on Sunday next. I have had to send out invitations for this civility & invitations for a dinner to meet Princess Mary on the 4th of April & ditto to meet Mr. Gladstone on the 29th instead of the 22nd on account of our dinner at Marlborough House. . . . We shall have enough of the King & Queen. Tonight dinner at Moley's [Lady Molesworth's] Saturday ditto the Prince of Wales', Tuesday ditto at Princess Mary's besides the luncheon here on Sunday.'

The Belgians, with whom Frances had been friendly since 1870, apparently enjoyed their luncheon as they stayed till 4.15 to the dismay of the levee regulars, who were further dismayed the following Sunday when the King again appeared. That time, however, Frances asked him to send back the royal carriage which so disconcerted her other visitors, and His Majesty had to return to the palace on foot. The dinner for Princess Mary was not the end, as the Prince and Princess of Wales proposed themselves for dinner the next day. Frances wearily apologized for her letters looking 'like a pack of cards with all the small ones left out'. At times she almost wished that Willie Harcourt had succeeded in filching her cook. Realizing that none of their own houses provided any means of escape, Carlingford insisted on spending Easter in an hotel at Tunbridge Wells.

On their return from Kent, Chichester and Frances spent a few days at Mentmore, the vast, splendid mansion Lord Rosebery had acquired with his Rothschild wife. Gladstone, whom Rosebery was to finance in the next electoral campaign for Mid-Lothian, was there with his wife and daughters. Except for the weather everything was delightful, but Lady Waldegrave had to cut the visit short as Prince and Princess Christian were to dine at Carlton Gardens a few days later and a musical evening had to be arranged for them.

At the beginning of May Frances and Chichester returned to Dudbrook where there were to be no parties until the end of the month. Normally the gardens were enchanting at that time of year, but the worst winter of all the ghastly winters during the seventies still continued. It had begun to snow at Chewton on November 1, and at Tunbridge Wells in the middle of April there was still snow. It had affected everyone's health, and Frances, who since Ward's death had a terror of neglected colds, was considerably worried as Chichester had for weeks been unable to rid himself of a sore throat. Her own magnificent vitality made her almost over-anxious about him, since she realized that he had not the constitution to live at the pace to which she was accustomed.

Dudbrook House was crowded at the beginning of June for the Whitsun holiday. The guest Frances was most pleased to welcome was Lady Strachey whom she had not seen for twenty months. Apart from her delight at seeing how much the long stay at Cannes had improved her friend's health, Lady Waldegrave was glad of the opportunity to discuss the question of Constance and Eddie. Constance was in great demand at balls and house parties, and any number of mothers were anxious to see their sons marry the all-powerful Lady Waldegrave's adopted daughter.

The difference in age appeared in no way to disturb the affection of the two young people, and although, as Eddie would not attain his majority till November, it was too soon for any official engagement, both Frances and Lady Strachey hoped to achieve their dearest wish before the latter returned to Cannes in the autumn.

The Whitsun party was a cheerful affair, everyone delighted at the news that their hostess's step-grandson, Lord Norreys, was the owner of the Derby winner. The guests stayed a week, and when they left Constance went with them to a house party for Ascot. To Chichester's great happiness it meant that he could spend ten days entirely alone with his wife before they went back to London.

It was during these days that Frances wrote to Lady Strachey: 'I had an inspiration the other day that it would be a good plan for the future to go to Strawberry Hill in the middle of April & stay there till the end of the first week in July & then come here until near the end of August when we are due at the Priory . . . so yesterday Hulse came from Strawberry Hill to arrange with Wilkinson that the Spring flowers should bloom at S. Hill & the Summer ditto here. When I lived at Nuneham the Spring garden was lovely at Strawberry & we can have the full enjoyment of it there. Here we leave it when it is in its greatest beauty & we leave Strawberry Hill when the summer garden is in perfection. This is a bore, so my plan is appreciated all round.'

The last day of their stay in Essex was fine enough for them to walk down to the summer house at the Navestock side of the park. As it was almost the first thing Frances had had built, she was devoted to it and liked to end each Dudbrook visit by taking sentimental leave of the little thatched cottage. On the various occasions when Dudbrook House was let, the summer house was never included in the lease. As they were walking home again up a gentle slope, Frances paused for a moment. In answer to Carlingford's look of enquiry she said, 'I'm sure I have something the matter with my heart.'

Her husband, to whom her least headache caused anxiety, could not help smiling at the absurdity of her remark. In spite of the years she so frankly admitted, her radiant vitality, her lovely colouring and the grace of her walk made *incessu patuit dea* as true as it had been twenty-eight years before. When, at Carlton Gardens, she changed for dinner in her little blue boudoir to save herself the climb upstairs, he invariably teased her about her laziness as he did about what she termed her 'little snooze' on the sofa in the library after dinner, if they were later going out.

Now he laughed softly at her with indulgent tenderness. She smiled back at him and taking his arm, they went on their way to the house.

Carlingford and his wife got back to Carlton Gardens on June 18. On the following day they were at the Gaiety where the *Comédie Française* was having a brilliant season, Coquelin and his son and Sarah Bernhardt were playing. It meant a very late arrival at Strawberry Hill, but they enjoyed the drive down, though the night air was wintry.

The following day came the horrifying news of the massacre of the Prince Imperial by Zulus, largely due to the disgraceful negligence of his commanding officer. Early in the year Frances had written of the young prince's determination to take an active part in the Zulu War:

'The Prince Imperial's letter to M. Rouher will make him very popular in this country & will astonish the Bourbons & Orleans family. One of the fine things in the late Emperor's character was his courage in owning his good feelings towards this country & his contempt for the French prejudice against it. The Orleans Princes have never had pluck to take the same line. *One* exception the Prince of Condé. If he had lived he would have done wonders.'

Her sympathy went out to the desolate Empress Eugénie and to poor little Princess Beatrice, whose engagement to the prince rumour had long since anticipated. Despite her loyalty to the Comte de Paris, Lady Waldegrave asked Algernon Borthwick to convey a message to the Empress.

Strawberry Hill was in 'tremendous beauty from Hawthorns and Laburnums and Acacias', and Frances was glad of a day or two's peace before her great party for the Crown Prince of Sweden. Mourning for the Prince Imperial would naturally make it a quiet affair, but she was full of plans for the huge fête on July 12 she was to give in honour of the Duc d'Aumale's visit to her. The Prince and Princess of Wales would also be present as they had proposed themselves for that Saturday to Monday.

In a letter about Aumale's visit Frances wrote that 'he talks of coming here the day before. I hope he won't as we are always in a bustle on these grand occasions, Fitch & Turner calling me "Y.R.H." in mistake & and their heads turned the wrong way!'

On the 22nd Frances and Chichester drove over to Pembroke Lodge to see Lady Russell who, they found, had aged very much since her husband's death the previous year. The next day Carlingford attended a meeting of the ex-Cabinet at Devonshire House and in the evening dined at the Crystal Palace with the former Liberal member for South Essex. There was a tremendous display of fireworks, though the weather was bad, and Chichester was able to assure his friend that the Liberal prospects were excellent.

At the same time, possibly on account of the weather or because he was never really happy away from his wife, he could not shake off a ghastly feeling of impending doom. He made an excuse to his friend and hurried back to Strawberry Hill to find Frances gay and delighted as a child at his early return. She challenged him to a game of billiards, won it with the greatest ease, and so dazzled him with her fascination that he found himself back in the ecstasy of their brief honeymoon.

On the 24th 'we had a most delightful dinner of Dudbrookites and Strawberry Hillites at the Mays'. The Duchess of Manchester, the Willie Harcourts, Hartington, Hayward, the Frank Stonors, Sir Henry James and Sir Charles Dilke were among the guests. 'I lost £4 at Poker but had much fun for my money. . . . We are off this afternoon to the French play and are due at Strawberry Hill for dinner. The weather has been & is still quite wretched & most trying for colds & rheumatic pains as we have tried to leave off fires & are now paying for this heroic & rather foolhardy experiment.'

Two days later Lady Waldegrave wrote that she was 'full of rheumatic pains in my chest & arms & back. I am not sure they are not neuralgia. We stupidly allowed Mrs. Northam to play at Summer & fill the grates with flowers & muslin. After 4 days of this tragic farce I told her to treat this June as if it were November & we are now in full blaze of Radstock coal, but my pains are not gone.'

The Crown Prince of Sweden's visit was most successful and on the first day, Saturday the 28th, even the weather improved. Doctor Du Pasquier had sent down some medicine which disposed of Frances's pains, and she thoroughly enjoyed her party. It brought back memories of that first visit to Drayton which had so influenced her life. Both old Sir Robert Peel's daughters were staying with her, Mrs. Stonor and Lady Jersey with whom, since her marriage to Captain Brandling, Frances had become very friendly.

She told Chichester how happy it made her that her few quarrels were all at an end. Sir Henry Ponsonby had brought his wife, the former Mary Bulteel, and the Willie Harcourts were there too, as if all the bitter feuds of the Nuneham days had never happened.

Lady Ailesbury was there, as good-humoured as ever, the Duchess of Manchester with Lord Hartington, and to the general confusion Sir Henry James, the ex-Attorney-General, and Mr. Henry James, a young American writer whose novels Frances greatly enjoyed.

By Monday the weather was again unspeakable. The year 1879 was one of the worst summers on record, so bad that at midnight on the day the Strawberry Hill party dispersed, the Poet Laureate wrote:

> *Midnight—and joyless June goes by*
> *And from the deluged park*
> *The cuckoo of a worse July*
> *Is calling through the dark.*

A young protégée of Lady Waldegrave's was painting both Carlingford and Frances, and on Wednesday they sat to her in the Round Room in front of a blazing fire, Frances, wrapped in a shawl, shivering and praying that the sitting would soon be over. She would have liked a day or two in bed to shake off her cold, but there was far too much to arrange for the double royal visit.

Before the end of the parliamentary session there was also a lot to settle. The fact that the last ex-Cabinet meeting had been held at Devonshire House instead of at Lord Granville's was itself a healthy sign. Granville, although a cousin of Hartington's, had for years felt it would be more advantageous for himself to give his allegiance to Gladstone. Meanwhile Hartington's position had strengthened and Gladstone had made himself even more unpopular at Windsor, a point that considerably influenced Granville.

Gladstone, even before he had resigned the leadership of the party, had assured the Queen that the defeat of his Government would mean his retirement from political life. When, therefore, the guests were invited to Prince Arthur's wedding early in '79, as only representative members of the Opposition were included, the Queen saw no reason to invite the Gladstones. 'The People's William' was furious and voiced his resentment. His remarks soon reached the Queen.

If Beaconsfield had to resign he would advise the Queen for whom to send and it would certainly be Lord Hartington. Frances therefore felt that it was essential to develop Hartington's political ambitions. Her great political influence had come about almost accidentally. Her devotion to old Sir Robert Peel and the boredom of the early years at Nuneham had begun it. Her friendship with the Duke of Newcastle and her desire to see him Prime Minister, the intimacy with the Clarendons and the old Duke of Bedford, the quarrel with Mary Bulteel, and her anxiety to help Chichester and then the Orleans family had little by little brought her such political knowledge and power that, had she wanted to—as she sometimes did—she could no longer have withdrawn from the political world. Too many of her nominees had come to rely on her for advice, and her influence in the embassies and legations as well as in the press made her too valuable for the Liberals to allow her to desert them.

On Thursday, July 3, Frances scribbled a note to Lady Strachey about a charity concert they were arranging at Chewton Mendip. 'I had such a bad night from the pain in my chest, that I have been fast asleep in my chair & now find the post is going.' That evening Chichester sent for the local doctor who gave her morphine to dull the rheumatic pains.

In the early morning of Friday, Chichester awoke to find his wife in great pain, but she reassured him. She remembered her father's illness and how ill morphine had made him. 'I'm like my father—I can't bear it.' During the day she insisted upon waiting until the ill effects of the morphine had worn off, before they drove up to Carlton Gardens to consult Doctor Du Pasquier.

They reached their town house early in the evening. Frances was too exhausted by the drive to be got upstairs to her room. A bed was prepared for her in the library and soon Doctor Du Pasquier arrived. He at once diagnosed congestion of the lungs and promised to bring Sir Andrew Clarke early the following day. Towards ten o'clock Frances, who had been in great pain, fell into a coma, greatly to Chichester's relief, as it meant a little respite for her from her suffering. He sat beside her through the night, convinced that her wonderful vitality would pull her through.

First thing on Saturday morning Chichester sent a note to his brother.

'My dear C.
Frances is very ill. I brought her up from S. Hill yesterday and

I have been very anxious about her since yesterday evening. I believe it is bronchitis. It is essential not to frighten her. I expect Du Pasquier directly & I believe he will bring A. Clarke. God grant they may do her good.

Yours affectly.

Cd.'

At nine o'clock the two doctors arrived. Frances was still in a coma. Chichester waited in his study until he heard Sir Andrew's footsteps. It was congestion of the lungs, but that brave, gallant heart was exhausted.

'She is in terrible and imminent peril.'

Somehow Chichester made his way to the bedside. She was still unconscious, but to relieve the agonizing sound of her breathing, he raised her slightly and sat in terror, supporting her with his arm. Dimly he heard the doctor giving instructions to the servants. He could hear a clock ticking through the tormenting gasps that seemed to fill the great room. A distant clock struck ten. For a moment the breathing against his shoulder seemed easier. There was an almost imperceptible movement and then utter quiet.

The last of the great ladies was dead.

POSTSCRIPT

In an over-furnished room in a chilly Scottish castle, a dumpy, plainly dressed, elderly woman rose to her feet with an inexpressible grace and held her hand out at a level for the tall, prematurely aged man before her to kiss. She was in as emotional a state as he, for they, the widow and the widower, had been discussing the only subject that absorbed them both—the happiness of their married lives.

In her beautiful clear silvery voice, gently she reminded him, 'You will not forget to send me a copy of the inscription and a photograph of your dear wife's memorial.'

Bending to touch her hand with his lips the Lord Privy Seal took leave of his sovereign.

*   *   *

From the memorial to Frances, Countess Waldegrave in Chewton Mendip church:

'Her brilliant gifts, her noble and beautiful character made her the centre of a wide and worthy influence, and attracted to her an extraordinary amount of friendship and affection. Owner for many years of the Waldegrave estates in the county of Somerset and elsewhere, she made herself a much loved home at Chewton Priory in this parish, with him who inscribes on these walls her dear and honoured name. The words, which kneeling here, she best loved to use were those of the thanksgiving—"Almighty God, Father of all mercies, we Thine unworthy servants do give Thee most humble and hearty thanks for all Thy goodness and loving kindness to us and to all men." Her body rests, as she desired, in this churchyard. This memorial is placed here by Chichester, Lord Carlingford, the record of a great happiness and a great sorrow, and a token of unspeakable gratitude and love,—"For where your treasure is, there will your heart be also".'

INDEX

T